Tools for Building and Zoning

Residential Zone Light Residential
Dense Residential

Signs

Commercial Zone Light Commercial
Dense Commercial

Query

Industrial Zone Light Industrial
Dense Industrial

Rotate Counter-Clockwise

Education School
College
Library
Museum

Rotate Clockwise

City Services Police
Fire Station
Hospital
Prison

Zoom Out

Recreation Small Park
Big Park
Zoo
Stadium
Marina

Zoom In

Center

FOR EVERY COMPUTER QUESTION,
THERE IS A SYBEX BOOK THAT HAS THE ANSWER

Each computer user learns in a different way. Some need thorough, methodical explanations, while others are too busy for details. At Sybex we bring nearly 20 years of experience to developing the book that's right for you. Whatever your needs, we can help you get the most from your software and hardware, at a pace that's comfortable for you.

We start beginners out right. You will learn by seeing and doing with our **Quick & Easy** series: friendly, colorful guidebooks with screen-by-screen illustrations. For hardware novices, the **Your First** series offers valuable purchasing advice and installation support.

Often recognized for excellence in national book reviews, our **Mastering** titles are designed for the intermediate to advanced user, without leaving the beginner behind. A **Mastering** book provides the most detailed reference available. Add our pocket-sized **Instant Reference** titles for a complete guidance system. Programmers will find that the new **Developer's Handbook** series provides a more advanced perspective on developing innovative and original code.

With the breathtaking advances common in computing today comes an ever increasing demand to remain technologically up-to-date. In many of our books, we provide the added value of software, on disks or CDs. Sybex remains your source for information on software development, operating systems, networking, and every kind of desktop application. We even have books for kids. Sybex can help smooth your travels on the **Internet** and provide **Strategies and Secrets** to your favorite computer games.

As you read this book, take note of its quality. Sybex publishes books written by experts—authors chosen for their extensive topical knowledge. In fact, many are professionals working in the computer software field. In addition, each manuscript is thoroughly reviewed by our technical, editorial, and production personnel for accuracy and ease-of-use before you ever see it—our guarantee that you'll buy a quality Sybex book every time.

To manage your hardware headaches and optimize your software potential, ask for a Sybex book.

FOR MORE INFORMATION, PLEASE CONTACT:

Sybex Inc.
2021 Challenger Drive
Alameda, CA 94501
Tel: (510) 523-8233 • (800) 227-2346
Fax: (510) 523-2373

SYBEX

Sybex is committed to using natural resources wisely to preserve and improve our environment. As a leader in the computer books publishing industry, we are aware that over 40% of America's solid waste is paper. This is why we have been printing our books on recycled paper since 1982.

This year our use of recycled paper will result in the saving of more than 153,000 trees. We will lower air pollution effluents by 54,000 pounds, save 6,300,000 gallons of water, and reduce landfill by 27,000 cubic yards.

In choosing a Sybex book you are not only making a choice for the best in skills and information, you are also choosing to enhance the quality of life for all of us.

Let us hear from you.

Talk to SYBEX authors, editors and fellow forum members.

Get tips, hints and advice online.

Download magazine articles, book art, and shareware.

Join the SYBEX Forum on CompuServe®

If you're already a CompuServe user, just type `GO SYBEX` to join the SYBEX Forum. If not, try CompuServe for free by calling 1-800-848-8199 and ask for Representative 560. You'll get one free month of basic service and a $15 credit for CompuServe extended services—a $23.95 value. Your personal ID number and password will be activated when you sign up.

Join us online today. Type `GO SYBEX` on CompuServe. If you're not a CompuServe member, call Representative 560 at `1-800-848-8199`.

SYBEX

(outside U.S./Canada call 614-457-0802)

SIMCITY

2000™

STRATEGIES

AND SECRETS

SPECIAL EDITION

SECOND EDITION

DANIEL A. TAUBER
and BRENDA KIENAN

SYBEX®

SAN FRANCISCO

PARIS

DÜSSELDORF

SOEST

Acquisitions Editor: Kristine Plachy
Developmental Editor: Gary Masters
Editors: Laura Arendal, Armin Brott
Project Editor: Michelle Khazai
Technical Editors: Erik Ingenito, David Hendee
Series Designer: Ingrid Owen
Endpaper, Part, and Chapter Opener Artist: Lucka Živny
Screen Graphics Artists: Aldo X. Bermudez, John Corrigan, Dan Schiff, Molly Sharp
PC Screen Graphics Created by Daniel A. Tauber and Brenda Kienan
Macintosh Screen Graphics Created by David Hendee
Desktop Publishing Specialist: Molly Sharp
Production Assistant: Taris Duffié
Indexer: Matthew Spence
Cover Designer: Archer Design

10 9

DEDICATION

For Mz Murphy

Foreword by Fred Haslam and Will Wright

DECEMBER 1990. MAXIS WAS HOLDING a first-ever company dinner for staff and associates. Will and I had recently finished SimEarth, so for the first time in a year I felt completely relaxed. During that festive event I was pitched two ideas.

The first was a quick-and-dirty project—installing new tile sets for the old SimCity. You know: medieval, future, Asian, etcetera. I said, "Give me 5 percent." They said, "Gee, we figured on a flat fee." A meeting of minds was not in evidence, so that project ended up being foisted on Mick Foley. The poor lad soon discovered that the project was dirty but not quick. Those tile sets turned out to be a morass of reprogramming that took him a year to complete. Whew!

The second idea was to write a sequel to SimCity. Will had spent five years on the original and was sick of it. He wanted nothing to do with writing the next one. I agreed to work on it because I loved the first game and had definite ideas on what should be in the second.

After eight months of hard work I had a game that was two-thirds complete. It had hills, rivers, sewage, power, a realistic water model, highways, rail, traffic, and five primary zones—residential, commercial, industrial, farming, mining. The graphics were overhead color tiles not unlike the original. Then tragedy struck.

Maxis contracted to work on a really cool game called "A-Train." It had a 3-D perspective that was gorgeous. It was decided by the powers that be that the new SimCity should have the same graphical style. I gritted my teeth and began working on my own 3-D view for SimCity 2000. As the old dictum goes: the first 90 percent of a project takes 90 percent of the scheduled time, the last 10 percent takes the other 90 percent.

I worked on the graphics for a full year and failed miserably to create anything attractive. My code crashed, my choice of viewing angle could not support large hills, my drawing method severely limited the graphics. I nearly had a breakdown. Finally, Will got back in the saddle. He started by importing the graphics code from "DollHouse," which he and Mick Foley had developed.

He also got back onboard to work on the simulation. He had ideas for SimCity 2000 that I frankly found boring and would not work on (don't tell him I said that). He got back in to make sure that the final code had those things he wanted. Maxis at this time offered to release me from the project to go work on other things. I politely declined their generous offer (all I could think was, "Fat chance!").

The last year of the project was a whirlwind of activity. Will and I had a synergy of ideas that created things neither of us had expected. Here is an example: We were having trouble laying down stuff on the terrain—it was difficult to tell where a mouse click would place an item. I noted that in "A-Train" the ground had a square grid to make this task easier. We included that. Then Will saw that we could replace the tiles with just the grid to get a look at the underground systems. Another example: Will wanted to include labels for locations. I wanted to induce connections to adjacent cities. His labels solved my problem of visually identifying the location of connections.

The last few months were especially intense. As we got closer to completion, opportunities arose for additional features. For example, once the stadiums were complete, it became possible to add news stories for the local teams' sporting events. And once the code for terrain editing had been finalized, I was able to include volcanos as a special disaster.

Let me talk about where some of the ideas for SimCity 2000 came from.

One of the first items I was given for this project was a printout of a bulletin board that had been dedicated to discussing ideas for a SimCity sequel. A lot of the ideas expressed there made it into the final game, but one topic especially caught my attention. At one point during the chain of messages, someone mentioned military bases and how they affect nearby cities. This idea engendered an explosion of response, mostly negative—some emphatically so. I felt that any topic with that much power just *had* to be included. I tossed in the flying hero to mollify the pacifists.

Will had certain ideas that he definitely wanted to include. His biggest was the microsimulations. He liked the idea that you could micromanage a police department if you wanted to. Unfortunately, while the microsimulations were included, we never got to add controls to them. His second-biggest idea was the underground view. Will had some books that showed what a city would look like if the earth it rested on were invisible. He loved that image, and we included it. His third-biggest addition was the arcologies, which allow your city to reach the exalted population of ten million. What a rush.

My best additions were free-zoning, the newspaper, and city bonds. Free-zoning is the second most-prominent change from the original SimCity (the first being hills and valleys). Allowing the free layout of zones gives the player more control without adding undue complexity. It is unfortunate that free-zoning created some problems that never got resolved vis-à-vis the growth of airports. The newspaper was included to replace the "Score" dialog box from the first game. I felt that as mayor, the player's feedback needed to be more realistic than a two-digit "approval rating." The final version turned out to be more entertaining than I had anticipated. City bonds were included for the sole purpose of expressing one of my pet beefs. In general I feel that if you float a bond, you will later regret it. To my chagrin, I found that you could actually use a bond to generate rapid growth that would offset the bond expense. How about that?

One last paragraph: the graveyard of dead ideas. Here is a list of some things that went into the game and were later stripped out for one reason or another. One-way streets—too hard. Mining & lumbering zones—undue complexity. Realistic water model—too much time. Farm zones—just useless. SimEarth terrain—lost in the shuffle. Tidal waves—plain ugly. Llamas—God, don't I wish.

—Fred Haslam

I FIRST STARTED WORKING ON SimCity back in early 1985 on a Commodore 64 computer. I now think of this early version as the first generation of SimCity, the Mac/IBM/Amiga versions of SimCity Classic being the second generation and SimCity 2000 the third. For ten years (on and off) I've been working on this game, and people keep buying it. This game, more than anything else, has made our company (Maxis) grow and succeed. It has kept me—as well as scores of others—gainfully employed and busy for many years. So it's about time I got something off my chest. I'm *sick* of SimCity! I really, really, really am.

No human should ever have to play one game as much as I've played this one. I've spent endless hours pouring over printouts, debugging code, designing land-valuation algorithms, studying textbooks on urban dynamics and, to top it all off, simulation tuning. Oh yes, simulation tuning. That obscure, obtuse black art that sucks the marrow out of your brain at 3:00 am. A process which, by its very nature, defies any analytic approach and twists your brain into as-of-yet-unheard-of topologies.

When people meet me now for the first time, they usually say, "So you're the guy who designed SimCity." I sometimes wish I knew enough about these other people to respond with, "Yes, and you're the person who just remodeled your bathroom," or some such thing. The only reason I bring this up is because the last three products I worked on were *co*designed by me. On two of those products, SimEarth and SimCity 2000, I shared the design responsibilities with Fred Haslam.

I won't go into how weird Fred is—this isn't the appropriate place. But I will say that we work well together, and I think the products we've designed reflect that. For some intangible reason, though, Fred never seems to get as much credit as he deserves for our designs. I'm always the one called for interviews, or book forewords, or emergency meetings with the president. On the other hand, I might also add that Fred manages to avoid much of the code-maintenance chores that I get stuck with. The brain-sucking tedium of digging through reams of debugging…never mind. So I'd like to thank Dan Tauber and Brenda Kienan for inviting Fred to coforeword this book with me.

Now that SimCity 2000 is out, what's next? Random people have started stopping me on the street; they tend to say, "Hey you. Yeah you, the guy who designed SimCity. What's next?" First I hit them, then I make them rephrase the question to: "the guy who codesigned SimCity along with Fred Haslam," then I stop and ponder a moment. A gleam comes into my eyes and rays of sun are cast from the heavens as I start to chant: "SimWorld, SimWorld, SimWorld." (And to nip any confusion in the bud right now, SimWorld != SimEarth, or for those "C"-impaired among us, SimWorld is *not* SimEarth. SimEarth is a game, SimWorld is a software architecture that is slowly being built around SimCity. It will not be ready for a while yet, but it will be wonderful.)

I stand straight and tall, point to the summit of yonder mountain (where the air is clear and the birds are singing), and reply, "SimWorld is like the mountain, persistent structure, parallel processing, fractal dynamics." Then as I point to the dark morass of linear media looming on the horizon I say "Beware, my daughter, that direction leads to the dark side: canned videos, low-interactivity, finite game states...."

[Editor's note: At this point, the forward Will wrote becomes quite disjointed and incoherent; we have decided to end it here to save on paper.]

—Will Wright

ACKNOWLEDGEMENTS

THANKS TO THE MANY PEOPLE who helped to produce this book. At Sybex, thanks go to developmental editor Gary Masters, who pointed us on our way; editors Laura Arendal and Armin Brott, who turned our occasionally upside-down phrasing right-side up; project editor Michelle Khazai, who kept it all on track the first time around with great finesse; and technical reviewer David Hendee, who apparently is ambidextrous and who checked everything on both the Mac and the DOS PC. Special thanks to Erik Ingenito for double-checking the Windows stuff and Kris Vanberg-Wolff for her invaluable assistance in the revision.

Many thanks to desktop publishing specialist Molly Sharp, artist Lucka Živny, production assistant Taris Duffié, and indexer Matthew Spence for their efforts. Thanks also to the assistant editors, without whom nothing would ever get into production.

Our appreciation also goes to Dr. R.S. Langer, Barbara Gordon, Chris Meredith, Kristine Plachy, and Celeste Grinage.

Thanks also to Sharon Crawford and Robert Williams for researching the AOL and Prodigy information.

We are indebted to those who frequent the Usenet games newsgroups, especially Chris Weiss, Kevin Endo, and Rich Holmes, for their insights and tips and the inspiration that came from their "frequently asked questions."

Many thanks to Don Walters at Maxis for being available to answer *our* frequently asked questions. Thanks also to Fred Haslam and Will Wright for creating a great game and an illuminating Foreword to this book.

Special thanks to family and friends who kept their patience and provided support throughout the writing of this book and others.

CONTENTS AT A GLANCE

TABLE OF CONTENTS

PART TWO: TECHNIQUES AND STRATEGIES FOR BUILDING A SIMCITY

PART THREE: WINNING THE MODEL SCENARIOS

PART FOUR: ADVANCED SIMCITY 2000

IN SIMCITY 2000, as in SimCity Classic, you are again the mayor of a simulated city where your role is to set the agenda for the city, build it, and manage it through whatever happens as a result of your actions. SimCity 2000 adds even more striking and dynamic graphics and animations to the simulation, and includes music and sound to augment your experience.

In this book, you'll get complete instructions for using SimCity 2000—the DOS and Windows PC versions and the Mac version. You'll also get loads of insider tips, winning strategies, and *Easter eggs*—special undocumented features included in the program that, if you can find them, contain surprises for the user.

SimCity 2000 Strategies and Secrets contains step-by-step instructions wherever necessary and is full of graphics and figures that show you just what to look for as you play SimCity 2000.

HOW THIS BOOK IS ORGANIZED

The book is divided into three parts.

- Part One, "The Big Picture," will orient you to SimCity 2000, describing the game and walking you through beginning a sample simulation, explaining your role, and telling you about the windows, menus, and tools you have at your disposal as you play.

- Part Two, "Techniques and Strategies for Building a SimCity," will take you through all the parts of a city, further explaining techniques for using the tools and providing in-depth strategies, tips, and tricks for making the most of your resources as you play.

- Part Three, "Winning the Model Scenarios," will walk you through winning strategies for each of the five model scenarios included with SimCity 2000.
- Part Four, "Advanced SimCity 2000," will show you how to use the Terrain toolbar to create or modify a landmass, how to create your own cities from scratch, how to hack the program by modifying the files, how to import and export SimCities, and how and where to trade SimCity 2000 know-how online (especially on the Internet).

In addition, an appendix at the end of the book will tell you how to install SimCity 2000 on a PC (DOS or Windows) or on a Mac.

CONVENTIONS USED IN THIS BOOK

SimCity 2000 Strategies and Secrets uses various conventions to help you find the information you need quickly and effortlessly.

SimCity 2000 Strategies and Secrets is meant to be a companion to the program. If you've never played the game, you'll be introduced to it through easy, clear descriptions. If you're already familiar with SimCity 2000 or SimCity Classic, you'll get new ideas, tips, and secrets to push your city up over the edge and help you win those scenarios.

Whatever your goal as SimMayor, you'll find a wealth of information in *SimCity 2000 Strategies and Secrets*.

Tips, Notes, and Warnings, as shown here, are boxed and placed strategically so you can find important information in a snap.

T I P

Here you'll find insider tips, short strategies, and information provided to help you use SimCity 2000 adeptly.

N O T E

Here you'll find reminders, bits of important information that should be emphasized, and references to other parts of the book.

W A R N I N G

Here, you'll find cautionary information about trouble spots you may encounter either in playing the game or in the program itself.

HERE'S WHERE YOU'LL FIND THE "EASTER EGGS," LONGER TIPS, AND SPECIAL EXPLANATIONS

In these boxed doohickeys, you'll find the "Easter eggs"—undocumented tricks that will net you quick cash or let you in on an inside joke (or an actual joke). The Easter egg icon you see here marks that sort of boxed text.

You'll also find boxed text *without* the Easter Egg icon. These boxes contain longer tips and strategies and special explanations about the game's background or features.

A CHAT WITH WILL WRIGHT

As the first edition of this book was going to print, we had the good fortune of talking with Will Wright. Among his comments, he said that Fred Haslam and he designed SimCity 2000 and created the Mac version, and that the Maxis team ported the game to DOS. Summarized here are Will Wright's comments:

- Most of the time spent in developing the game involved redoing the model, which was rewritten from scratch.

- Development was done on a Mac. The original SimCity was written in machine code for a Commodore C64 (8-bit) in 1986. Maxis published a second-generation (16-bit) SimCity in 1989. SimCity 2000 is a 32-bit application.

- The scenarios were done by Don Walters. To do this, first topographical and zoning maps were acquired for the cities. Then, using the Terrain editor, land was mapped for each one. A special version of SimCity 2000 was used to zone and build the city according to the scenarios' requirements. Finally, each scenario was fine-tuned to make it playable.

- Political and environmental factors are taken into account when designing a Maxis game, but game playability outweighs other factors. Accuracy is sometimes sacrificed for playability.

- The limit of 150 microsimulations was imposed so the game would run on 4-MB machines. (Microsimulations take up a lot of memory.)

- Version 1.1 gets over the previous population limit by using the average population of all arcos that have microsimulators as the population for arcos that do not have microsimulators.

- The llama was chosen by Maxis employees as the Maxis mascot.

- Maxis is planning to support other platforms: Amiga and OS/2 in the near future.

- Maxis is also looking into creating a SimCity toolkit, but the product is not yet firm enough to talk about its contents.

- Other follow-up projects include SimWorld—where you can take a city created by SimCity 2000 and look around in it. Another will allow you to (virtually) walk around a SimCity. Will's working on that one.

ONE MORE THING...

As the Easter eggs and cheats become commonly known, Maxis changes them. If you have 1.1 and your pal has 1.0, they might include different cheats. In our conversation with Will Wright, we learned a new one for the Mac version 1.1: First, display the Map window. Type **pirn**. Then click on the Info box. Type **topsguzzardo**. You'll find your coffers lined with cool cash.

Typing **ardo** alone after this will get you even more cash.

By the way, Will himself does not know the megacheat in the DOS 1.0 or 1.1 version. He said he saw it once, but it was too involved to remember.

CONTACTING THE AUTHORS

If you'd like to contact us, you can either post a message on Sybex's CompuServe forum or send Internet e-mail to simcity@sybex.com.

PART ONE

THE BIG PICTURE

CHAPTER ONE

GETTING TO KNOW YOUR VIRTUAL WORLD

SIMCITY 2000 IS AN URBAN PLANNING and simulation game that makes you the mayor of a simulated city. You can create your own city, or you can use one of the sample cities provided. Either way, your city will have the same needs, potential for growth, and increasingly sophisticated urban structure as a real city. Your challenge will be to make your growing city a place where *Sims* (the citizens of a SimCity) can be safe and prosperous.

> **NOTE**
>
> **Our goal here is to get you playing. If you already have SimCity or SimCity 2000 experience, you may want to skim this chapter for tips, then move on to later chapters.**

In this chapter, you'll get a quick look at a SimCity 2000 simulation, or "game." We'll run a sample simulation—we'll create and develop a small city—so you can see just what SimCity 2000 is and how it works. In later chapters, we'll go into the more involved aspects of SimCity management.

WHAT IS SIMCITY 2000?

SimCity 2000 allows you to plan and build a simulated city, and, as time goes on, watch it grow and develop or fall into disuse. There are many variables for you to control in SimCity 2000. The simulation uses more than one hundred rules to govern the interaction of various parts of the city as you create it. The unemployment rate—determined by the jobs available compared to the number of residents—affects property values. Property values, in turn, affect the population level, which, in turn, affects industry and, again, the unemployment rate. By using a large set of relations—everything from traffic and pollution to employment and land value—SimCity 2000 creates a realistic model of urban life.

SimCity 2000 was preceded by SimCity (now called SimCity Classic), which was developed by Will Wright and Fred Haslam and became the flagship game of the Maxis line. SimCity 2000 incorporates four years' worth of suggestions from users of the original SimCity, which was a best-seller in its own right.

SimCity 2000 comes in three versions:

- The DOS (PC) version
- The Windows version
- The Mac version

Almost everything you do in SimCity 2000 is the same, whether you're using the DOS, Windows, or Mac version. Two exceptions are installing SimCity 2000 and starting the program. (Most of the other differences are merely cosmetic—for example, the floating info box in the DOS and Mac versions of the game has become a status bar at the bottom of the screen in the Windows version.)

> ### N O T E
>
> **The appendix at the back of this book describes installing SimCity 2000 on a Mac and on a DOS or Windows PC.**

STARTING SIMCITY 2000

You'll start SimCity 2000 slightly differently depending on which version you have.

ON A DOS PC

Assuming you've installed SimCity 2000 in the default directory on your hard drive, at the DOS (C:) prompt type **cd \sc2000** and press ↵, then type **sc2000** and press ↵ again. The Maxis logo will appear for a moment, followed by a dialog box showing the version number of the program and to whom the software is registered (presumably you). To clear this message and continue, click anywhere within the dialog box (Figure 1.1).

Next, the SimCity 2000 opening menu appears, also shown in Figure 1.1.

ON A WINDOWS PC

When you installed SimCity 2000 for Windows on your computer, a group in Program Manager was created and named *Maxis*. In this group you'll find an icon for SimCity 2000.

To start SimCity 2000 for Windows, just double-click on that icon.

SimCity 2000
for Windows

This copy of SimCity 2000 is the
exclusive registered property of:

Brenda Kienan

Tauber & Kienan

FIGURE 1.1   *Click anywhere on the registration dialog box (left) and you'll see the Sim-City 2000 opening menu (right).*

ON A MAC

If you have a Macintosh computer, open the folder into which you installed SimCity 2000 (if you installed according to the instructions in Appendix A of this book, that folder will be called "SimCity 2000"). Double-click on the SimCity 2000 icon.

The Maxis logo will appear, followed by the registration dialog box and the SimCity 2000 opening menu.

> **NOTE**
>
> **The Maxis logo screen, registration dialog box, and opening menu will all look the same in the DOS, Windows, and Mac versions.**

START A NEW GAME BY STARTING A NEW CITY

Let's run through a quick sample simulation to show you around SimCity 2000.

THE OPENING MENU

In SimCity 2000 for the DOS PC or for the Mac, the opening menu gives you five options as shown in Figure 1.1. In our sample, we want to create a city from the ground up, so click on the Start New City button.

A message appears indicating that SimCity 2000 is creating a landmass. (In the Windows version, the dialog box message reads "Terrain Generation.") The landmass that appears is randomly generated, with a mix of hilly and level terrain; streams, lakes, or rivers; and other geographic attributes. In Chapter 22 we show you how to use the Terrain toolbar to modify the land as you prefer and to specify the percentage of hills, water, and trees to be included in the terrain that's generated, but for now, we are going to use the land just as it was created.

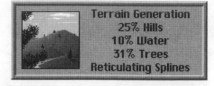

Terrain Generation
25% Hills
10% Water
31% Trees
Reticulating Splines

Once land is created, a message box appears (Figure 1.2) asking for the name of the new city and other basic information—like the level of difficulty and the starting year.

> **NOTE**
>
> The model scenarios are covered in Part Three of this book. Each model scenario presents a developed city that has some challenge built into it. Check out the material in Part Three—you'll find strategies for "winning" the model scenarios *and* tips for meeting the challenges presented in creating and managing your own city.

NAME THE CITY

First, the city must be named. Click on the text box that contains the phrase "New City." "New City" will be highlighted; just type a new name over it. We named our city Puyallup (pronounced "Pile-up").

> **NOTE**
>
> If you'd like, you can follow along on your machine as we play out this game. If you do, keep in mind that your results will differ from ours because the landmass you are dealt will be quite different from the one we used in this chapter.

SELECT A LEVEL OF DIFFICULTY

As we'll discuss in a minute, a very important aspect of managing your city is setting up and maintaining the budget. It stands to reason, then, that the most visible difference between levels of difficulty is how much money is available as you begin the game. There are three levels of difficulty from which you can choose:

Easy	$20,000
Medium	$10,000
Hard	$10,000 bond (debt)

FIGURE 1.2 *Type in a name for the new city and choose your level of play.*

For our sample, we'll select Easy. That'll give us enough money to get our new city up and thriving.

SELECT THE YEAR

Now you can select the year in which your simulation will begin. Again, this affects your level of challenge, because certain technologies—such as nuclear fusion—become available only in later years. These more advanced technologies take a bigger bite out of your budget, so it's easier to get your city going if you start in an earlier era.

Choose 1900 as the starting year. This will give you a chance to accumulate money before expensive new developments—like subways and alternative energy sources—start to appear.

After you've entered a name for the city, selected Easy as the game level, and chosen 1900 as the game's starting year, click the Done button to start the game. A newspaper will flash onto your screen (Figure 1.3), heralding the founding of your city.

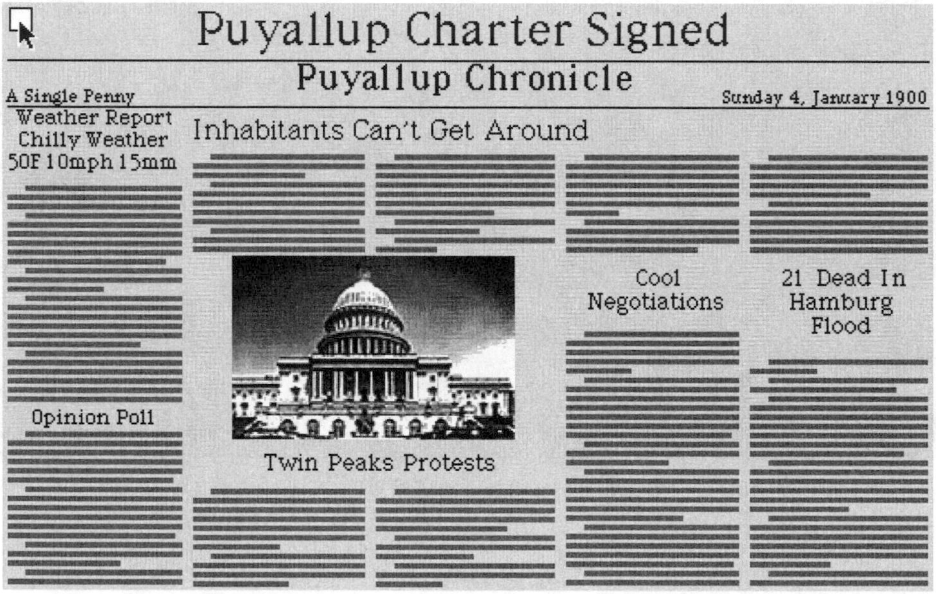

Puyallup Charter Signed
Puyallup Chronicle

A Single Penny   Sunday 4, January 1900

Weather Report
Chilly Weather
50F 10mph 15mm

Inhabitants Can't Get Around

Cool
Negotiations

21 Dead In
Hamburg
Flood

Opinion Poll

Twin Peaks Protests

FIGURE 1.3   *The Puyallup Chronicle*

WHAT'S THE NEWS?

SimCity 2000 newspapers play an important role in keeping you informed. The headlines will tell you directly how you're doing as mayor (in the form of opinion and popularity polls) and what sorts of problems the Sims in your city are

> **TIP**
>
> Newspapers in SimCity 2000 take the place of the opinion polls in SimCity Classic. Watch the newspaper for repeating stories to see which issues are affecting your Sims the most.

experiencing. Opinion and popularity polls appear in the lower-left corner of the paper, while other news is scattered about the page. To read any story, click on its headline.

You can have newspapers delivered on screen regularly, only when something special happens, or never. If you don't want to be disturbed by the newspaper, pull down the Newspaper menu and deselect all the options (click on them until they all have *no* check marks). If you have turned off the newspaper but want to see what is in the latest issue, pull down the Newspaper menu and select a particular newspaper. (The number of different newspapers published in your city will depend on the size of your city. You'll often find some combination of the *Chronicle,* the *Herald,* the *Times,* and the *Picayune* available at the beginning of a simulation.)

> **N O T E**
>
> If you are playing SimCity 2000 on a Mac and your papers "go on strike," the problem is not with your SimPublishers or SimUnion. Your machine is out of memory. As the city grows larger, the program uses more memory. Saving your city and restarting the game should help.

To close the paper when you're finished reading it, in the DOS or Mac version, click on the close box; in the Windows version, click on the OK button. (Either the close box or the OK button will appear in the paper's upper-left corner. In Figure 1.3, the cursor is shown on the close box.) An unobstructed view of your landmass will fill the window.

> **N O T E**
>
> In the Windows game the terrain takes up the entire game window, but in the DOS and Mac versions the landmass first appears in a small window in the center of your screen. It's a lot easier to see what's happening if you maximize that window so it fills the whole computer screen. If you want to follow along step-by-step, click on the zoom box in the upper-right corner of your screen to maximize the on-screen display of your landmass so it matches our illustration.

LOOKING AT THE LAND SURFACE

You'll build your city on a landmass with some combination of level terrain, hills, trees, and water (rivers, lakes, and sea coast). Take a look at Figure 1.4 to get familiar with different aspects of the screen display and how you use them when playing SimCity 2000.

FINDING A LOCATION

Cities do well on large, flat areas of land near a water supply. Pull down the Speed menu at the top of your screen, select Pause, and take a minute to look around your landmass for an appropriate location.

> ### N O T E
>
> **You can play the landmass you've been dealt, or you can alter it to make it easier or more challenging. In Chapter 22, you'll learn to control or change the features of a landmass.**

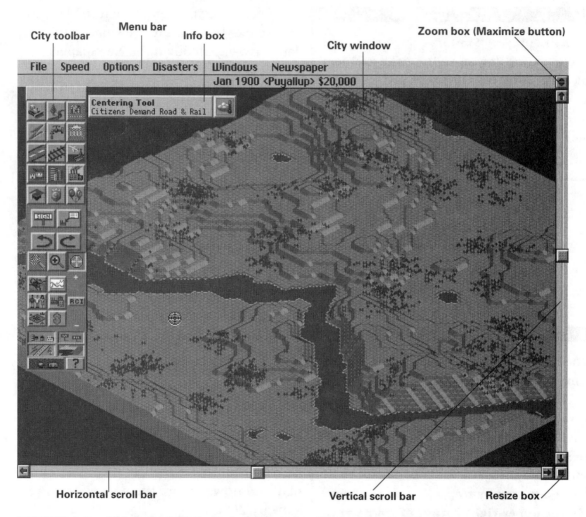

FIGURE 1.4   *This is the DOS version's main window. The basic parts of the main window in the Windows and Mac versions are very similar to what you see here. One difference, though, is that the Info box that appears in the DOS/Mac versions is instead a status bar at the bottom of the screen in the Windows version.*

ZONING AND BUILDING YOUR CITY

As an urban planner and mayor, your goal is to plan and build a thriving city. This will involve zoning and building. You'll zone areas for industrial, residential, and commercial use, and, if you've zoned wisely, you'll soon see industrious Sims live, work, and do business in those areas. The Sims will, at various times, need and ask for such civic services as police protection, fire protection, hospitals, and schools. (You can anticipate these needs and build the facilities before they're demanded if you like.) You can build these structures where you want, but remembering your goal of a thriving SimCity, you should place them where they'll do the most good.

> **NOTE**
>
> In the DOS and Mac versions there's an Info box in the upper-left portion of your screen, just above your view of the landmass. At the beginning of the simulation, you should see a message there saying that a power plant is needed. You might see a message instead that says the Sims demand road and rail. Go for the power plant first. In the Windows version you'll see the same information displayed in the status bar along the bottom of the main window.

The first structure you'll need to supply your city with—before you do anything else, in fact—is a power plant. Pull down the Speed menu again and select Turtle, the slowest speed, to begin.

BUILDING A POWER PLANT

Immediately after the newspaper announcing your new city's founding, you'll need a power plant (Figure 1.5).You are still in the early 1900s, so your choice of power plants is limited to:

- Coal
- HydroElectric
- Oil

FIGURE 1.5   *Before you zone or build, you'll need power.*

Later, sophisticated alternatives like solar power, nuclear power, and fusion will be developed and announced in the newspaper.

Selecting a Power Plant

To select a power plant, follow these steps:

1. Click and hold down the mouse button with the pointer on the City toolbar's Power icon.

> **N O T E**
>
> **You'll build other civic structures in the same basic way you build a power plant.**

2. A menu will appear listing the two items related to power you can build at this time.

3. Hold down the mouse button and pull the pointer down to the Power Plant icon until it looks indented. Then release the mouse button. You will see the Select Powerplant window, showing the types of power plants available now.

Given the time period and the resources available, you will have the most success now with a Coal power plant. It's dirty, but it's relatively cheap for what it puts out, and it'll last 50 years—until more alternatives become available.

> **N O T E**
>
> **Click on the Info button above each plant to see important information describing that plant's capacity, durability, and potential for creating pollution. Consider this, along with the cost of the plant, when you choose the plant that best suits your purposes.**

4. Click on the type of plant you wish to build. The mouse pointer will turn into a little lightning bolt, and if you drag it around your landmass, you'll see a large dark shadow falling under the pointer. The shadow indicates the size of the power plant: 4×4 tiles. *Don't click anywhere just yet.*

Having indicated *what* you want to build—a power plant—you must now decide *where* you want to build it.

Placing the Power Plant

> **T I P**
>
> **Although you cannot build a power plant on the edge of your landmass, you can place it very near the edge. Building the plant at the edge reduces the impact the plant's pollution will have on your Sims.**

Your power plant should be relatively near, but not in the very center of, the largest flat area available—the area you've chosen for your city. (Your city should also be near a water supply, but you don't want to pollute the water, so don't put the power plant next to the water.)

To place the power plant:

1. Move the mouse pointer until the shadowed area falls where you want to place the plant (Figure 1.6).

2. Click once and the power plant will appear, as shown in the close-up in Figure 1.7.

FIGURE 1.6 *Place your power plant at the edge of a large, flat area, near but not right next to a water supply.*

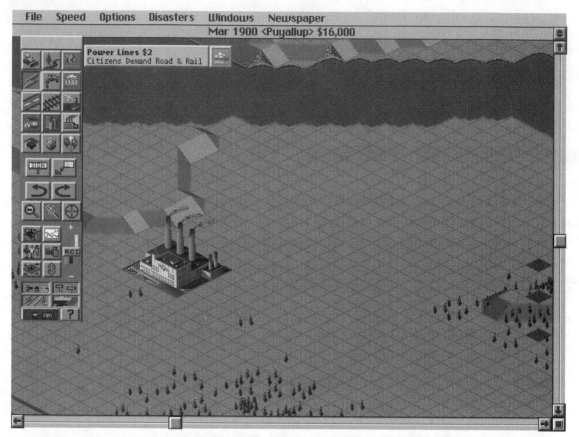

FIGURE 1.7   *To see a close-up of your power plant after you place it, click twice on the Zoom In tool's icon (the magnifying glass with the + sign in it).*

Your power plant will provide spark to your city. Soon you'll zone industrial and residential areas, build some roads, and watch your city grow. But first, a word about the budget. If you're following along, pull down Speed again and select Pause.

MINDING THE MONEY

The city budget is a major factor in building a successful SimCity. We'll go into detail about budget strategies and the Budget window in Chapter 7. Right now, we want to get your city going, so let's just take a quick look at the Budget window.

NOTHING LASTS FOREVER

To illustrate the basic workings of development in SimCity 2000, we'll give you a peek at the future of your city: power plants last a finite number of years, then they fail and must be rebuilt. Assuming you have enough money to cover the cost and that you have disasters disabled as we do in this chapter, SimCity 2000 will automatically rebuild your power plant with one of the same type when it fails. As your power plant nears its death, the newspapers will warn you. You can either let the plant die and be replaced or take the initiative to replace it yourself. By then your city will have become somewhat developed, so you'll probably want to move the thing anyway. You can select and build a new plant that's more powerful, or cleaner, or both, in a location that's better suited for further development. To do this, use the same techniques you used to select and build your first power plant. Once you've built the new plant, you can bulldoze the old one and zone the land for some other use. Clearing an existing structure like a power plant is covered in Chapter 3. More details on power plants can be found in Chapter 4.

On the menu bar, pull down the Windows menu and select Budget. The Budget window, shown in Figure 1.8, will appear.

Note that each budget category has a default percentage of 100%. This does not mean that 100% of the city's financial pie goes to each budget category, but rather that you are funding each budget category to 100% of its own maximum.

Your city doesn't need or have a lot of services or much of an infrastructure yet. You could, if you wanted to, adjust the funding levels shown in the Budget window. (Not too much—if you underfund roads, for example, you'll soon see potholes around town.) But the simulator does not deduct costs for services that don't exist, so there's no point in fidgeting now.

In addition to setting funding levels in the Budget window, you can pass your own city laws. Click on the book to the far right of the City Ordinances line, and in the window that appears (Figure 1.9), click on the

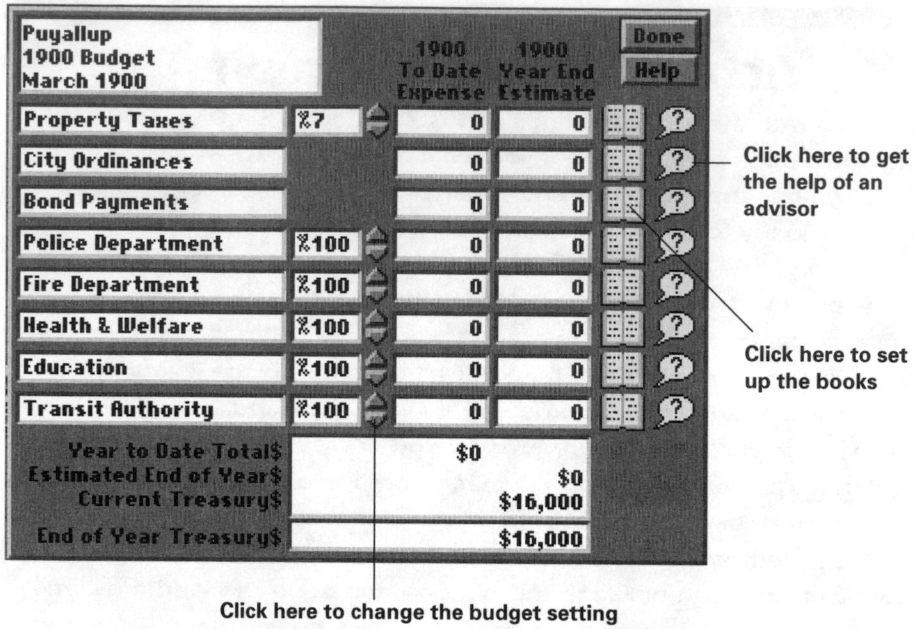

Puyallup 1900 Budget March 1900			1900 To Date Expense	1900 Year End Estimate		Done / Help
Property Taxes	%7	⇅	0	0	▦	⑦
City Ordinances			0	0	▦	⑦
Bond Payments			0	0	▦	⑦
Police Department	%100	⇅	0	0	▦	⑦
Fire Department	%100	⇅	0	0	▦	⑦
Health & Welfare	%100	⇅	0	0	▦	⑦
Education	%100	⇅	0	0	▦	⑦
Transit Authority	%100	⇅	0	0	▦	⑦

Year to Date Total$	$0
Estimated End of Year$	$0
Current Treasury$	$16,000
End of Year Treasury$	$16,000

Click here to get the help of an advisor

Click here to set up the books

Click here to change the budget setting

FIGURE 1.8   *The Budget window*

check boxes for Neighborhood Watch and Volunteer Fire Dept. This will compel SimVolunteers to provide these services to your small city at a very small cost to your budget. Now click the Done button, and the Budget window will reappear.

In a moment, when you turn up the speed and resume the game, you'll see an annual profit indicated in the Budget window's Estimated End of Year $ line. If you had passed more ordinances and made changes to funding levels, you'd see the financial results of those changes reflected here as well. As it is, only a small amount for road maintenance and for the volunteer services you implemented will be deducted from your budget. You're in the black, and as long as you don't overexpand, your money will increase every year. Click the Done button to close the Budget window.

The Budget window will reappear on your screen every January for annual review. To keep it from distracting you for a while, pull down the Options menu and select Auto-Budget.

Finance			Safety & Health		
1% Sales Tax			Volunteer Fire Dept.	✓	0
1% Income Tax			Public Smoking Ban		
Legalized Gambling			Free Clinics		
Parking Fines			Junior Sports		

Education			Promotional		
Pro-Reading Campaign			Tourist Advertising		
Anti-Drug Campaign			Business Advertising		
CPR Training			City Beautification		
Neighborhood Watch	✓	0	Annual Carnival		

Other			Estimated Annual Cost	
Energy Conservation			Finance	0
Nuclear Free Zone			Safety & Health	0
Homeless Shelters			Education	0
Pollution Controls			Promotional	0
			Other	0

Done		YTD Total$	0	EST Total$	0

FIGURE 1.9 *Click on the check boxes for Volunteer Fire Dept. and Neighborhood Watch to provide these services to your small community.*

LOOKING INTO YOUR POWER PLANT

You can find out more about an individual structure, like your power plant (or a citywide system, once you have systems), using the Query

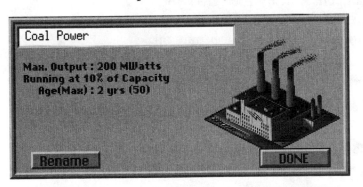

Coal Power

Max. Output : 200 MWatts
Running at 10% of Capacity
Age(Max) : 2 yrs (50)

Rename   DONE

tool. The easiest way to use the Query tool, which we describe in detail in Chapter 4, is to hold down Shift and then click with the mouse pointer on whatever you want to investigate. When you do this on a Coal power plant, you'll see an info box containing various statistics that will help you to know in detail what's going on down in the streets of your SimCity. When you're finished looking over your power plant's statistics, click anywhere in the info box to close it.

MICROSIMULATIONS: CITYWIDE STATISTICS VS. INDIVIDUAL STATISTICS

Some items in SimCity 2000—power plants, schools, and the like—produce statistics for the individual item, while others—libraries, bus depots, etc.—provide statistics for the citywide system.

This is because, in addition to the big simulator that creates your perception of the whole city, the program includes a number of microsimulators that allow smaller simulations to take place. You'll see evidence of the microsimulations in the form of statistics for individual items, for example. The program's ability to create microsimulations is limited, though, so the game is limited to including 150 microsimulations at any given time. The designers of SimCity 2000 grouped some items together into citywide systems to reduce the number of microsimulations necessary. (More on this in later chapters.)

When your city exceeds 150 microsimulations, SimCity 2000 stops reporting individual statistics about new items that you build.

A WORD ON DISASTERS

In SimCity 2000, as in life, disasters happen. SimCity 2000 gives you floods, fires, earthquakes, and even monsters. When you're up for a challenge, overcoming them is part of the fun. For now, let's concentrate on building a city without unexpected interruptions. From the menu bar, pull down Disasters and select No Disasters. Then pull down Speed and select Turtle again to resume the game.

ZONING INDUSTRIAL AND RESIDENTIAL AREAS

SimCitizens must have jobs and homes. At first, the economy will be industrial; later it will move toward commercial. Right now, though, you'll have to provide an industrial zone in which the Sims can work.

In the City toolbar, click on the Industrial Zone icon and hold down the mouse button. A menu will appear, allowing you to choose Light Industry or Dense Industry. Pull the pointer to Light Industry on the menu and release the mouse button.

The mouse pointer will be shaped like a tiny factory. Move to an area along the edge of the power plant, and click and drag an area three tiles deep and six tiles long (see Figure 1.10). Watch the cost of zoning this area mount as you click and drag. Note, too, that the cost is being deducted from the total funds available to you, as shown at the top of your screen. When you're finished, let up on the mouse button. Small yellow dots will appear on the tiles you zoned to indicate that they are zoned for Light Industry.

> **N O T E**
>
> A basic principle for building a successful SimCity is to start small and build to denser populations.

Now add some housing for your SimCitizens. Select the Residential Zone icon and hold the mouse button down. A menu will appear, allowing you to choose Light Residential or Dense Residential. Pull the pointer to Light Residential on the menu and release the mouse button.

The mouse pointer will be shaped like a little house this time. Leaving a one-tile strip (for a road) in between, click and drag to zone a 3×6 residential area (Figure 1.11). Small green dots will appear on the tiles to indicate that they're zoned Light Residential.

> **N O T E**
>
> SimCitizens simply will not walk more than three tiles. When you're planning zoned areas, you can take advantage of this by making them a maximum of three tiles deep—or six deep if you have a road on each side of the six-tile-deep area.

LAYING DOWN A ROAD

Having created zones in which your Sims can work and live, you now need to provide a way for them to get from one place to another. Roads are cheap to build, and at this stage they offer the advantage of simplicity. (Later, you'll want to build rail and subways, perhaps even highways, to carry your Sims.)

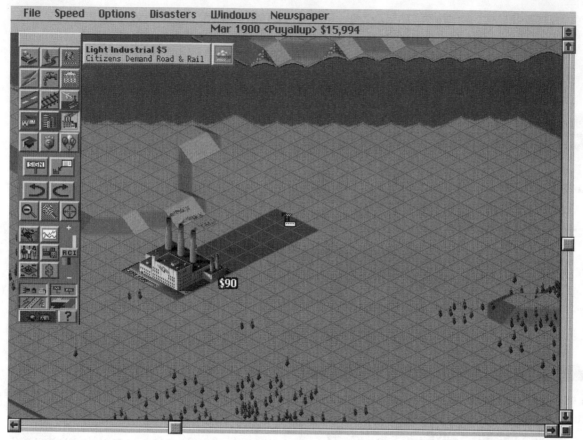

FIGURE 1.10 *Click and drag an industrial zone into place next to the power plant. (It's going to cost you 90 bucks.)*

To build a road between your industrial and residential zones, click on the Road tool in the City toolbar and hold the mouse button down. The menu that appears this time will allow you to choose from several types of transportation (more on this in later chapters). Pull the pointer to Road on the menu and let up on the mouse button.

The mouse pointer will be shaped like a piece of roadway. Move to one end of the one-tile-wide strip between your residential zone and industrial zone, click, and drag to the other end. A road will appear.

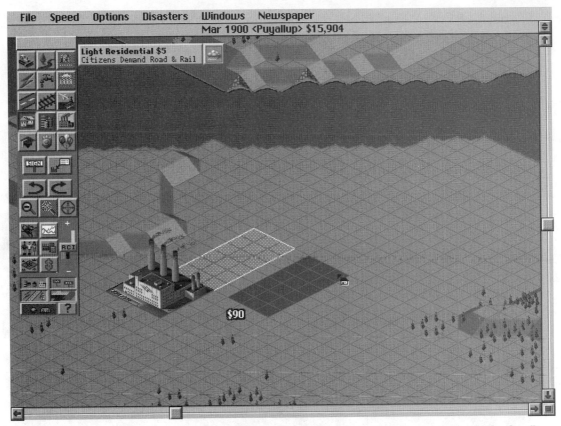

FIGURE 1.11 *Click and drag a residential zone into place. This will cost you another 90 bucks. (It cost us a dollar on top of that because we made a mistake and had to demolish/clear one tile at a cost of $1. You can see at the top of the screen that we're down to $15,904 total available funds.)*

PLACING A POWER LINE

The industrial area next to your power plant gets power just because it's next to a powered area (the power plant itself), but the residential area doesn't have any power. No power, no building. No building, no place for Sims to live. You need to place one power line spanning the road to make a power connection to the residential area.

To do this, click on the Power tool icon (the one with the little lightning bolt on it) just as you did to select your power plant. This time, from the menu that appears, select Power Lines. (Check the Info box to make sure that's what you've selected.) Then move the mouse pointer to a roadway tile and click once. A tiny power line will appear. Until power is transmitted, you'll see it flashing with a yellow and red lightning bolt (Figure 1.12).

The power line will soon stop flashing, and in a few seconds you'll see industries and homes being built. Then cars will appear on the roadway, carrying SimCitizens to and from work and home (Figure 1.13).

SAVING YOUR CITY FOR THE FUTURE

You can save the city you've set up by pulling down the File menu and selecting Save City. Your city will be saved, and a small window will appear with the file name, as shown here.

Game Saved As:
PUYALLUP.SC2

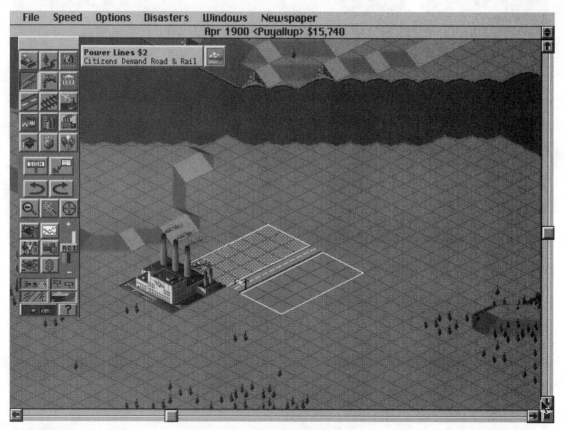

FIGURE 1.12 *A very small town is laid out for the Sims.*

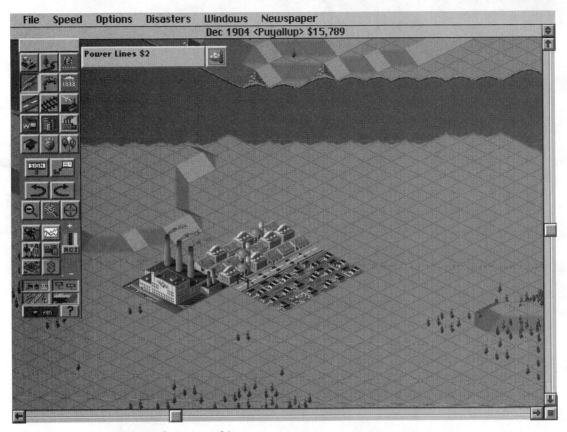

FIGURE 1.13 *The Sims have moved in.*

Click on the window, and your city will be available to you in the future, exactly as it is now.

MOVING ALONG

As you go on, you'll want to balance the city's needs by providing the right zoning and services and by keeping a good, sound budget so you can do those things. In the rest of this book, you'll find detailed information about all the elements of successful urban planning with SimCity 2000.

CHAPTER TWO

YOU'RE THE MAYOR

AS MAYOR, YOU'LL ENGINEER AND manage a city that may grow into a huge megalopolis or wind up a ghost town. The city is all yours, and because there is no opponent and no specific end result to achieve, *you* set the agenda for winning. You can increase your city's size without regard to the environment, or you can try to find ways to maintain a city without creating excess pollution. You decide whether to build a cheap (but dirty) coal-burning power plant or to splurge on a cleaner gas one. You decide whether your Sims will have colleges, museums, parks, and a stadium or whether they can live with less. (The Sims, on the other hand, decide if they want to live in your city or not—they'll move out if they don't like the way things are going.)

WHAT YOU'RE RESPONSIBLE FOR

As mayor, you have two main responsibilities:

- To guide the development of your city
- To respond to disasters and urban problems

> **NOTE**
>
> **You'll find out the best ways to respond to disasters in Part Two of this book, where we talk strategies, and in Part Three, where we describe ways to win the model scenarios.**

Of course, you also have to watch the budget, keep the Sims happy, *and* have a good time yourself. That's part of being a civic leader.

PLANNING

Your most fundamental city-management task is to plan development. That's what you're doing when you zone areas as residential, industrial, or commercial and when you place civic services like police stations and hospitals. In Chapter 1, we covered the basics of how to zone and build. You can use the same methods for zoning and building all the parts that make up your SimCity.

> **NOTE**
>
> **In Part Two, we'll go into detail about the types of zones and how they work.**

CITY INFRASTRUCTURE

As mayor, you must provide for the city's *infrastructure*: the roads, power lines, water supply, and so on—all the stuff that makes up the city. The infrastructure grows as your city's needs grow. For example, when you start your city, you won't have to worry about water; just power, a road, and some basic zoning will do. But as soon as your city reaches a certain size—and not a very large one at that—a message will appear in the Info box in the upper-left portion of your screen (or in the status bar if you are playing the Windows version), alerting you to the city's need for water. To provide water, you'll place pumps near a water supply (river or ocean) and lay pipes to your city. (More on this in Chapter 9.)

CITY SERVICES

Sooner or later, your citizens will demand services: fire and police protection, hospitals, and schools, for example. As your city grows, the Sims will want more and more services. If crime rises to an uncomfortable level, they'll demand prisons. Messages describing which services they want will appear ("Citizens Demand Hospitals" is common), and the newspapers that flash on your screen periodically will report on what services the Sims want you to provide. (You can also anticipate the wishes of your Sims and give them the services you think they'll want before they demand them.) Sims like the good life, and the more services you provide, the more Sim-Citizens your city will have.

> **TIP**
>
> **Services cost money. Keep an eye on your budget and add services only as they're warranted.**

Remember, though, that conceding to the wishes of the citizens is not always what's best—for them or for you. One SimCity 2000 user tells the real-life story of his grandfather, who was elected mayor of a small city on the promise that he'd have Main Street paved, then ousted from office for raising taxes to pay for the paving.

THE HEALTH, HAPPINESS, AND PROSPERITY OF YOUR PEOPLE

As mayor, your job is to ensure the well-being of your citizens. Your citizens will thrive in a balanced setting where they can work, live, shop, and get around. They'll behave in all the ways anyone would—preferring to drive rather than take the train, tending to move out of town if unemployment goes up too high, wanting more police in high-crime industrial neighborhoods, and so on.

In SimCity 2000, commerce, crime, pollution, education, and employment are all interrelated. When you zone industrial zones to create employment, you also increase pollution. When you build large residential areas without providing enough industrial zoning, employment goes down and the crime rate goes up. Your challenge is to strike the right mix so your Sims will be healthy, happy, and productive.

YOUR CITY'S BASIC NEEDS

As mayor, you must use the tools available to you to balance the needs of your citizens with the resources you have available. The program calculates internally such factors as city growth, population density, crime, pollution, traffic levels, tax revenues, land value, and the city's economy. Through your actions in zoning and building, you affect the balance of these factors both directly and indirectly. You also have control over factors like the budget, city services, tax rates, transportation, and the generation and transmission of power. You can encourage some kinds of industry in your city and discourage others. You have influence over land value, pollution, and the health and prosperity of your citizens. You have no control over factors like the external economy and the occurrence, location, and intensity of disasters (unless, of course, you turn off the disasters option).

As we've said before, simply responding to every request of your Sims is no guarantee that you will "win," but if you ignore your citizens' demands altogether, you are sure to get bounced out of office.

THE CRY OF THE DEPRIVED (OR IS IT DEPRAVED?)

In the DOS and Mac versions, if you have sound capability, type **porn** and you'll hear a groaning voice say, "Can't get *enough*!" We hear it's the voice of another of those fun-loving Maxis employees just goofing off.

ZONING

It is important that you build your city with a balanced mix of industrial, residential, and commercial zones. This will allow your city to prosper and your citizens to thrive. Zoning property does not ensure that the property will be used. It merely means you have designated the property for that purpose. The property has *potential*, not actual value. The property gains value as industry, Sims, or commerce move in—and this is exactly what you want. Sims are important to your city. They form the work force, they pay property taxes, and they vote. (Without their votes, in the form of the approval ratings you see in the newspapers, your city will fail and you'll be out of office.)

> ### TIP
>
> While there is no hard rule for the best proportion of industrial to residential zones, maintaining a ratio a bit higher than 1:1 will help your city develop, especially in its early years.
>
> Remember, too, that land will develop fastest when you mix zones. Sims prefer to live near where they work and shop.

POWER

Power is necessary to spark and maintain the growth of zoned areas. Without power, a neighborhood or industrial area will decline. Power can become interrupted or terminated by disasters, accidental bulldozing, or the death of your power plant. You should fix damaged power lines immediately, and in some cases you may want to duplicate power lines as a kind of insurance (though unnecessarily long or redundant power lines are inefficient and will in themselves cause power shortages).

Your power plant will not last forever (see Chapters 1 and 4), and without power your city will be a wasteland, so keep an eye on the life and output of your power plant and maintain your power lines.

TRANSPORTATION

In SimCity 2000, rail and other forms of public transit create less pollution. Sims love to drive, however, and roads are cheap to build and maintain. But watch out: roads can fill to capacity quickly.

> **TIP**
>
> One user has suggested building two identical cities on the same landmass, one using mainly public transit and the other using mainly roads, then watching the two cities develop. This will quickly show you the effects of your transportation choices.

It is critical to the success of your city that transportation be appropriately placed. The Sims must be able to travel from home to work or commerce (shopping and business), from commerce to home or work, and from work to home. If the distance from one of these areas to another is too great, the Sims will not go there and the transportation route, along with the too-distant area, will go into decline or simply never develop at all.

POLLUTION

Pollution has an adverse effect on land values, the quality of your citizens' lives, and other factors. Pollution is caused by industry, sea- and airports, certain power plants, congested traffic, and radioactivity released from damaged nuclear power plants.

Pollution can be controlled, as described in Chapter 15.

INDUSTRY, COMMERCE, AND EMPLOYMENT

As mentioned previously, it is important to seek a balance between the industrial, residential, and commercial populations of your city (as represented by the amount and density of occupied areas zoned to be industrial, residential, and commercial). The jobs in your city are industrial and commercial. If you have an overabundance of industrial/commercial areas and not much in the way of residential areas, industry and commerce will fall off, decreasing the tax base. If you have too much residential and not enough industrial/commercial areas, unemployment will rise and commerce will fall further.

The number of Sims residing in your city is influenced by the birth rate, which is always positive; unemployment; land values; taxes; and the quality of life, as indicated by pollution, crime, the availability of services, and educational and recreational facilities. Industrial growth is affected by taxes, the presence of sea- and airports, and the external economy.

> **N O T E**
>
> **The external economy impacts SimCity 2000 in ways over which you have no control.**

Commercial development is influenced by industrial and residential development, taxes, and the overall growth of the city. At a certain level of growth, the city's economy will turn from industrial to commercial in nature.

CRIME

Crime tends to occur in denser industrial, commercial, and even residential areas. Unemployment and low land values also contribute to rising crime. Because land values near industrial areas are lower, crime flourishes there as well as in dense residential areas near industrial areas. Falling land values and rising crime rates are so intertwined that they feed on each other, sending your city into a downward spiral.

The best way to deal with crime is to prevent it by keeping land values up and placing police protection strategically in denser areas where crime flourishes.

LAND VALUES

Developing and maintaining land values is a crucial element of SimCity 2000. The desirability of land will encourage Sims to move in and will increase tax revenues, allowing you to develop the city further. Basically, in the same way lower land values inspire higher crime rates and

> **T I P**
>
> **To increase land values, build your city closer to forests, rivers, and the ocean, and provide plenty of educational and recreational facilities.**

ultimately put the city into a downward spiral, higher land values raise the quality of life and bring prosperity.

Land value will be increased especially through the presence of nearby educational and recreational facilities, trees, and bodies of water.

In general, your best bet for increasing land values is to plan zones wisely, maximizing usage and avoiding widespread unemployment.

WINNING SIMCITY 2000

SimCity 2000 is neither violent nor adversarial. To "win" the game, you set a goal for yourself and achieve it. Your goal might be high population, low pollution, a large cash reserve, extensive city services, or the encouragement of some kinds of industry over others. You may pursue some combination of these goals or something altogether different. You do have one obvious objective—to stay in the Mayor's office—but beyond this minimal requirement, you determine what type of city is a winning city. You can attempt to build Megalopolis or to maintain Smallsville. It's up to you.

When you play one of the five model scenarios included in SimCity 2000 and described in Part Three of this book, you will be addressing a predefined challenge. Your goal will be to overcome the problem built into that scenario within the allotted time. If you succeed, you win.

When you play a simulation that involves building a city from the foundation up, you will set the agenda, and you will make the big decisions that win or lose the challenge you've set.

In either case, you'll need a firm grounding in the various elements that make a SimCity what it is. In the next two chapters, we'll look at the gizmos available for you to work with in SimCity 2000. Then in Part Two, we'll look at the components of a SimCity.

CHAPTER THREE

GETTING AROUND IN SIMCITY 2000'S MENUS AND WINDOWS

NOW THAT YOU UNDERSTAND THE basic elements of a simple city, you'll need to learn how *you* interact with the SimCity 2000 simulator. In this chapter, we'll go over the ways you control SimCity 2000. We'll also tell you how to gain information about the status and history of your city. This current and historical information is vital and will help support you in making decisions as mayor (and chief city engineer).

THE MENUS

Once SimCity 2000 starts running, a menu bar appears across the top of the main screen (see Figures 3.1, 3.2, and 3.3).

To access choices on the menu bar, maneuver your mouse pointer to the choice you want and *click* (press the mouse button—the *left* one if you're using a mouse with multiple buttons). A drop-down menu will appear, listing various items depending on which menu you selected.

The menus in SimCity 2000's menu bar are as follows:

File	Commands that relate to your SimCity data file
Speed	Commands that change the speed at which time passes
Options	Commands that change options in the simulator
Disasters	Commands that allow or disallow disasters from occurring and with which you can force disasters
Windows	Commands that open and control different windows
Newspaper	Commands that allow or disallow the display of newspapers
Help (Windows version only)	Accesses the online Help available in the Windows version of the game

Later in this chapter, we'll cover each of these menus in turn and explain its options. (You can also control SimCity 2000 using tools on the City toolbar. See Chapter 4 for more on this.)

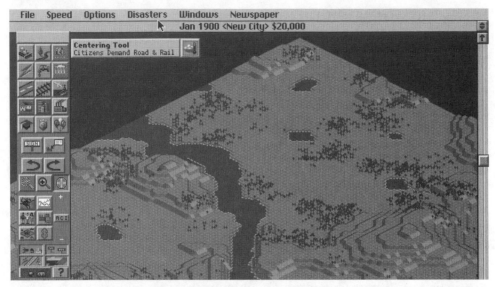

FIGURE 3.1   *The SimCity 2000 for DOS main screen*

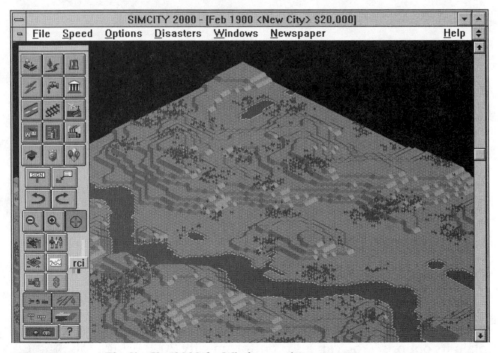

FIGURE 3.2   *The SimCity 2000 for Windows main screen*

FIGURE 3.3   *The SimCity 2000 for the Mac main screen*

FILE

The File menu holds commands that relate to your SimCity 2000 file. From this menu, you can create a new city, save your current city to a file, load a saved city, and more. The options on this menu are

Load City	Allows you to load a previously saved SimCity Classic or SimCity 2000 file into the simulator
New City	Generates a new land mass and allows you to start a new game on that land
Edit New Map	Lets you edit the terrain of your current city, create a randomly generated land mass, or create a land mass with the percentages of hills, water, and trees you've specified
Load Scenario	Loads one of the five predefined SimCity 2000 scenarios for you to play
Save City	Saves your current city to a disk file

Save City As   Saves your current city to a disk file, prompting you first for a new file name

Quit   Exits SimCity 2000

See Part Three to find out more about winning the model scenarios. Refer to Chapter 22 for information on changing a land mass with the Terrain toolbar.

SPEED

The Speed menu allows you to set the speed at which the simulation will run. When you start a new game, the speed is set to the default—Llama (the second-fastest setting). The speeds at which you can run the simulator are:

- Pause (stopped)
- Turtle (slow)
- Llama (medium)
- Cheetah (fast)

> **TIP**
>
> Save your city from time to time under different names. Then, if and when you run into trouble, you can go "back in time" and replay the simulation more knowledgeably, having learned from your mistakes.

> **NOTE**
>
> The actual speed at which SimCity 2000 will run on your computer depends on two factors: the speed of your computer's CPU and the speed of your computer's video system. When you run very large cities, you'll notice that things start getting slower, and you'll *really* see the difference between a slow 386 or LC machine and a fast Pentium or Quadra.

You may occasionally want to pause SimCity 2000 to allow you to make plans. For example, when a disaster strikes, you might need some time to figure what to do about it. When things are going well, though, you may want to run the simulator at its fastest speed.

OPTIONS

The Options menu allows you to control how SimCity 2000 operates. The most useful of the options you can set here is Auto-Budget. When Auto-Budget is on, the budget will be dealt with automatically each year, and you won't have to tend to it.

> **TIP**
>
> When you have Auto-Budget toggled on you should still review the city budget every once in a while.

But because exercising control over the budget is a powerful way for you to manage your city, you probably won't want to keep Auto-Budget on all the time. (See Chapter 7 for more on Auto-Budget.)

The choices available on the Options menu are

Auto-Budget	Toggled on, allows you to avoid dealing with the budget as it comes up each year
Auto-Goto	Moves the displayed part of the city automatically to show you where a disaster has happened
Sound Effects	Toggles sound effects on or off (SimCity 2000 uses sound effects to highlight certain events in the game, such as airplane crashes)
Music	Toggles on or off the SimCity 2000 "score"— music that was written just for the game

DISASTER

The disaster menu allows you to

- Allow disasters to occur
- Force disasters to occur
- Disable all disasters

You can toggle disasters individually or in combination. If you toggle a disaster on, it will occur immediately. If you toggle on No Disasters, there will be none during your game. (You'll need to do this if you want to leave the game running unattended.) The types of disasters that will occur right away if you select them from this menu (and might crop up any time if you haven't turned on No Disasters) are

- Fire
- Flood
- Air Crash

TIP

Once you have a balanced city (even a small one) that can maintain itself and produce a profit from taxes every year, you can beef up the city's treasury by selecting No Disasters on the Disaster menu, turning off the newspapers, setting the speed to Cheetah, and then just letting the simulation run overnight.

- Tornado
- Earthquake
- Monster
- Hurricane
- Rioters

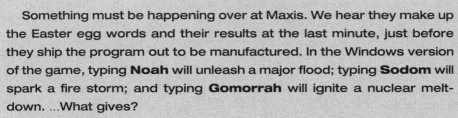

WHAT THE H—?

Something must be happening over at Maxis. We hear they make up the Easter egg words and their results at the last minute, just before they ship the program out to be manufactured. In the Windows version of the game, typing **Noah** will unleash a major flood; typing **Sodom** will spark a fire storm; and typing **Gomorrah** will ignite a nuclear meltdown. ...What gives?

WINDOWS

SimCity 2000 displays the large city map and a lot of information in various windows. (In SimCity 2000 for DOS, the windows function much like the windows in Windows, or for that matter, the windows in SimCity 2000 for the Mac.) To close a window,

- In the DOS or Mac versions, click in the control box in the upper-left corner of the window.
- In the Windows version, *double-click* in the control box in the upper-left corner of the window.

Most windows, with the exception of those showing newspapers, the budget, and ordinances in SimCity 2000 for DOS and the Mac, can be dragged around the screen; to do this, click the mouse pointer on the window's title bar (the bar on the top of the window, which often actually does *not* contain any title) and drag it where you want it. Figure 1.4 in Chapter 1 shows the parts of a SimCity 2000 window.

From SimCity 2000's Window menu, you can open various windows that will allow you to control the simulation and get information about the status of your city. Items listed on the Window menu include

- Budget
- Ordinances
- Population
- Industries (in the Mac version) or Industry (in the DOS and Windows versions)
- Graphs
- Neighbors
- Map
- Help

Budget

The Budget window is pretty much what it sounds like: the place where you make and keep the budget. The Budget window (Figure 3.4) appears in January of every year, unless you have toggled Auto-Budget on.

If Auto-Budget is toggled on, or if it is off and you just want to see the budget, you can select Budget from the Windows menu or click on the Budget tool on the City toolbar. (The City toolbar is described in an upcoming section.) The Budget tool icon is shown at left.

The Budget window allows you to control your city's finances. Within it, you can

- Set the general tax rate
- Allocate money to different city departments
- Check in with advisors
- Issue and repay bonds

As an example, to set the Property Taxes (general tax) rate, open the Budget window (Windows ➤ Budget). Then, in the Property Taxes budget item line, locate the amount box (it shows a percentage). You can repeatedly click on the downward-pointing arrow next to the amount

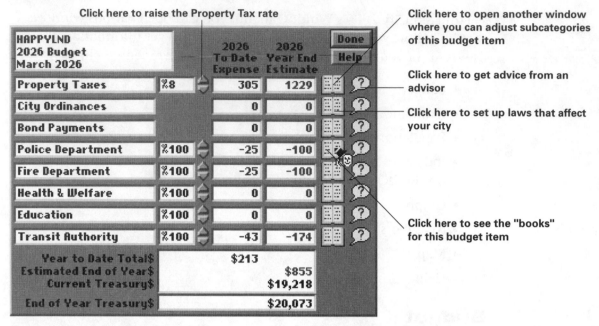

FIGURE 3.4   *In the Budget window, you set up and maintain your city's budget.*

box to lower the tax or the upward-pointing arrow to raise the tax. The default tax rate is 7%; you can raise it to as much as 20% if you want, but that will drive Sims from your city and ultimately lower land values and increase crime. You can lower the tax rate to as little as 0%, but then your city will have no income. (The safe range for taxation is 6%–8%.)

Advisors   The Budget window provides on-screen advisors to help you make important choices that affect your city's business. To get help from an advisor, click on the question mark on the far-right side of the budget item that interests you. A window will appear showing the advisor's face and a message. You don't have to ask for or follow the advisor's advice, but you should be aware that the advisor is often speaking on behalf of the Sims.

Books   Click on the Books icon to the right of each budget item to get more detailed information or greater control over the settings. In some cases (Police, Fire, and Health & Welfare), when you click on the Books icon, a window will appear (like the one in Figure 3.5) detailing the

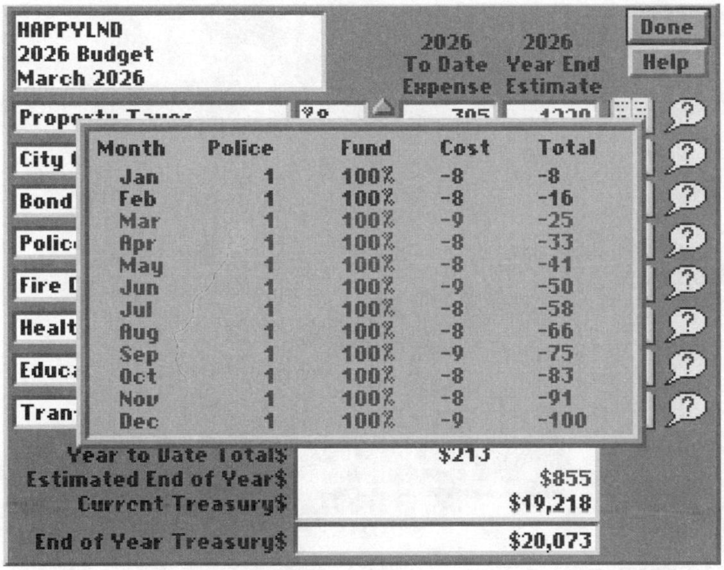

```
HAPPYLND                    2026     2026      Done
2026 Budget              To Date  Year End
March 2026               Expense  Estimate    Help

Property Taxes         0         305     4220         ?

City     Month  Police   Fund    Cost   Total        ?
          Jan      1     100%     -8     -8
Bond      Feb      1     100%     -8     -16          ?
          Mar      1     100%     -9     -25
Polic     Apr      1     100%     -8     -33          ?
          May      1     100%     -8     -41
Fire      Jun      1     100%     -9     -50          ?
          Jul      1     100%     -8     -58
Healt     Aug      1     100%     -8     -66          ?
          Sep      1     100%     -9     -75
Educa     Oct      1     100%     -8     -83          ?
          Nov      1     100%     -8     -91
Tran      Dec      1     100%     -9     -100         ?

      Year to Date Totals        $213
   Estimated End of Year$                $855
        Current Treasury$             $19,218

     End of Year Treasury$            $20,073
```

FIGURE 3.5 *This subwindow of the Budget window's Police Department line is merely informational.*

results of your budgeting. Click anywhere within this type of window to close it or click the OK button if you are playing the Windows version.

In some other cases—the Property Taxes Books window shown in Figure 3.6, for example—you can review the tax rates over the past year and change any or all of the industrial, residential, or commercial tax rates, again by clicking on the upward- or downward-pointing arrows. As you change the tax rate, the projected revenue estimates will be changed to reflect the new tax rate. SimCity will update the tax rate number. When you're finished, click on the Done button or OK to close the window.

Ordinances

In the City Ordinances window (Figure 3.7), you get to wield some real mayoral power by passing your own *ordinances* (laws). You can use city ordinances to raise revenues (by setting income taxes and parking fines), to encourage or discourage certain behavior in your Sims (reading or smoking, for example), or to provide for the public health (through special programs like CPR training). Some ordinances, like advertising for tourists, will cost you money to put into effect.

HAPPYLND
2026 Budget
March 2026

		2026 To Date Expense	2026 Year End Estimate

| Done |
| Help |

Month	Residents		Commerce		Industry		Total
Jan	8%	47	8%	17	8%	37	101
Feb	8%	46	8%	18	8%	39	204
Mar	8%	46	8%	17	8%	38	305
Apr	8%	47	8%	18	8%	38	408
May	8%	46	8%	18	8%	39	511
Jun	8%	47	8%	18	8%	38	614
Jul	8%	46	8%	18	8%	39	717
Aug	8%	46	8%	17	8%	38	818
Sep	8%	47	8%	18	8%	38	921
Oct	8%	46	8%	18	8%	39	1024
Nov	8%	47	8%	18	8%	38	1127
Dec	8%	46	8%	17	8%	39	1229

Res% **8%**   Com% **8%**   Ind% **8%** | Done |

Estimated End of Year$	$855
Current Treasury$	$19,218
End of Year Treasury$	$20,073

FIGURE 3.6 *In this subwindow of the Budget window's Property Taxes line, you can change the rates by clicking on the upward- and downward-pointing arrows.*

Finance		
1% Sales Tax	✔	26
1% Income Tax	✔	69
Legalized Gambling		
Parking Fines		

Safety & Health		
Volunteer Fire Dept.	✔	-23
Public Smoking Ban		
Free Clinics		
Junior Sports	✔	-17

Education		
Pro-Reading Campaign		
Anti-Drug Campaign		
CPR Training		
Neighborhood Watch	✔	-23

Promotional		
Tourist Advertising		
Business Advertising		
City Beautification		
Annual Carnival		

Other		
Energy Conservation		
Nuclear Free Zone		
Homeless Shelters		
Pollution Controls	✔	-57

Estimated Annual Cost	
Finance	96
Safety & Health	-40
Education	-23
Promotional	0
Other	-57

Done		YTD Total$	0	EST Total$	-18

FIGURE 3.7 *In the City Ordinances window, you can pass and adjust various public laws and policies.*

Population

The Population window displays statistical information about your city's population. When it first appears, this window contains a bar graph showing the age range of the Sims in your city. The two vertical lines in the age-range bar graph point out the portion of the population that is in the work force. At the top of the window, you'll see a number representing the percentage of the total population in the work force.

Notice three buttons (check circles in the Windows version) at the bottom of the window. One—the Population button—is selected (indented or checked). The other two are labeled Health and Education. Click on the Health button, and you'll see a graph showing the life expectancy of the population (Figure 3.8). Click on the Education button, and you'll see another graph, this time showing the educational level of the population (again, Figure 3.8).

In the Educational Level graph, the number shown (the EQ) represents the average educational level of the Sims in your city. Higher numbers describe higher levels of education. A high school education for every Sim perks the EQ to 90; the SimNational average is 100, and if you have a lot of college-educated Sims in town, it'll hover around 140. (See Chapter 12.)

Industries (or Industry)

The Industries (or Industry) window provides information about each sector of industry in your city and allows you to encourage or discourage various types of industry by changing the tax rates on an industry-by-industry basis. For example, if you want to encourage the Petrochemical industry (probably because it is shown in the Demand window to be in demand), you can lower its tax rate.

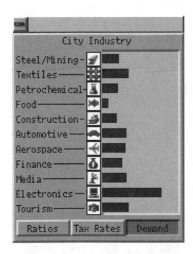

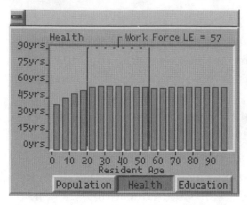 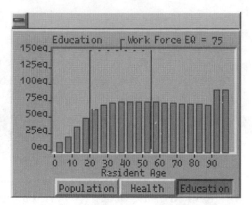

FIGURE 3.8 *Click on the Health button in the Population window, and you'll see info on the life expectancy of your Sims. Click on the Education button and you'll see the educational level of Sims of various age groups.*

Click on one of the three buttons (or check circles) at the bottom of the window to see these types of information:

Ratios — The amount of each type of industry compared to the amount of other types of industry

Tax Rates — The tax rates for each type of industry listed

Demand — The current demand for each type of industry listed

Graphs

The Graphs window shows you how your city is doing in a number of areas. When you first open the Graphs window, you'll see the following graphs displayed:

- City Size
- Residents
- Commerce
- Industry

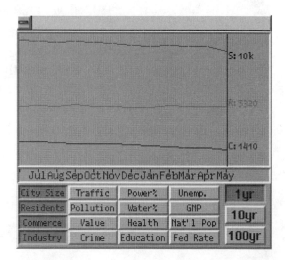

To toggle any of these graphs on or off, click on the button (or check circle) for that graph. You'll see the buttons or check circles along the bottom of the window. You can display any or all of the following types of graphs in the window:

City Size	The total population of your city
Residents	The population that is not part of the job market
Commerce	The number of Sims employed in commercial business
Industry	The number of Sims employed in industry
Traffic	The amount of traffic
Pollution	The amount of pollution
Value	The total value of all land in your city
Crime	The crime rate
Power%	The percentage of capacity at which your power plants are running
Water%	The percentage of capacity at which your water system is operating
Health	The health level of your city's residents
Education	The educational level of your city
Unemp	The unemployment rate in your city
GNP	The SimNation's Gross National Product (the amount of stuff created in the entire SimNation, which includes your city and neighboring cities)
Nat'l Pop	The population of the entire SimNation
Fed Rate	The rate the Fed will charge for a loan if you issue a bond—this also affects both industrial and commercial ventures

Note the time-frame buttons at the bottom-right side of the Graphs window. You can view graphs for one-year, 10-year, or 100-year periods to get different perspectives on the information.

Neighbors

The Neighbors window displays a map showing the population of your city along with the population of neighboring cities and the population of the entire SimNation.

You can also display the Neighbors window by clicking on its icon (shown here) on the City toolbar.

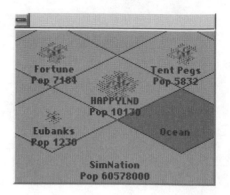

Map

The Map window shows a scaled-down view of your city with an overlay of information graphically displayed to help you quickly pinpoint the locations of problems—or where you are doing things right. To see the Map window, pull down Windows ➤ Map. In the DOS or Mac versions, the map that appears will be small; you can increase its size by clicking on the zoom box in the Map window's upper-right corner. When you're finished with it, close the Map window by clicking on the close box in the upper-left corner.

In the Map window, you'll see that trees are green and water is blue (clever, eh?). You can determine the height of land by its shading of brown: higher land is lighter in color. A white rectangle frames the area of the city that is currently visible in the City window (the main screen). You can change the area displayed in the City window by clicking anywhere in the Map window. This will move the outline and update the City window to display the area bounded by the new rectangle.

> ### N O T E
>
> **Many of the tools that appear as icons on the City toolbar are the equivalent of options under the Windows menu we've just discussed. Some of the tools on the City toolbar, however, are *not* equivalent to items under the Windows menu. You can activate and use those tools only by clicking on their icons in the City toolbar. These unique tools are described in Chapter 4.**

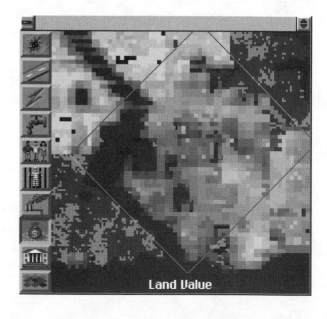

Along the left side of the Map window you'll see a number of icons. Each of these icons represents a different type of map window you can look at—everything from crime rate to land values to traffic density can be seen here. To see the map you long to view, click on its icon. Often you'll find that under the icon there's a menu listing even more map options.

As you look at different types of maps, the display will change. In maps that represent density of this or that throughout the city, darker shades of gray correspond to denser areas. For example, in the Police Power map, the more concentrated areas of police power are darker.

You can change the display of the City window to show the same information you see in the Map window (Figure 3.9). To do this, click on the Map Mode icon, shown here, which appears at the bottom of the column of icons. To switch back to the usual city view, click again on the Map Mode icon. (This won't close the Map window, it will just change how the city is displayed in the City window.)

In the sections that follow, we'll look at the maps that result from using each of the icons in the Map window.

 City Form Displays a menu allowing you to choose between Structures and Zones. When you select Structures, you'll see the structures that have been built in your city. Select Zones, and you'll see the zoned areas.

 Roads Displays a menu with three items: Roads, Rails, or Traffic Density. Roads or Rails will show you the location of all the roads or rails within your city. Traffic Density shows traffic density.

 Power Grid Displays a map showing power lines as white lines, powered zones as yellow areas, and unpowered zones as red areas.

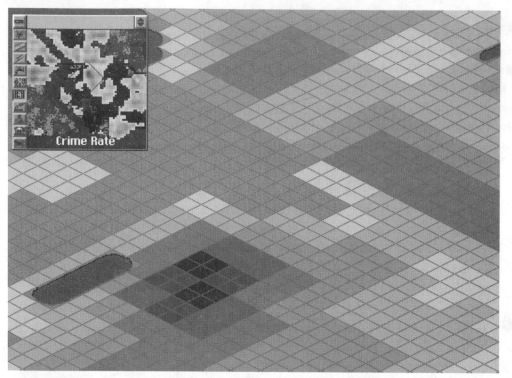

FIGURE 3.9 *The Map window and the City window, with the City window in map mode*

Water System Displays a map with water pipes appearing as white lines, zones with water as yellow areas, and zones lacking water as red areas.

Population Displays a menu with two choices: Density or Rate of Growth. Density shows which areas of the city are more or less populated. Rate of Growth tells you which areas of your city are growing fastest. Areas with a positive rate of growth are blue—darker blue represents a higher rate of growth. Areas going down are displayed in red, and darker red means a greater population loss.

Crime Displays a menu with three choices. Crime Rate shows the crime rate with areas of higher crime darker. Police Power shows crime-fighting power as it radiates out from police stations. Police Stations appear as white dots on the map. Note that the locations of police stations will correspond to the more concentrated (darker) areas of police power.

 Pollution   Displays a map showing levels of pollution throughout your city. The darker the gray is in an area, the more that part of your city is polluted.

 Land Value   Displays a map indicating land values around your city. The darker gray an area is, the more it is worth.

 City Services   Displays a menu of four items: Fire Power, Fire Depts, Schools, and Colleges. Fire Power represents your fire-fighting power throughout the city, with areas that have more fire coverage appearing darker. Fire Depts, Schools, and Colleges all show locations (as white dots) of their respective buildings.

Help

The Windows version of SimCity 2000 provides sterling online Help via the Help menu. It's just like the help system you get in every other Windows program, so it's probably a pretty familiar feature, but we thought we'd mention it here just to be complete.

NEWSPAPERS

This menu item allows you to select whether the program displays newspapers regularly, occasionally, or never, as shown below.

How Often You Want the Paper	Why You Want to Do It That Way	What You Should Select
Regular delivery	A lot of important events are occurring	Subscribe
Occasional delivery	Nothing much is occurring, but you want to be notified if it does	Extra!!!
No delivery	Whatever happens, you don't want to hear about it	Nothing; toggle off all options

There are alternative newspapers published in your city; they're listed at the bottom of this menu and you can click on the name of any of them to read that newspaper. (As your city grows larger, the number of alternative papers increases.)

When a newspaper is displayed, you can read any article in it by clicking on the headline or the article itself with the mouse pointer (see Figure 3.10).

When you've read the article, close it by clicking on it again. To close the newspaper itself, click on its close box in the upper-left corner.

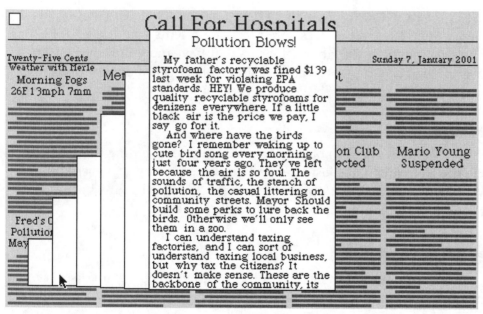

FIGURE 3.10   *The newspaper articles are always informative and often very amusing.*

THE INFO BOX AND THE STATUS BAR

You'll see important information and messages in the Info box that appears at the top of the main window in the DOS and Mac versions. The same info appears in a status bar at the bottom of the window in the Windows version. It is in these places that you can look to verify that the little bulldozer icon (Figure 3.11) represents Demolish/Clear (meaning that structure will be razed but the underlying land will not be altered) and not Level Terrain (meaning that the land will be leveled).

When a disaster strikes, you'll see it here even before it hits the papers. And this is where you'll see messages telling you what the citizens are currently demanding (roadways, hospitals, or police protection, for example).

The little weather icon at the far right end of the Info box will change frequently, showing you the current state of the weather. (In the Windows version, the state of the weather is indicated in the status bar, where a word will appear rather than a picture.)

You can drag the Info box to a more convenient location on your screen, but you cannot close it. The Info box or status bar will be your constant visual advisor.

FIGURE 3.11 *The Info box (DOS/Mac; shown on the top), or the status bar (Windows; shown underneath) will tell you what you're doing to your city, what your citizens are demanding, what disasters are brewing, and even the current weather.*

CHAPTER FOUR

THE CITY TOOLBAR

THE CITY TOOLBAR APPEARS WITH the City window along the left side of the screen. Each of the icons in the City toolbar allows you to zone or build something or displays a window containing information about your city. In this chapter, we'll cover the icons in the City toolbar and provide how-to instructions for using each of them. You'll find tips and insights here, but this is not a strategy chapter. For strategies, turn to Part Two of this book.

> **TIP**
>
> **You can move the City toolbar around the screen by clicking on its title bar and dragging it wherever you want.**

USING THE CITY TOOLBAR

To activate a tool in the City toolbar, click on its icon with the mouse. Depending on which of the tools you click, either the mouse pointer will change to a new shape to indicate what it now represents (a piece of road, a small factory, a bulldozer, etc.), or a new window will appear.

Icons that are grayed or dimmed on the toolbar are unavailable due to lack of funds or lack of necessity. You cannot use these dimmed tools.

When you select a tool from the City toolbar, helpful information about that tool will appear in the Info box or (in the Windows version) the status bar on your screen. You'll always see the name of the tool; you may also see its cost—when you zone, build on, or change a tile, there is a cost attached. Get in the habit of looking to make sure you've selected what you want (accidents do happen) and that you're willing to pay the price. If you choose to go ahead, the cost will be deducted from your total funds, which appear at the top of your screen.

> **NOTE**
>
> **Some of the tools represented by icons in the City toolbar are also available through the menu bar. (See Chapter 3.)**

TOOLS FOR BUILDING AND ZONING

Here, we'll go over each of the tools you'll use for zoning and building your city. These tools are represented by icons on the City toolbar.

Bulldozer

When you click and hold down the mouse button on the Bulldozer tool icon, a menu will appear, listing the actions you can perform using the Bulldozer tool:

- Demolish/Clear
- Level Terrain
- Raise Terrain
- Lower Terrain
- De-Zone

You'll use the bulldozer to demolish any structures that have been built in your city. To do this, click the Bulldozer tool icon, then select Demolish/Clear from the menu. The mouse pointer will turn into a little bulldozer, and you'll see the cost-per-tile indicated in the Info box. Click and drag the mouse pointer across whatever you want to demolish. You'll see the effects of demolition on screen—smoke or dust will billow up, and the tile will be littered with rubble. You will have to click and drag over the tile again to clear the rubble (at an additional cost per tile). The tile will then return to its predeveloped state, either as bare land or with its zoning indicated by patterns of colored dots. Demolish/Clear can be very useful to free up space for a road, railway, water pumps, or urban redevelopment.

Four other options on the Bulldozer menu—Level Terrain, Raise Terrain, Lower Terrain, and De-Zone—allow you to change the land on which your city is built. You can remove or create hills with Level Terrain or Raise Terrain. To level hilly

---

TIP

Changing your landmass during the game by using the Bulldozer tool is very costly. Modify the land, if you wish, *before* a game starts—you won't spend any of your city's money if you use the Terrain toolbar, but you'll spend a bundle using the Bulldozer. See Chapter 22 for details on how to create land with the Terrain toolbar for your own private utopia.

TIP

In the Windows and DOS versions of SimCity 2000 you can quickly demolish tiles without using the Bulldozer tool with this little trick: point at the tile you want to demolish, hold down the Ctrl key, and click. Whatever is underneath the pointer at the time will be cleared away just as if you'd used Demolish/Clear.

land, for example, select the Level Terrain tool and click and drag the mouse pointer over the hilly area. The land will lower to be level with the surrounding area. To raise a hill, select Raise Terrain from the menu, then click and drag until the hills are as you want them to be. To lower the land (until, perhaps, you hit the water table and a lake forms), select Lower Terrain from the menu and click and drag as usual until the land is as low as you want. You can return land to an unzoned state by selecting De-Zone and clicking and dragging.

Landscape

The Landscape tool allows you to place water and trees wherever you like in your city or its surroundings. Again, this is more expensive than doing the same thing before the game using the Terrain toolbar, so you should do that instead if you can. When you select this tool's icon and hold down the mouse button, a menu will appear listing the two types of Landscaping you can place in your city: trees and water.

> **WARNING**
>
> In version 1.1 and the Windows version, the Bulldozer tool should always default to Demolish/Clear instead of the last tool you selected. In version 1.0, when you want to bulldoze an area or structure, be sure you have Demolish/Clear selected and not one of the other menu options. If you have by accident selected Raise Terrain or Lower Terrain, you can do a lot of damage.

Again, the pointer will change shape to reflect what you've chosen. To actually place the trees or water, click and drag over the area where you want it to appear.

Emergency

This tool, which is available only when disaster strikes your city, allows you to dispatch police, fire protection, the National Guard, or the military to respond to the emergency. (If you don't have police or fire stations, one unit of the National Guard will be available.) The more police and fire stations you have, the more police officers and fire fighters you'll be able to dispatch to respond to a disaster when it occurs.

You can send out military units to deal with disaster only if you have a military base in your city. (The SimNational government will ask if you want a military base in your city when the population surpasses 60,000. You don't have to accept the offer—military bases may offer protection in the event of disaster, but they also bring their own problems.)

To respond to a disaster, click on the Emergency tool icon and pick the response team (Police, Fire Protection, or Military) you want to send. Then click on the location in your city to which you want to dispatch the response team. (See Chapter 5.)

Power

With the Power tool you can build new power plants and lay power lines around your city to give it spark. When two buildings are next to each other, the Sims take care of connecting the power between them. If empty or unpowered squares are between a new structure and the nearest powered area, you must lay power lines to make a connection.

When you click and hold down the mouse on this tool's icon, a menu will appear that allows you to pick between Power Lines and Power Plant. To lay power lines, just select Power Lines and then click and drag where you want to place them. (See Chapter 5.)

> ### TIP
> Be sure to zoom in on the area where you're placing power lines—it's easy to miss that one last, vital link if you aren't close enough to see what you're doing.

The amount of time it takes for power to start flowing through your power lines is proportional to the size of your city—the more things the program is tracking, the longer it takes power to start flowing.

If you select Power Plant, you will see a dialog box showing you all the types of power plants that are currently available. You pick one of these plants by clicking on its picture. You can find out more information about any of the power plants by clicking on the Info button above the picture. Your choice of power plants is dependent on the era in which you are building the plant. Different types of power become available at different times in SimCity 2000. (See Chapter 5.)

Water System

Using the Water System tool, you'll build a system of pumps and underground pipes to lay out your city's water supply. While a water shortage will not immediately cripple your city (as a power shortage would), it is a serious problem that will slow down development.

As your city develops, you might consider adding water towers to your system to allow storage of fresh water that can then be used during droughts or dry summers.

Fairly early in the passage of time, technological developments will be announced in the newspaper that will add to your water-system options. For example, you'll be able to add a water-treatment facility to process waste water, which reduces pollution, or a desalinization plant to turn ocean water into fresh, usable water.

When you select the Water System tool and hold down the mouse pointer, a menu will appear listing

- Pipes
- Water Pump
- Water Tower
- Treatment
- Desalinization

> **N O T E**
>
> **Like power plants, treatment facilities and desalinization plants are technologies that develop as you play—you won't see them in the year 1900. They are, however, available fairly soon into the game, so we've included them here.**

As usual, the mouse pointer will change shape to reflect what you've chosen. The techniques used for placing pumps or towers, however, differ slightly from those for placing piping.

To get their maximum benefit, place pumps near a fresh water supply. The edge of a river is best, but a lake or pond will do. (If necessary, resort to ocean water with desalinization included in your water system.) Keep in mind that it's best to place water pumps side by side and not at angles to each other (this makes it easier to provide them with power). Having chosen those tiles on which you want to place pumps, point and click once on a tile for each pump you want to place. You must connect the pumps via power lines to a power source or powered area. Figure 4.1 shows water pumps placed strategically and all powered up.

This leaves you with water pumping, but no piping connections to your city.

Pumps

FIGURE 4.1   *Water pumps strategically placed to pump water for the city's use*

Click and hold again on the Water System icon in the City toolbar. This time, select Pipes. Note that the icon changes shape, *and the map of your city changes, too*. The view that appears now represents the *underground* map of your land mass and city. Figure 4.2 shows the underground view of the same area shown in Figure 4.1.

In the underground map, you will see that the Sims have been busy underground as well as above: In developed areas, they have been building pipelines, which now appear as grids of empty piping. (You can tell they're empty because they're gray and not running blue water.) You'll also see the water pumps you've placed represented by heavier pipelines running blue water. Your task, then, is to connect the gray, empty piping to the pumps running blue water.

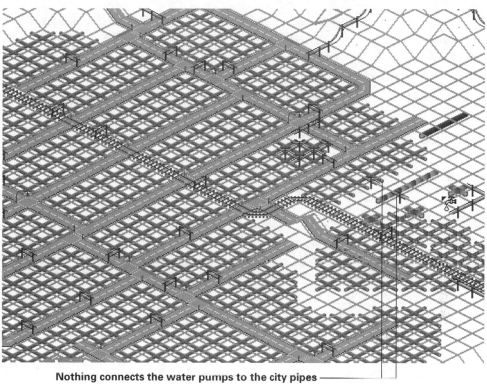

Nothing connects the water pumps to the city pipes ─────────

FIGURE 4.2   *You can see here that the Sims built pipes in developed areas, and that water pumps (represented by heavier pipelines) are in place, but that nothing connects the pipes to the pumps.*

To lay pipelines, while you are viewing the underground level of your city, and with Pipes selected from the Water System menu, simply click and drag along the squares where you want pipes to be placed. Note that when your laying of pipes is successful—meaning that the pipes have been connected—the pipes in the developed section will turn from gray to blue. You'll actually see water running through them. Note, too, that you will have to lay pipelines under roads and rails to make the connections in your city complete.

   When you're finished laying pipes, click on the Show Underground icon shown here to switch back to the aboveground view of your city.

To place water towers, treatment facilities, or desalinization plants, use the same techniques you used to place pumps. Note, however, that you can place a tower almost anywhere; you must place a desalinization plant near the ocean, where it will do some good; and any of these pieces of your water system are just that—pieces—and must be linked to the whole system via piping.

The water system is discussed further in Chapter 9 of this book.

Rewards

If you're doing well as mayor, you'll be rewarded. The Rewards icon will then turn from dimmed to active in the City toolbar, and you'll be able to build structures that glorify you as mayor. These range from a mayor's house, city hall, and a statue, to the wild, futuristic Braun Llama Dome, and more (see Chapter 14).

Rewards are tied to gaining a certain population level. Watch the newspaper—it'll clue you in to when you can build a reward—and watch for the Rewards tool to become active.

> **N O T E**
>
> **You do not absolutely have to build rewards when they're available. You may be the more modest type of mayor. If you do not build a reward when it is first available, you can always build it later.**

Roads

With the Roads tool, you can build roads and highways. You can also build tunnels and public transit (bus depots). When you click and hold on the Roads tool icon, a menu with these options will appear:

- Road
- Highway
- Tunnel
- Onramp (for Highway)
- Bus Depot

Roads allow cars to travel about the city—they're cheap to build, and Sims love to drive. Soon after you build a road, you'll see little blue cars zipping up and down it as Sims travel from home to work and back again. The drawbacks to roads are that cars cause pollution, and because Sims love to drive so much, roads are frequently—and quickly—used beyond capacity. Highways, which are higher-capacity roads, allow more cars to travel greater distances without overstressing the road system. To use a highway, you must build on ramps at strategic locations to connect it to other roads.

> **NOTE**
>
> Where are the *off* ramps? Well, they're part and parcel of the *on* ramps. Maybe they should be called *on and off ramps*, but they aren't.

Placing a road or highway is a simple matter of clicking and holding the Roads tool icon, selecting what you want to build, and clicking and dragging along the length of squares where you want to place the road or highway. You can build roads up and down hills; when you do, the road will snake along the most viable path. Note however, that if a ramp is needed to make the path more viable, it will be built, and that sometimes those ramps can appear at a different angle than you'd planned. If that should happen, you can demolish the problematic piece of road using the Bulldozer tool ➤ Demolish/Clear option and rebuild the road the way you want it.

You may sometimes want to tunnel your road *through* a hillside rather than letting it take up valuable land snaking across the hills. Just click and hold the Roads tool icon, then select Tunnel from the menu and click on the side of the hill you want to tunnel through. Either a dialog box will appear showing you the cost of the tunnel and asking if you want to build the thing—the cost is related to the length of the tunnel— or a message will appear from the SimEngineers saying you cannot build a tunnel under this hill. Note that a tunnel cannot cross other tunnels, subways, or water pipes. Also, both sides of the hill have to be suitable for the tunnel entrance and exit.

You can encourage the use of public transit by placing bus depots around your city. The buses themselves will of course use the regular roads and highways. For best results you should place your depots at busy intersections.

For more on the strategies involved in laying out roads, highways, and other transit system options, see Chapter 8.

Rails

Railways—both aboveground and below—are an alternative to roads and highways. The presence of railways and underground subways in your city will encourage use of public transit, reduce the burden of car and truck traffic, and reduce pollution. Remember that railways can also move freight, while subways can carry only passengers.

To build a railway or subway, you must lay down tracks and build stations.

First click and hold the Rails tool icon, then select which of these options you want to build:

- Rail
- Subway
- Rail Depot
- Sub Station
- Sub <—> Rail

As always, the pointer will change shape to reflect what you've chosen, and its cost will appear in the Info window. Use the same click-and-drag method for laying down rail lines as for roads. Use the point-and-click method described earlier for placing rail depots. (Note that you must provide power to rail depots.) The more rail depots you build, the larger the capacity of your rail system will be, and the greater its benefits in reducing traffic and reducing pollution.

Subways are trackways that go below your city primarily to move people. When you build a subway line, you must also place subway stations aboveground to allow your Sims access to the underground. For best results, place subway stations near busy road intersections and in high-density residential, commercial, and industrial areas.

To build a subway system, first plot visually where you're going to place the stations and the subway lines. (Remember that the lines themselves will be underground.) Now place the subway stations. To do this, click and hold the Rails tool icon, then select Sub Station. The pointer will change shape, and the cost of the subway station will appear in the Info box. Point and click to place your subway station in the location you planned for it. Don't forget to provide power to your subway stations.

Now click and hold the Rails tool icon, then select Subway. The underground view of the city will appear, just as it did when you laid pipelines to supply your city with water. Use the click-and-drag method to indicate where you want the subway lines to go—between the subway stations you just built. An underground "tube" will appear where you have indicated (Figure 4.3). When you are done, click the Show Underground icon on the City toolbar to switch back to the aboveground view.

The final rail transport option presented on the Rails tool menu, Sub <—> Rail, allows you to link together your surface rail system and your underground subway system with a special station. (The sub <—> rail station appears on screen as a small aboveground building with

FIGURE 4.3 *You can click and drag subway tubes (the wide black lines) into place underground between the subway stations.*

an opening to allow surface trains access to subway tracks.) Building a sub <—> rail station allows trains to move between the surface and underground and provides maximum flexibility for your rail and subway transit system. Use the techniques for placing a rail or subway station, described above, to place a sub <—> rail station.

Ports

Using the Ports tool, you can build either a seaport or an airport. When you click and hold the Ports tool icon, a menu will appear. Before the invention of the airplane is announced in the newspaper, you'll be

offered only the option to build a seaport. For most of the game, however, the Ports tool menu will offer both options.

To create either a seaport or airport, first zone a piece of land at least 4×4 tiles in size for a seaport and at least 1×5 tiles for an airport. If you zone less land than that, your port might not develop.

Click and hold the Ports tool icon. From the menu that appears, select the type of port you wish to build. The pointer will change shape to reflect your choice, and the cost will appear in the Info box. Click and drag the pointer to indicate where you want to locate the port. Remember, you must connect power to the port. After that, the port should appear and become active within a short time.

> **TIP**
>
> When you have the No Disasters option selected in the Disasters menu, planes will crash but they will not cause fires. If you are planning to play an entire game with No Disasters set, you can go ahead and build an airport in the middle of a large city.

> **NOTE**
>
> Sometimes you will find that you've plotted an area large enough for your port and provided it with power, but the port doesn't develop. This may be because there is a problem with the location—your airport may be too close to a hill—or something may be out of whack with the economy. See Chapter 10 for more on developing ports.

Residential Zones

Using the Residential Zone tool, you can zone either lightly or densely populated residential areas for your Sims. Both types of residential zones can have a place in your city—you just need to figure out the proper balance. (More on this in Chapter 6.)

To use the Residential Zone tool, click and hold that icon, then select the type of residential zone you want from the menu that appears. The pointer will change to reflect your choice, and the cost for that choice will appear in the Info box. Click and drag across the area you want to zone. Connect power lines and pipes, provide the area with transportation (road, rail, or something else) so the Sims can get around, then watch the Sims build their homes and move in.

Commercial Zones

Using the Commercial Zone tool, you can zone for either light or dense commercial areas. A balanced and more livable city (meaning, ultimately, one with higher property values) will include both types of commercial zones. (Again, see Chapter 6 to find out more about this.)

To use the Commercial Zone tool, click and hold that icon, then select the type of zone you want from the menu that appears. The pointer will change to reflect your choice, and the cost for that choice will appear, as usual, in the Info box. Click and drag across the area you want to zone. Connect power lines and pipes and provide the area with appropriate transportation. Busy Sims will soon begin to flock to your commercial zones.

Industrial Zones

The Industrial Zone tool allows you to zone for either light or dense industry. You should mix the two types of industry in your city, as each affects different parts of your city's economy. (More on this in Chapter 6.)

To use the Industrial Zone tool, click and hold that icon, then select the type of zone you want from the menu that appears. The pointer will change to reflect your choice, and the cost for that choice will appear in the Info box. Click and drag across the area you want to zone. Connect power lines and pipes. Provide the area with transportation so the Sims can get to work and home again. Soon you'll see evidence of happy Sims making their way to and from their jobs and homes.

Education

The Education tool allows you to place institutions of learning around your city.

You can build any of the following learning centers:

- Schools
- Colleges
- Libraries
- Museums

To use the Education tool, click and hold its icon. From the menu that appears, select the type of learning center you want to build. The pointer will change to reflect your choice. The cost for that choice will appear in the Info box. Point and click where you want the learning center to appear. (You can place learning centers in or near any zone, though aesthetics suggest you probably won't want to put them in industrial areas.) Connect power lines and provide transportation, if you have not already done so, for the zone in which you're placing the learning center.

City Services

With the City Services tool you can build the various services your city provides to keep the Sims healthy and safe. (See Chapter 11.) These services include:

- Police Stations
- Fire Stations
- Hospitals
- Prisons

To use the City Services tool, click and hold its icon. Then, from the menu that appears, select which type of service you want to provide. The pointer will change to reflect your choice and the cost for that choice will appear in the Info box. Point and click where you want the service's building to appear. Connect power lines and provide transportation, if necessary.

Recreation

Using the Recreation tool, you can build places for your Sims to play. Play is a good thing. Play improves your Sims' quality of life, and so it reduces crime and increases property values. (See Chapters 6, 7, and 13.) You can choose to build the following types of recreational areas:

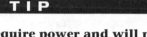

> **TIP**
>
> **Parks do not require power and will not transmit power to surrounding areas.**

- Small Park
- Big Park
- Zoo
- Stadium
- Marina

To use the Recreation tool, click and hold its icon. From the menu that appears, select the type of recreational facility you want to provide. The pointer will change to reflect your choice, and the cost for that choice will appear in the Info box. Point and click where you want the facility to appear. Connect power lines and provide transportation, if necessary.

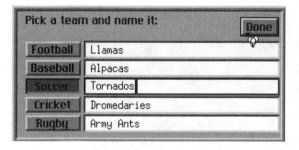

If you're building a stadium, a menu will appear after you've placed the stadium. In the menu, you can select which type of sports team you wish to have (Figure 4.4).

Choose the type of sports team you want either by clicking on the correct button (DOS and Mac) or by making a selection from the bottom list box (Windows). Next, select a name for your team. You can either accept the name that appears in the text box or type in a new name. Click on Done to finish.

Signs

To highlight a point of interest in your city, you can place a specially written sign. To do this, click and hold the Sign tool icon on the City toolbar, then click the mouse pointer where you want to place the sign (this can be anywhere in your city).
A dialog box will appear.

Type the text for your sign into the text box in the dialog box. Press ↵ and the sign will appear as you placed it. Figure 4.4 shows a sign pointing out the home of the Turista Tornados.

Query

Using the Query tool, you can investigate specific information about the areas or structures in your city. The information, which appears in a small info box on screen, will vary depending on the type of item you're investigating. For example, when you click on a power plant, the info box will tell you its maximum output, the percentage of its capacity at which it is running, and its age. When you click on a tile that's zoned residential, the info box will tell you what type of residences have been built there (cheap apartments, for example) and more.

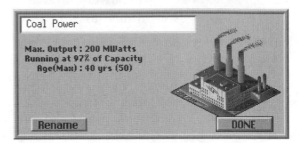

FIGURE 4.4   *This stadium is obviously the home of the Turista Tornados.*

To use the Query tool, click on the Query tool icon, then point and click on the item you want to investigate. An info box will appear, identifying the item and showing a variety of facts. To close the info box when you're finished, click anywhere within it.

Rotate Counter-Clockwise

To use the Rotate Counter-Clockwise tool, just click on its icon and the city will turn counterclockwise. This is very helpful when you cannot see behind a hill or tall building. Figure 4.5 shows a city viewed from one vantage point, then rotated to a new vantage point.

Rotate Clockwise

To use the Rotate Clockwise tool, click on its icon, and this time the city will turn clockwise.

Zoom Out

Click on the Zoom Out tool icon to give you a more expansive view of the land mass that contains your city. When you have zoomed out as far as the program will allow, this Zoom Out tool icon will be dimmed.

Zoom In

Click on the Zoom In tool icon to get an extreme close-up. When you have zoomed in as close as SimCity 2000 will allow, the Zoom In tool icon will be dimmed. Figure 4.6 shows the same city— from afar and then zoomed in.

FIGURE 4.5   *The city as you see it before and after rotating*

Center

The Center tool allows you to center the window. Just click on the icon, then point and click on the place you want to be centered in the window.

T I P

In the DOS and Windows versions, you can do the same thing by clicking the right mouse button.

TOOLS FOR QUICKLY SEEING INFORMATION WINDOWS

These are tools to let you see quickly those windows and maps that are also available through the menu bar. To see or use these items, you can either click on the tool's icon in the City toolbar or use the pulldown menus in the menu bar at the top of your screen. Here, we'll just list them and tell you what they do. We'll also tell you how to get to them via the menus, but for more information on using menus, turn to Chapter 3.

Maps Window

Select the Maps Window tool icon to display the same maps you can see by using the Maps menu in the menu bar (Windows ➤ Maps).

FIGURE 4.6 *The city seen from a distance and then up close and personal*

Graphs Window

Click on the Graphs Window tool icon or use the menu bar (Windows ➤ Graphs) to display the Graphs window.

Population Window

Click on the Population Window tool icon to display the Population window. This can also be accomplished with the menu bar (Windows ➤ Population).

Industry Window

Select the Industry Window tool icon to see information about your city's industries. This can also be done with the menu bar (Windows ➤ Industries or Windows ➤ Industry).

Neighbors Window

Click on the Neighbors Window tool icon on the City Toolbar to compare the population of your city with those of neighboring cities in Sim-Nation. You can also select Windows ➤ Neighbors from the menu bar to do this.

Budget Window

Select the Budget Window tool icon on the City toolbar to display the Budget window. You can also select Windows ➤ Budget from the menu bar to do the same thing.

TOOLS FOR SEEING SELECTIVELY AND GETTING HELP

These tools will let you pinpoint certain aspects of your city for a closer view of particular items or special help.

Show Buildings

You can toggle the Show Buildings tool on or off by clicking on its icon. You may occasionally want to toggle off Show Buildings so you can see more clearly the roads, rails, and power lines in your city.

Show Signs

Again, you can toggle Show Signs on or off to see signs you have placed either displayed or not displayed in the City window. (You can place signs in your city by using the Sign tool on the City Toolbar, discussed earlier in this chapter.)

Show Infrastructure

Toggle the Show Infrastructure tool on or off by clicking on its icon. You may want to toggle this tool on to display the roads, rails, and power lines that you have placed in your city.

Show Zones

Toggle the Show Zones tool on or off by clicking on its icon. You may want to toggle this tool on to see more clearly the pattern of zones in your city.

Show Underground

Click on the Show Underground tool icon, and you'll see the underground level of your city. This is where your water pipes and subways are located. Click on the icon again to return to the aboveground view.

Help

In the Dos and Mac versions, you can select the Help tool in the City toolbar and a small message will appear telling you to hold down the Shift key and click on anything in the game to get additional information on that item. This is an invaluable tool—you'll find yourself using it all the time.

In the Windows version, select the Help tool and you'll access the online Help system, just as if you'd selected Help from the menu bar.

N O T E

When you Shift-click on a building or land in the City window, you'll see the same information that is displayed when you use the Query tool.

PART TWO

TECHNIQUES AND STRATEGIES
FOR BUILDING A SIMCITY

CHAPTER FIVE

PROVIDING POWER

FROM THE ALARM CLOCK THAT wakes you in the morning to the computer that simulates your SimCity, the common thread that runs through modern life is *power*. You'd be lost without it. In fact, the need for power is so basic that in SimCity 2000, you must build a power plant before you do anything else. Which power plant you choose, where you locate it, and how wisely you use it will be among the most important decisions you'll make as you play SimCity 2000.

CHOOSING A POWER PLANT

At first, your choice of power plants will be limited. But as time goes by, new technologies will appear and be announced in the newspaper. There are a number of factors to consider in choosing your power plant.

PRACTICAL AND PHILOSOPHICAL CONSIDERATIONS

When you choose a power plant, you must consider two basic practical variables: the life span of the power plant's generator and the amount of electricity it can produce. You must also think about the drawbacks involved in using the type of power plant you're considering.

Consider also the agenda you've set for your city: you may be trying to expand your city as much as possible, or you may be trying to build an ecologically sound city. If you're planning to build a large city and you don't mind using resources, you may want to start with a coal plant, which makes a lot of pollution but is economical to build and operate. On the other hand, you might want to start with hydroelectric power, which is clean but not very efficient.

> **TIP**
>
> To build a large city, the best—meaning the most economical and expedient—sequence might be coal → nuclear → fusion. To build a small city with an ecologically safe power source, the best sequence might be hydroelectric → wind → solar, with each augmenting, rather than replacing, the other.

Over the course of time, these types of power plants will be available:

Power Plant	Year Invented (+/- 10 Years)	Output in Megawatts	Cost
Coal	1900	200	$ 4,000
Hydroelectric	1900	20	400
Oil Power	1900	220	6,600
Gas Power	1950	50	2,000
Nuclear	1955	500	15,000
Wind Power	1980	4	100
Solar Power	1990	50	1,300
Microwave	2020	1,600	28,000
Fusion	2050	2,500	40,000

If you were to consider only the amount of power it generates per dollar spent, your best bet in choosing a power plant would be coal or hydroelectric (both cost $20 per megawatt) until the 2020s, when microwave becomes available (at a cost of $17.50 per megawatt). Then, a few years later, fusion (which generates power at a cost of $16 per megawatt) will become available and economical.

> **NOTE**
>
> The "cost" of each power plant refers to the initial construction cost. The subsequent cost of rebuilding it when it dies out is the same.

Power plants have *hidden costs*, in the form of lowered property values if the plant produces a lot of pollution (like coal, which burns a fossil fuel), or loss of power during brownouts if the plant is not a constant source (like solar, which depends on the unreliable presence of sunlight). Your choice of power plant impacts your city in a number of ways that might not be immediately obvious.

DEATH OF A POWER PLANT

The life span for each power plant, except hydroelectric and wind, is 50 years. A hydroelectric power plant or wind power plant will last forever without needing replacement or maintenance. When an aging power plant is about to fail, the newspaper will announce the upcoming problem with alarm. If you are playing with No Disasters toggled on, and if you have enough money available, you can sit idly by through all the warnings. At the moment it fails, the old power plant will be automatically replaced by a new one of the same type. If you are playing with disasters enabled, you'll have to act quickly to rebuild the power plant when it dies to avoid widespread business and industry failure resulting from the lack of power.

As an alternative, when an aging power plant is about to die, you can choose a new type of power plant from the more sophisticated options that have become available in the 50 years since you built the old one. Quick, while there's still time, find a new location for the new plant (presumably a little farther away from your growing metropolis), and build the new plant before the old one keels over. Then have some real fun blowing up the old one yourself. (You can use Demolish/Clear under the Bulldozer tool icon to do this.)

Finally, you'll have the option to rezone the tiles that used to be occupied by the aging power plant. You can incorporate them into your overall city plan in any way you like.

TYPES OF POWER PLANTS

In the following sections, we'll describe each of the types of generators that appear in SimCity 2000 and go over their advantages and drawbacks.

Coal

Coal power plants burn fossil fuel to generate electricity. In the early half of the 1900s, coal is cheap and easy to get, so this somewhat-primitive technology is a good choice—especially in the early years of a simulation.

Advantage: Coal power plants are cheap to build and maintain and are available at the beginning of the game. In SimCity 2000, coal power plants pose no real danger of disaster—they don't have meltdowns, for example—and they're not dependent on the presence of a water source. In addition, because they're not dependent on sunlight, they're not subject to a lot of brownouts. Coal power is inexpensive, steady, and reliable.

200 Mw $4,000
Coal Power

COAL POWER - coal plants generate large amounts of vile black smoke that will cover your buildings in soot. Your citizens may start complaining when they have to repaint their buildings every two years.

Disadvantage: Burning coal is a dirty way to produce power; coal-burning plants throw off a lot of smoke, which you can see blowing across the landmass or (yikes!) your city. Pollution lowers the quality of life for your Sims, and thus, property values.

Strategy: Build one coal power plant at the beginning of the game, when it's a cheap and expedient way to get rolling. Be sure to build it away from any area you're planning to zone as residential. When your growing city needs more power than a single coal plant can produce, replace it with a more powerful and cleaner plant.

Hydroelectric

Hydroelectric power is generated very inexpensively by plants that process the movement of water into electricity forever. That's right—*forever*. Most of the other power plants in SimCity 2000 must be replaced every 50 years, but a hydroelectric power plant will work until the end of the game. You will never have to pay to replace it, because it will never wear out.

20 Mw $400
HydroElectric

HYDRO ELECTRIC - water generators are very clean and efficient, but require a large investment of capital. They require only minimal maintenance.

Advantage: Hydroelectric power plants are cheap to build and use, they do not use fossil fuels and so do not create pollution, and they are not vulnerable to accidents. They're also available at the beginning of a game, so if you want to build a city that's ecologically less damaging than a coal or oil power plant would allow for, hydroelectric's your ticket.

Disadvantage: Unfortunately, hydroelectric power plants don't provide much electricity—each plant generates only 20 megawatts of power. You have to build quite a few of them to power even a small city. (It takes 25 hydroelectric power plants to produce the same amount of power as a single nuclear power plant.) Also, they must be built on waterfall tiles, which are rare in SimCity 2000.

TIP

Before you start a simulation, you can use the Terrain toolbar (which we cover in Chapter 22) to create a custom land form that includes plenty of waterfalls. During a simulation, you can use the Landscape ➤ Water/Trees tool to add water to an existing hillside to create waterfall tiles, or you can use the Bulldozer tool's Raise Terrain option to create a hill and then use the Landscape ➤ Water/Trees tool to add water to the new hillside. This is *very* expensive, however. It's best to make changes to terrain before you start a simulation, when changing the landmass is still free.

Strategy: If you're lucky enough to come up with a landmass with waterfall tiles, or if you've created one, in the early part of the game you can place a few hydroelectric power plants on the waterfall tiles.

As your city grows, you can add hydroelectric power plants incrementally. This will not only be ecologically sound, it will also avoid having wasted capacity. (Coal power plants, for example, will produce more power than your early, small city will need at first.) Alternatively, as your city grows larger, you can add other types of power plants while retaining the hydroelectric power plants you built early on.

Oil

Oil power plants burn oil—also a fossil fuel—to generate electricity. In the early 1900s, using an oil power plant may represent an expensive, but viable, compromise between coal and hydroelectric.

Advantage: Oil power plants are a bit cleaner than coal, and they're available at the beginning of the game. Oil power plants are not dependent on the presence of sunlight, which is unreliable, or waterfall tiles, which are rare.

220 Mw $6,600
Oil Power

OIL POWER – the use of oil power fluctuates with the cost of petroleum. It is marginally cleaner than coal power.

Disadvantage: Oil power plants are not as cheap to build and maintain as coal or hydroelectric. If you choose to build an oil power plant at the beginning of a simulation, it's going to drain away almost half of your available cash ($20,000 if you're playing at the Easy level). Oil power plants produce almost as much pollution as coal power plants, and they're even more expensive.

Strategy: You may have your own reasons for using an oil power plant, but in general we think coal is a more economical alternative, especially at the beginning of a simulation. Later on, you'll have more alternatives, so why bother with an oil power plant?

Gas

In the 1950s the invention of gas power will be announced in the newspapers, and gas power plants will become an option. Gas power plants burn natural gas, which is cleaner than coal or oil.

Advantage: As mentioned, gas power plants are cleaner than coal or oil. Gas power plants are available fairly early in the game, so they provide an alternative to coal or oil that will allow you to reduce pollution.

50 Mw $2,000
Gas Power

GAS POWER – natural gas is much cleaner than coal, but very expensive. Many cities save their gas plants for reserve power due to their cost.

Disadvantage: The initial cost to build a gas power plant is twice that of an equivalent coal power plant.

Strategy: If you have the cash available, you may want to replace your aging coal or oil power plant with a new, cleaner gas power plant. (See "Death of a Power Plant" earlier in this chapter.)

Nuclear

Nuclear power becomes available in 1955. It has fairly extreme advantages and disadvantages (remember Chernobyl?), but there is a way to use a nuclear power plant in SimCity 2000 with no risk at all (see "Strategy" below).

Advantage: A nuclear power plant produces a lot of electricity and generates no pollution whatsoever—unless it melts down, in which case it will lay waste to a large area. Fortunately, the chances of a meltdown are very low.

500 Mw $15,000
Nuclear

NUCLEAR POWER – nuclear power is clean, efficient and relatively cheap. Unfortunately, there is always the risk of a deadly meltdown.

Disadvantage: To build a nuclear power plant, you'll spend more up-front capital than you would to build more traditional power plants. A nuclear power plant costs $15,000. Compared to a coal power plant at $4,000 or a gas power plant at $2,000, that's a hefty price to pay.

If a meltdown does occur, fires will ravage the nearby land and little radiation symbols will litter a widespread area of now-radioactive tiles (see Figure 5.1). You'll have to put out the fires, and you'll never again be able to build on the radioactive tiles. It's a pretty big mess.

Strategy: Some people consider this a cheat, but if you pull down Disasters on the menu bar and turn on No Disasters, your nuclear power plant will never melt down and you'll have a pollution-free source of energy with no risk.

FIGURE 5.1   *A nuclear power plant meltdown is hard to get over.*

Wind

Wind power plants (really just sophisticated, modern windmills) last forever and will provide you with an inexpensive, risk-free, pollution-free source of power—but at a hidden price.

Advantage: Wind power plants, available beginning in 1980, are inexpensive to build and maintain. They'll provide you with a pollution-free source of electricity that does absolutely no damage to the ecology and presents no risk. Like hydroelectric power plants, they never need to be replaced. Using them will also show you to be politically correct.

4 Mw $100
Wind Power

WIND POWER - very clean and relatively reliable, wind power is more cost-effective than solar power.

Disadvantage: First, let's talk about the unreliability of the wind: When there is insufficient wind to drive your wind power plants, they won't make much electricity and your Sims will experience brownouts.

Also, while other power plants incur expenses through higher start-up and maintenance costs, and through the effects of pollution, wind power costs *land* (see Figure 5.2). You can place only one wind power plant per tile of land, and you'd have to devote 125 tiles of land to wind power plants to generate the same power provided by the 16 tiles taken up by a nuclear power plant.

Strategy: If your goal is to build a small, ecologically sound city that does little damage to the resources and land, your best bet is to start

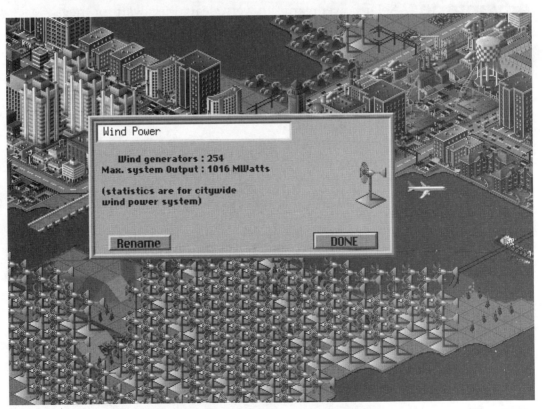

FIGURE 5.2 *It takes a lot of wind power plants to juice this city.*

with hydroelectric, as mentioned before, and augment that with wind when it becomes available. Build your wind power plants high on hills or in other areas that will allow them to catch a good strong breeze.

But if your grand design involves building a very big city, forget wind power plants—they take up too much land and don't produce enough to provide your city's energy needs.

Solar

Solar power plants, which become available in 1990, harness power from the sun without burning any fuel. Like wind power plants, they create no pollution, but the power they generate costs more than that generated by other forms of power plants.

Advantage: Solar power plants are very clean. Megawatt for megawatt, they take up less room than wind power plants, and they're safe.

50 Mw $1,300
Solar Power

Disadvantage: Every time clouds cover the sun, the sunlight necessary for a solar power plant is diminished, and your Sims will experience a brownout. Solar power plants are expensive to build and maintain, and they produce less power than other types of plants that take up the same amount of land.

SOLAR POWER – solar power is clean and cheap but unreliable. Cloudy seasons will leave your citizens shivering without light.

Strategy: Again, if your goal is to build a small city that does little damage to the resources and land, you can start with hydroelectric, augment that with wind when it becomes available, and add solar after 1990. Build solar power plants in areas away from tall buildings and high hills to maximize the sunlight available to the plant.

If you build a large city, you can augment your power plant system with solar if you like. Just don't rely on it as your primary energy source.

Microwave

Microwave technology, which comes into play in 2020, involves an orbiting satellite that collects solar energy and beams it down to the microwave power plant, which then supplies the energy to your city.

> **NOTE**
>
> While microwave technology as a power source might seem a little farfetched right now, it is an idea that in real life is being explored as a potential energy source.

1600 Mw $28,000
Microwave

MICROWAVE RECEIVER DISH - launch a satellite to collect solar power, then beam it down to Earth. Microwave power is very efficient, clean and reliable. Unfortunately, the effects of a mis-targeted beam are as yet unknown.

Advantage: Microwave power plants are relatively inexpensive and clean and do not create pollution of the usual types.

Disadvantage: Microwave power-plant technology is prone to some pretty unpleasant accidents: The microwave beam can miss the plant and hit nearby buildings instead, torching them. These missed transmissions will also result in a loss of power emanating from your microwave power plant, so your Sims will experience brownouts.

Strategy: Some people—adventurous people—will want to try out microwave power-plant technology in SimCity 2000. To those people, a few words of advice: don't build a microwave power plant near your city's center. Keep the thing far from buildings, roads, and parks.

You can, if you don't think it's cheating, pull down the Disasters menu and turn on No Disasters to avoid accidents. Then your microwave power plant will at least be safe, if not entirely reliable.

Fusion

Fusion, which makes its appearance in 2050, is the much changed replacement for nuclear fission. Through a process of combining atoms, fusion takes small amounts of hydrogen from water and makes it into helium and energy. Fusion creates large amounts of energy with very little waste. Unlike most other power plants, which often consume large amounts of costly fuel to make energy, a fusion power plant uses only small amounts of water as its fuel source.

Advantage: Using a fusion power plant will provide you with a highly productive source of electricity that produces no pollution. Fusion power plants aren't as dangerous as microwave power plants, and they produce much more energy than any of the other power plants.

2500 Mw $40,000
Fusion

FUSION POWER - Fusion energy is clean, reliable, efficient, and expensive. Accidents may destroy the plant but will not spread radioactive havoc.

Disadvantage: Fusion power plants are unreliable; the Sims will experience frequent brownouts. They are also *very* expensive to build.

Strategy: Because fusion power plants are not dangerous, you can build them closer to the city—even *in* the city. This will reduce stress on the power lines (it takes a lot of energy to make energy travel long distances over lengthy power lines) and thus minimize brownouts.

SELECTING A LOCATION FOR YOUR POWER PLANT

Choosing a good location for your power plant is also important. You probably wouldn't want to live near one—with its pollution and chances of accidents—and neither do your Sims. Find a location

> **TIP**
>
> One good strategy is to place your power plant near a corner of your map (but not right at the edge). This will limit the area that can be affected by pollution or accident.

that is not at the center of the area you plan to develop for commercial or residential use. (It does not hurt to zone and build industrial areas near most types of power plants.)

In general, you can't place power plants on the edge of your landmass, and you should place them near enough to areas you plan to zone and develop so that the power lines are not overburdened. For specific tips on different types of power plants, refer to the sections earlier in this chapter. For more on choosing a location, see Chapter 1.

JUICING UP THE PLACE WITH POWER LINES

Having built your power plant, you will have to place connecting power lines to transmit the electricity to zones and buildings.

To lay power lines, click on the Power icon tool, then, from the menu that appears, select Power Lines. The mouse pointer will change shape to represent what you've chosen, and the per-tile cost of power lines will appear in the Info box or (in the Windows version) the status bar. Move the pointer to where you want the power lines to begin, and click and drag to where you want them to stop. New power lines will flash with red and yellow power bolts at first (to indicate that power is not being transmitted), but they will soon stop flashing, thus indicating that power is traveling along the lines.

> **NOTE**
>
> **If you string power lines through an undeveloped zoned area or through an unzoned area, and you later develop that area, the power lines on any given tile will be replaced by the buildings that appear.**

Power is transmitted through developed areas—you do not have to place power lines *through* developed areas, only between them. If, for example, your nuclear power plant is a good, safe distance from your nearest zoned area, you'll have to stretch power lines all the way from the power plant to the zoned area. If your coal power plant is butt up against an industrial (or other) zoned area, you will not have to place connecting power lines from the plant to the zoned area.

Power does not cross roads, railways, or highways. When a road or railway divides two zoned areas—as is often the case—you must connect the two zoned areas, crossing the road or railway with a single piece of power line.

Power lines also do not cross water; when you are stringing power lines and you encounter a waterway, you will be offered (by a dialog box) the opportunity to build raised wires to cross the water. The cost of the raised wires will depend on the width of the waterway. To go ahead and build the raised wires, click on Raised Wires in the dialog box. Raised wires will be strung across the waterway, suspended between two "ramps" of land. If you don't want the raised wires, click on None.

> **TIP**
>
> You can encourage quick growth of newly zoned areas by crisscrossing power lines through the area.

ALL THE BENEFITS OF RAISED WIRES WITHOUT THE UNSIGHTLY WIRES

Raised wires do allow ships to pass underneath them, but they're very unsightly and they take up two tiles of valuable waterfront land for those unattractive suspension ramps. You can get all the benefits of raised wires—without any of the drawbacks—using a simple trick.

First, run your power lines up to the edge of a waterway at least three tiles wide. When the raised Wires dialog box appears, click on Raised Wires to build the crossing. Then use Bulldozer ➤ Demolish/Clear to blow up the raised power lines strung across the water. When you do this, the two suspension ramps will vanish, too, leaving flat land tiles jutting out into the water in their place. Surprisingly, you'll find that power still flows across the water—even without power lines. You can select Landscape ➤ Water and click on those two land tiles if you want to restore the body of water to its original condition.

When you place a structure—like a police station or hospital, marina or zoo, school or museum, and so on—you'll have to provide it with power. If you place it in a developed area that already has power, it will not be necessary to hook it up to power separately. But if you place it in an undeveloped zoned area or an unzoned area, you'll have to connect it via power lines to the nearest powered area or power source.

Big and small parks do not require power, and they do not transmit it. You probably won't want to cross your parks and green areas with power lines, so think about where you're placing parks in relation to the power needs of surrounding areas.

MANAGING YOUR POWER SYSTEM

Your power system is one of the most fundamental aspects of your city, and as such, you'll want to manage it closely. The power system usually is not something you just put into place and forget (though you can do that if you just keep enough cash on hand to allow for automatic replacement of the power plant and if for some reason you don't need to build new or additional power plants).

The newspaper will alert you when your aging power plant is about to fail. If you have several power plants and you want to know which one is going to blow, click on the newspaper's headline about the power plant's upcoming death and read the article that appears (Figure 5.3). It will tell you what *type* of plant is nearing its death, and from there you can use the Query tool (as described below) on individual plants of that type to figure out which one is oldest.

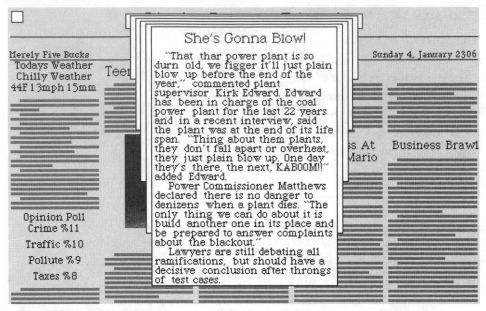

She's Gonna Blow!

"That thar power plant is so durn old, we figger it'll just plain blow up before the end of the year," commented plant supervisor Kirk Edward. Edward has been in charge of the coal power plant for the last 22 years and in a recent interview, said the plant was at the end of its life span. "Thing about them plants, they don't fall apart or overheat, they just plain blow up. One day they's there, the next, KABOOM!!" added Edward.

Power Commissioner Matthews declared there is no danger to denizens when a plant dies. "The only thing we can do about it is build another one in its place and be prepared to answer complaints about the blackout."

Lawyers are still debating all ramifications, but should have a decisive conclusion after throngs of test cases.

Merely Five Bucks

Todays Weather
Chilly Weather
44F 13mph 15mm

Opinion Poll
Crime %11

Traffic %10

Pollute %9

Taxes %8

Sunday 4, January 2306

FIGURE 5.3 *You can read in the newspaper which type of power plant is nearing the end of its life span.*

You don't have to wait for the newspaper to tell you how things are going, of course. To check on the status of any power plant at any point in the game, you can use the Query tool. Just move the mouse pointer to that power plant, hold down the Shift key, and click the mouse pointer. An info box like the one on the right will appear to tell you all about that particular power plant.

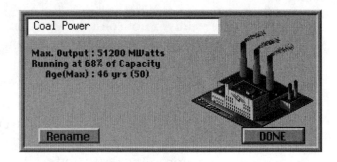

Coal Power

Max. Output : 51200 MWatts
Running at 68% of Capacity
Age(Max) : 46 yrs (50)

Rename

DONE

DEALING WITH BROWNOUTS

As your city grows larger it will need increasingly more power. Even with power plants that are not inclined to brownouts, your Sims might experience brownouts if the power plant is running over its capacity.

T I P

The buildings in your city must be connected via power lines to a power plant or be in contact with other powered areas. However, once they are—once you have established a power grid—adding a new plant *anywhere on the map* will increase the power in the power grid, even if the new power plant is not actually attached to the power grid.

Brownouts are indicated by flashes of red and yellow power bolts—just like the ones you saw when you first placed the power lines, but often more widespread. Sometimes large areas of the city will be flashing, indicating a widespread power outage. (Note that if this situation does not rectify itself or if you do not quickly intervene to solve the problem, Sims will move out in droves and that area will become abandoned.)

If you find that brownouts are occurring regularly in a given area, check the capacity at which your power plant is running. You may want to add another one.

CHAPTER SIX

ZONING

ZONING IS THE PROCESS BY which certain types of buildings are allowed to be built in certain areas. For example, a city planner (*you* in Sim-City 2000) might want to encourage a healthy mix of residential, commercial, and industrial areas, thereby stimulating a high quality of life for the residents and encouraging economic growth. To do this, the city planner would set aside certain areas of land for specific purposes—that's what urban planning is all about.

In SimCity 2000, you—as the mayor (and city planner)—won't actually *build* the buildings in zoned areas. The Sims do that. If you zone wisely, the Sims will move in quickly and build bigger and better things. If you zone poorly, the Sims will move in reluctantly or not at all. They may even move in, then move out in droves, leaving blocks of abandoned shells where a thriving neighborhood once existed.

In Chapter 1, we described basic techniques for the first steps in zoning and building a new city. In Chapter 4, we described how to use the Zoning tool in the City toolbar to actually do zoning. In this chapter, we're going to talk about zoning strategy.

BASIC ZONING GUIDELINES

First, let's go over some basic elements in zoning strategy.

TYPES OF ZONES

There are three fundamental types of zones in SimCity 2000:

- Residential
- Industrial
- Commercial

Each of these comes in two flavors:

- Light
- Dense

When your goal is to build a large city, dense zones seem like an attractive option—they really pack in the population, whether it's residential, industrial, or commercial—but they have hidden costs: dense urban areas foster higher crime rates and generate more pollution. This does not mean you should completely avoid zoning dense areas, nor that you should necessarily mix dense areas with light areas. Rather, it means that you should be aware of the downside of zoning dense areas and plan to address the issues (crime and pollution) that are bound to come up. (More on this as we go along.)

THE IMPORTANCE OF LAND VALUES

In SimCity 2000, you, as the Mayor, set the city's agenda. You have a great deal of control in setting goals and choosing the path and tools to get where you want to be. You don't *have* to build an industrial megalopolis—you can build a little, green EcoUtopia if you want. You can try to make tourism your city's leading industry. You can try to build a city that relies exclusively on public transit. You name it.

One thing you *can't* do is get by with lowered land values. Let's face it: a city can't survive without an income, and income in SimCity 2000 comes in the form of taxes, which are based on land values. Without good, solidly high land values, your city won't be able to maintain roads (they'll develop potholes before your eyes) and won't be able to support civic services (your Sims will scream about that). The whole city will start spiraling down a path of stunted commerce and industry and higher unemployment and crime rates, which will drive land values even lower, and so on.

All this talk about zoning is really talk about land values—about the tricks of balancing and mixing zones in the proportions and ways that will boost your city's income and make for a robust economy, whatever other goals you may want your city to achieve.

PRINCIPLES TO ZONE BY

Remember the following rules of thumb as you zone your city.

Select a large, flat area for your city. Don't think you're going to build suburban tract housing (aka Light Residential) on those attractive slopes just out of town—Sims can't build on hillsides. You can place power lines and lay pipes up hill and down dale, and doing that, you can successfully zone and develop the *flat* parts of hilly land, but it won't be an efficient way to go—you'll have to run a lot of power lines and pipes to supply juice and water to a relatively small population.

Zone areas of land the same type of zone. It's just a fact of life that Sims, like real people, prefer to live in residential *areas*, and do not like to live on an isolated residential *tile* in an industrial area or even *next to* an industrial tile.

Remember the "three-tile" rule. Sims won't walk more than three tiles. They won't bother to build anything more than three tiles from the nearest transportation. Transportation means (in this context): *road*, or subway or train *station*. You can zone an area six tiles wide, bound by roads on either side, and make it as long as you like, and Sims will build on it. But if you make that area seven tiles wide, the strip in the middle will go unused.

> **NOTE**
>
> **The three-tile rule is not absolute: Sometimes when you zone a dense area, a multitile building will appear on a group of tiles that are not all within three tiles of transportation.**

The simplest thing to do, because of this, is to zone areas that are basically 6×6 tiles. You do have some latitude—for example, 6×10 or 6×15, bound by roads, will work.

One of the sample cities (Lakeland) included with SimCity 2000 uses an ingenious system of making 9×9 tiles, with a small lake dug in the four tiles at the center of the 9×9 square, so that every zoned tile in the 9×9 group has access both to transportation and to water—all of which increases land values. That sample city's clever system is described at the end of this chapter.

Place residential, industrial, and commercial areas near each other. Sims don't like to commute long distances, so you should zone residential areas near industrial and commercial areas. Placing residential zones next to industrial zones lowers land values, however, so you should try to buffer those areas from each other.

Watch the path of pollution. Not only don't Sims like to live *next* to pollution-producing industrial zones, they don't like to live anywhere *near* them. This may seem contradictory to the idea that the Sims don't want to commute very far. Thus described are the challenges of urban planning. You'll find strategies to resolve this as we go along in this chapter.

Trees and water raise land values. Sims *do* like trees and water in all their various forms. Residential areas will have higher land values if they're placed near "empty" spaces filled with trees or on any kind of waterfront. Placing big or small parks, marinas, small lakes, or other open areas in or near residential areas will also raise land values. (See Chapter 13 for more details.)

LOOKING INTO YOUR CITY (ABOVEGROUND)

To help you make decisions and strategize, SimCity 2000 provides you with a number of tools for viewing and evaluating your city.

LOOKING AT ZONED AREAS

As your city grows, it will take on the appearance of a bustling metropolis. Buildings will sprout up all over, and the little dotted squares that indicate zoned tiles will no longer be visible. The visuals in SimCity 2000 are wonderful—a great improvement over SimCity Classic—but sometimes you'll want to see your original zoning patterns.

To see your city's industrial, residential, and commercial zones without buildings (except city services buildings), click on the Show Zones button, shown here.

All the buildings in zoned areas—except city services buildings like police stations, schools, and so on—will vanish. You'll be able to see clearly the pattern formed by your zoning efforts. Figure 6.1 shows a busy city; Figure 6.2 shows the same city viewed using the Show Zones feature.

Another way to look at zoning is via the Map window (see Chapter 3). Click on the City Form icon in the Map window and then on the Zones button. In the City window you'll see a very cool map showing the zoning in your city.

LOOKING AT INDIVIDUAL STRUCTURES

Having zoned an area and watched buildings start to appear, you may wonder what kinds of buildings those are. You can find out this and other useful information by using the Query tool on the City toolbar.

You can use the Query tool in one of two ways:

- Select the Query tool icon from the City toolbar (see Chapter 4) and click the left mouse button on any item within the City window.

- Just hold down the Shift key and click the left mouse button on anything within the City window.

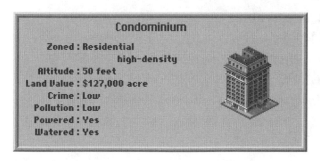

Depending on what you click on when you use the Query tool, you'll see different information. Here you can see information that was displayed about a condominium building, which was, of course, built in an area zoned for high-density residential use.

FIGURE 6.1 *It could be easier than it is here to see the pattern of zoning.*

Different types of buildings look different in SimCity 2000. As your city grows, watch for some of these interesting buildings:

 A drive-in showing the movie *Ants*. (Maxis also makes the game SimAnt, so this is an inside joke.)

 The Maxis headquarters building, which can be identified by the Maxis sign on the side.

 A historic office building.

FIGURE 6.2 *The same city shown in Figure 6.1, viewed after clicking the Show Zones button on the City toolbar.*

USING THE DEMAND INDICATOR

NOTE

The Demand Indicator does not distinguish between Light and Dense zones—it just tells you which of the three basic types of zones are in demand.

Using the Demand Indicator in the City toolbar, you can see how much demand (or lack of demand) exists at any given moment for the three types of zones: Industrial, Residential, and Commercial. Each bar represents one of the three types of zones. The farther upward the bar

moves, the greater the demand for that type of zone; the farther down-ward the bar moves, the less need there is for that type of zone.

Here you can see that there is too much Residential compared to In-dustrial. This, of course, means that unemployment is a problem.

A FEW WORDS ON ABANDONED BUILDINGS

As you play SimCity 2000, you may notice some buildings becoming dark, empty-looking shells. These buildings have been abandoned by your Sims. Sometimes this is just part of urban development: Often, an abandoned building will be replaced by a newer, more suitable—and perhaps much larger—building. That's nothing to worry about.

Sometimes, however, the Sims had good reason to clear out. For ex-ample, Sims will let a building go vacant when the demand for a par-ticular type of zone has gone way down. They will also stop using a building if it loses its access to transportation, or if, in residential areas, pollution rises to unbearable levels.

You can verify that a building is abandoned using the Query tool, as described in detail in Chapter 4.

One strategy for dealing with abandoned buildings is to demolish them and let the Sims rebuild. This does not address the root cause of your problem, though, and will cost you bulldozing fees.

A better solution is to determine *why* an abandoned building is not being used and remedy the situation. First, check to be sure the build-ing is within three tiles of access to transportation and that the pollution levels aren't too high. Then check the Demand Indicator (see "Using the Demand Indicator") to see if you've let your mix of zones get way out of balance.

Finally, here's a quick tip: Adding a park next to an abandoned apart-ment building always helps bring the building back to life.

The one basic principle to remember here is that you do not want any of the bars in the Demand Indicator to slip downward and stay there. If one does, that will mean you've built too much of that type of zone. You especially do not want all three bars to fall down into the "no demand" end of the Demand Indicator—that means your city's in trouble.

You *do* want to build what is shown to be in demand. If, for example, the Residential bar is way up and the Industrial bar is lower (closer to the middle), it means there are more jobs than people and you should zone more residential areas.

It is okay if all the bars in the Demand Indicator are way up—even for a period of time. That just means your city wants to grow.

WHAT SIMS WANT AND WHAT THEY SHOULD GET

The Demand Indicator does not tell you what other sorts of services or structures the Sims want—it tells you only what sorts of zones are in demand (or out of demand) in the city. To find out what the Sims want, watch the Info box and the newspapers and check in with your advisors from time to time. Look in those places for messages saying that your Sims are demanding this or that: Sometimes they want a hospital or stadium, sometimes they want police, sometimes they want you to stop tearing down the forests to build industrial areas.

When the Sims demand something, you should consider building it, but you don't *have* to build it. Sometimes Sims demand things that aren't what's best for them. Zones are a different matter, though—when a demand exists for one kind of zone over the other two, it's in the best interests of a balanced, growing city to zone land for that type of area.

ZONING STRATEGIES

Now, with some basic principles under our belts and a good understanding of the tools to use, let's look at specific zoning strategies.

ZONING LIGHT OR DENSE AREAS

Light and Dense areas are just that: light or dense. When you are thinking of placing Light Residential zones, you probably want single-family homes to be built. In a Dense Residential area, you're going to get high-rise condo and apartment buildings. In a Light Commercial zone, you'll get one-story storefronts; in a Dense Commercial zone, office towers…. You get the picture, right?

There are numerous workable strategies for using light and dense zones of all types. In a mature city, you may want a mix of these elements. In a brand new city, the tried and true approach is to start with areas zoned light and replace them with denser areas later.

ZONING INDUSTRIAL AREAS

Industrial zones are where your Sims build factories and industry. The presence of at least one strong industrial area is essential to a successful city. Without an industrial base, your city will never develop because having an industrial base creates jobs which, in turn, will encourage Sims to move into your city.

Remember that when you start a new city, you must first zone industrial areas to attract Sims. They won't move into your city if they aren't going to have jobs.

When you select the Industrial tool from the City Toolbar, you can zone either Light or Dense Industry. Keep in mind the following pointers as you zone industrial areas.

> **N O T E**
>
> As the population increases, you'll begin to notice that the Demand Indicator less often shows a high demand for Industrial and more often for Commercial—this is because as time goes on, an increasing amount of economic activity in your city will shift from industrial to commercial in nature. As this happens, fewer jobs will be available in industry and more in commerce, so you should switch your emphasis in zoning.

A new city may start growing faster if you zone for light industry. If you plan to grow your city into a large one, however, you'll need more dense industrial zones as the city becomes established.

Try to maintain more industrial zones than residential zones in the beginning of the game. A 3:1 ratio is generally good.

Industrial areas produce pollution. Light industry tends to generate less pollution than dense industry.

Sims do not like to live next to industry. Placing Industrial zones right next to residential zones will reduce the value of the residential zones and reduce your city's income from taxes. To resolve this, maintain a buffer zone of commercial areas, or some other structures, or preferably parks between industrial zones and residential zones.

> ### TIP
>
> To keep crime rates down and raise land values in nearby residential areas, checker your industrial areas with police stations.

To summarize, it is important, especially when your city is new, to create a lot of industrial areas. It is on the parts of your city that are zoned Industrial that your Sims build the factories that provide them with jobs. If Sims do not have jobs, they will move someplace else to find them, and enough of this will collapse your carefully built SimCity.

ZONING RESIDENTIAL AREAS

 Residential zones are where Sims live. You can build either Light or Dense Residential zones, depending on your purposes. Areas zoned Light Residential will contain single-family homes that will allow fewer Sims to live in the area but will also have lower crime rates and less pollution (because there will be fewer cars in the area). Areas zoned Dense Residential will contain densely packed, high-rise condominium and apartment buildings. A large, robust city can have a mix of both types of residential zones. Building a dense downtown and less-populated outward area is one strategy that tends to work well.

When you're zoning areas Residential, keep in mind the following thoughts.

Sims like to live *near* where they work and shop. That means near industrial and commercial zones. Sims do not, however, like to live *next to* industrial and commercial zones—especially not next to industrial zones.

The presence of water and trees in or near a residential zone will raise land values. Sims just love water and trees. Try zoning a lot of waterfront property Residential and watch those land values skyrocket.

You can take advantage of this by placing industrial areas far from waterfronts and snagging all that coastline and riverfront for residential areas. In fact, you can try tricks along these lines:

- To revive a sagging residential area, place a park or marina nearby.
- Plant a few trees with the Landscape ➤ Trees tool in an unzoned area near a residential area and watch the Sims move in and be happy.
- Apply the "buffering principle" by placing a row of parks between a residential area and industrial or commercial area.

Place schools, libraries, and recreational facilities in or near a residential zone to encourage Sims to move in and to raise land values. Sims want their kids to have better educations and they want to have more fun. To attract more Sims into your city's residential areas, sprinkle the areas with schools and recreational facilities.

Forget building dense residential areas on the edge of the landmass. Teetering out there on the edge of the world-as-we-view-it, Sims will never build anything bigger than a single-family dwelling. A better alternative is to shift your vision one tile inward by placing a road on the very edge and the residential areas inside of that.

Avoid rising crime rates and pollution levels. When a residential area in your city has a high crime rate or a high pollution level, Sims will leave; if it gets too bad, they'll go in droves. To combat high crime rates, place police stations in that area, or better yet, prevent it from happening in the first place by keeping land values up and unemployment down.

Pollution, once it's upon you, is harder to fight. You can pass the Pollution Control Ordinance (see Chapter 7's sections on establishing ordinances) to reduce citywide pollution. You can also remove any nearby industrial zones, but that's troublesome and expensive.

Again, it's best to prevent this problem before it gets started. Make sure your power plant and industrial areas aren't too close to a residential area. Cars are big contributors to pollution, so to prevent pollution, place train depots, bus depots, or subway stations in the area when you zone.

N O T E

Once you have zoned a residential zone and the Sims have built there, you can Shift-click on any given tile in that area to use the Query tool to get an idea of what the place is like. With the Query tool you can not only see what kind of building the Sims have built on the land, but also how that part of your city is doing in regard to crime and pollution.

The best thing to keep in mind as you're zoning for Sims is that they like and dislike all the same things where they live that you do. Make them a nice, clean, safe environment with good schools and fun things to do when they're not working, and they'll be perfectly happy to pay their taxes and allow you to keep zoning and building and reaping rewards.

THE APPEARANCE OF CHURCHES

From time to time, without warning, Sims will decide to build a church in an area you have zoned for residential use. When a church is built in a residential zone, the land that it sits on becomes unzoned. It also becomes land on which no taxes are paid, which, if it's high-land-value waterfront property, for example, can be very inconvenient. You can, if you wish, use Bulldozer ➤ Demolish/Clear to get rid of the church. (In SimCity Classic, if you did this, your city would be visited by a devastating tornado.) You'll find that another church will pop up somewhere nearby to replace the one you demolished. You can only hope that the new church will be more conveniently located, or you can try this trick: Zone a 2×2 residential area nearby, where you want the church to be. Then blow up the church. It will probably appear where you want it.

In an even more devious scheme, you can instead build an 8×8 industrial area with a road leading to an empty 2×2 area in the center. Now blow up a church and quickly rezone the 2×2 spot residential.

ZONING COMMERCIAL AREAS

In commercial zones, your Sims conduct their commercial business—shopping and banking, for example. When you start a new city (as you

did in Chapter 1), you don't actually need commercial zones; until Sims are working and living in your city, there's no need for shopping and banking.

You will see this lack of demand reflected in the Demand Indicator on the City toolbar. It's only after you zone some residential and industrial areas and after the Sims start building that you'll see a demand for Commercial begin to appear. That's when you should start to zone commercial areas in your city.

In the early years of your city, you'll notice far greater demands for industrial zones than commercial zones. This is because your city, in its early history (just as it would be in real life), is an industrial economy. As your city matures and time passes, the economy will shift to one that is commercially based. Your Sims will need more commercial zones and fewer industrial zones.

Sims drive their cars to and from commercial areas (unless they take public transit), but the type of business they conduct in these areas does not spew pollution out into the city. The activity that takes place in commercial zones pollutes your city far less than does industrial activity. There is also less of a crime risk in commercial areas than in industrial areas.

Because of this, commercial areas can act as a buffer between industrial and residential areas, as discussed earlier in this chapter.

> **N O T E**
>
> **Many of the principles that drive land values up and down in industrial and residential areas are also at work in commercial areas; for extra insight into making areas that are zoned Commercial live up to their potential, look also at the sections of this chapter on zoning industrial and residential areas.**

WATCH YOUR LANGUAGE

In the DOS version, if you type **damn**, you'll soon find yourself punished—all your residential areas will develop dotted with an overabundance of churches. You can fix this by quitting the game and restoring your city from a saved file. Similarly, typing the words **darn** and even **heck** can get you into trouble.

NOTE

Most of the cities whose zoning patterns we're going to look at come with SimCity 2000. You can open up those cities' files and take a look at the zoning patterns on screen if you like. To view a sample city, from the menu bar select File ➤ Load City, click on the name of the sample city from the list that appears, and then click the Load button. When the City window appears, displaying the sample city, select Speed ➤ Pause and then click the Show Zones button. To view a scenario city in the same manner, select File ➤ Load Scenario from the menu bar, click on the name of the scenario city from the list that appears, and then click the Load button. When the City window appears displaying the scenario city, you must immediately select Speed ➤ Pause or press Alt-P to stop the action. Then click the Show Zones button.

ZONING PATTERNS

As you gain experience in SimCity 2000, you'll see patterns develop in the zones that catch on and those that don't. To start, it is best to zone in rectangles or squares in large, flat areas. Be sure that you follow the "three-tile principle"—that each tile in the zoned area is within three tiles of a road or access to other transit.

Figure 6.3 shows zoned areas that have not yet developed. Notice that each zoned area consists of a group of 6×6-tile blocks bounded by roads so that each tile in the block is only three tiles from the road. Notice, too, that each block of tiles contains one unzoned corner, which has been set aside for use as a subway station or bus depot later.

Let's take a look at some patterns in zoning that have led both to successful cities and to cities with specific problems.

Zoning Patterns in Happyland

Happyland, a sample city included with SimCity 2000, is a small, pleasant town on a nice, flat area. Figure 6.4 shows Happyland as it appears in the City window. Figure 6.5 shows Happyland's zoning pattern. Notice the area to the left, zoned Dense Industrial, with a police station between it and the area zoned Dense Residential right next to it. This illustrates the principle of placing police stations strategically to lower crime rates.

Notice, too, that the Dense Residential area, in more or less a large "C" pattern, surrounds a large Dense Commercial area bisected by four big parks. The whole effect allows the Sims in Happyland quick access to where they work, live, and shop.

FIGURE 6.3 *These areas have been zoned for different types of usage. Notice that every tile is within three tiles of a road and that space has been saved at most intersections for a subway station or bus depot (to be placed later).*

Some distance from the city, you can see two solar power plants and several hydroelectric power plants, which, while they provide adequate power for a small town like this, do not create pollution.

Near the waterfront, notice the marina surrounded by an area zoned Light Residential. The whole scene here is one of tranquil, productive existence in a small, happy town. M-m-mm.

FIGURE 6.4   *This is Happyland.*

FIGURE 6.5   *This is Happyland's zoning pattern.*

Zoning Patterns in Lakeland

Lakeland, another sample city that comes with SimCity 2000, is shown in Figure 6.6. In Figure 6.7, you can see Lakeland's zoning pattern. This sample city is very cleverly designed to use the three-tile principle along with the Sims' love of water and trees to best advantage.

In Lakeland, industrial, residential, and commercial areas are all dense, and they are far more mixed than is usual. The really ingenious thing here, though, is the way each 9×9 block of tiles has a small lake at its center. This means that each tile in the block is only three tiles from the surrounding road, *and* that many tiles are in close enough proximity to water and trees so that their land value is jacked up as high as it can go.

This clever system offsets the dangers of an industrial or commercial area being too close to a residential area.

Note, too, that the city has a stadium, zoo, college, and marina, centrally located along with its police and fire stations near a larger downtown lake, with a library and a museum nearby.

These Sims should be very happy campers.

Zoning Patterns in Turista

Turista, which is not included with SimCity 2000, was developed by a SimCity 2000 user. In Figures 6.8 and 6.9, you can see Turista and its zoning patterns. We included Turista here because it shows an example of the buffering principle at work: notice the area zoned Dense Commercial providing a buffer between an area zoned Dense Industrial and another zoned Dense Residential.

The Dense Residential area, as you can see, is taking advantage of a waterfront location that really jacks up land values.

Note, too, that the nuclear power plant in Turista is within the city limits—this can only be done if you turn on No Disasters in the Disasters pulldown menu on the menu bar so you can place the nuclear power plant anywhere without endangering nearby buildings.

FIGURE 6.6 *Lakeland, one of the sample cities that come with SimCity 2000.*

FIGURE 6.7 *Lakeland's zoning pattern shows very clever usage of water, trees, and the three-tile principle.*

FIGURE 6.8   *This is Turista.*

FIGURE 6.9   *Turista is an example of the buffering principle at work.*

Zoning Patterns in Hollywood

Never mind that monster in the picture, take a look at how Hollywood is laid out. Hollywood is the city in one of the sample scenarios that come with SimCity 2000. In Figure 6.10, you can see Hollywood with all its buildings, and in Figure 6.11, you can see Hollywood's zoning pattern.

NOTE

See Part Three for tips on winning the model scenarios, including Hollywood, Charleston, and Flint, MI.

The SimCity 2000 version of Hollywood is laid out in a very interesting manner, with a big cross of areas zoned Dense Commercial as its primary feature, and blocks of dense residential areas surrounding the cross. Large areas zoned Dense Industrial are shunted over into corners of the landmass. Some smaller areas of Light Residential and Light Commercial rest on the opposite side of the river from all this, but most of the zoned areas are bunched together.

Another interesting aspect of this layout is the group of water towers—southern California, as everyone knows, is a dry place, with long, drought-like summers. (This may be just a cosmetic effect, but it sure increases realism in the Hollywood scenario's looks.)

Zoning Patterns in Charleston

Charleston, a city about to be consumed by flooding in the wake of a major hurricane, is nonetheless a model of urban balance, with light and dense zones of all types. (Charleston is one of the scenarios that come with SimCity 2000.) In Figures 6.12 and 6.13, you can see a beautiful mix of zones. Note here the oft-used buffer principle hard at work, keeping industrial and residential areas away from each other; this effect is not as pronounced in Charleston as it was in Turista, but it's definitely visible.

Zoning Patterns in Flint, MI

Flint, MI, one of the scenarios that come bundled with SimCity 2000, is a great example of zoning doomed to disaster. In Figures 6.14 and 6.15, you can see a lot of areas zoned Light Residential spanning large areas of the city, but notably little in the way of Light or Dense Industrial.

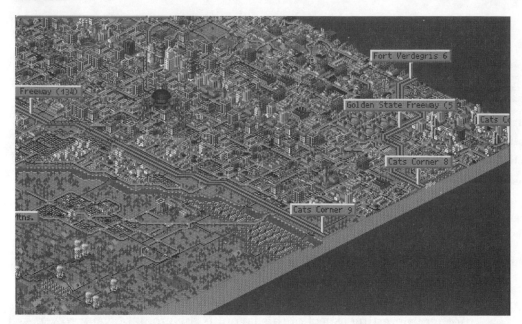

FIGURE 6.10   *Hollywood in a moment of high drama.*

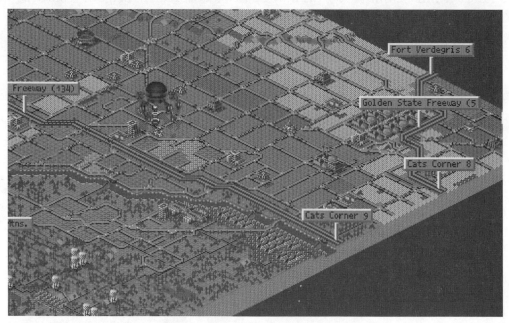

FIGURE 6.11   *Forget the monster; look at Hollywood's zoning pattern.*

FIGURE 6.12   *The charming and gracious town of Charleston, just as the flood begins.*

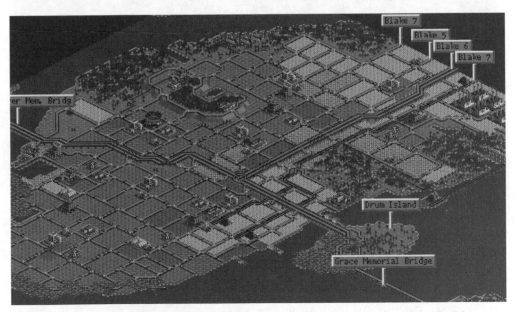

FIGURE 6.13   *Charleston's charming and gracious zoning pattern shows wonderful balance.*

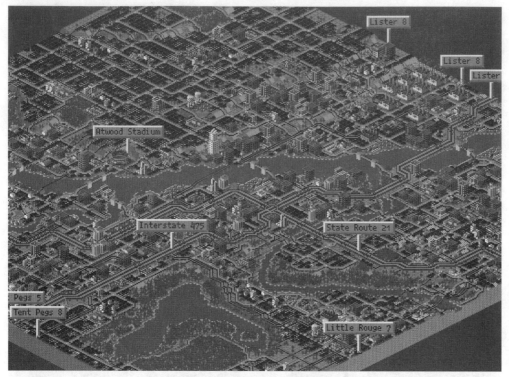

FIGURE 6.14 *Flint, MI, is dotted with abandoned buildings.*

Where can these Sims work? It's no wonder they're moving out of town—Flint in SimCity 2000 is awash with high unemployment, low land values, and diminished tax income.

Just take a look at the Budget window—the city has only $57 in income per year! It's a disaster. This could happen to your city, too, if you don't zone enough industrial areas so your Sims will all have jobs. Keep an eye on that Demand Indicator, and you can avoid a mess like this.

Flint 1974 Budget September 1974		1974 To Date Expense	1974 Year End Estimate	Done Help
Property Taxes	%7	1218	1951	
City Ordinances		37	64	
Bond Payments		0	0	
Police Department	%100	-333	-533	
Fire Department	%100	-250	-400	
Health & Welfare	%100	-62	-100	
Education	%100	-113	-182	
Transit Authority	%100	-463	-742	
Year to Date Total$		$32		
Estimated End of Year$			$57	
Current Treasury$			$19,498	
End of Year Treasury$			$19,555	

FIGURE 6.15 *In the SimCity 2000 version of Flint's zoning pattern, you can see the seeds of the city's doom.*

MAXIMIZING POPULATION

If building a really big city is your goal, you'll need to understand a few things to help you maximize the density of your areas. First, take a look at this listing of the occupied structures Sims will build in residential areas:

Structure	Size in Tiles	Population per Tile
Lower-class homes	1×1	10
Middle-class homes	1×1	10
Luxury homes	1×1	10
Churches	2×2	0
Cheap apartments	2×2	80

Structure	Size in Tiles	Population per Tile
Apartments	2×2	80
Nice apartments	2×2	80
Condominiums	2×2	120
Condominiums	3×3	360
Large apartment buildings	3×3	450

Basically, to maximize population you need a lot of 3×3 buildings in your city. That's not just because they are big and tall and hold large populations, it's also because 3×3 buildings don't use any more power than smaller buildings. And—here's the real benefit—*you get more tax revenue from bigger buildings*.

The building of 3×3 structures, however, is not entirely up to you: Remember, you zone, the Sims build. You can, however, set up circumstances that encourage the building of 3×3 structures. These buildings will be built when your overall land values are high and where roadway intersections are present.

These principles do not apply only to residential structures; even in industrial and commercial areas, if you want to build a bigger city, 2×2 and 3×3 buildings will give you more bang for your buck.

"ZONING" SEAPORTS AND AIRPORTS

To establish seaports and airports—vital links to the outside world that will help your city's economy flourish—you use techniques very similar to those you use for zoning industrial, residential, and commercial areas. For example, to create a seaport or airport, you use the Ports ➤ Seaport or Ports ➤ Airport tool and then click and drag an appropriately sized area, just as you use the zoning tools to click and drag an area to be zoned industrial, residential, or commercial. However, seaports and airports are not, strictly speaking, zoned areas, and they have their own special issues. Turn to Chapter 10 for info on seaports and airports.

GETTING THE RIGHT MIX

As your city grows, and as you add one sort of zoned area or another, the mix of zones will change. Watch the Demand Indicator on the City toolbar to see which zones are in demand, and you can build to suit demand.

Getting the right mix of industrial, residential, and commercial zones is one of the keys to winning in SimCity 2000.

Another key issue is money. In Chapter 7, we'll talk about taxes, budgets, and ordinances—the city's coffers.

CHAPTER SEVEN

THE CITY BUDGET AND ORDINANCES

IN SIMCITY 2000, AS IN LIFE, money makes things happen. You'll start a new game with a set amount of money (the amount will vary depending on the level of play you select at the beginning of the game). As the game progresses, you'll have to establish an income and balance spending against that income.

> **TIP**
>
> To get around what would have been a programming nightmare, SimCity 2000 uses a clever trick to relate the amount of property tax collected to the value of property. Instead of making a simple calculation based on the value of each building in your city as you might expect, the program calculates property tax based on *population*. When you maintain high land values, you actually are maintaining higher populations, which increases the amount of property tax collected. As a rough guide to the amount collected, you can figure: Tax collected = 1.29 × {[T(residential) × P(residential)] + [T(commercial) × P(commercial)] + [T(industrial) × P(industrial)]} where T is tax rate and P is population.

Your city's income will come primarily from property taxes. You'll be able to set the property tax rate, and you'll want to maximize the value of property in industrial, residential, and commercial zones so your city is raking in as much money as possible. You'll also get to decide whether your city will or will not collect a 1% sales tax, a 1% income tax, and parking fines. To garner additional income, you can allow legalized gambling, and if you are desperate for a large amount of quick cash, you can issue a bond.

Everything you develop in SimCity 2000 will cost you—you not only pay for zoning and building, but often for maintenance as well. Your ongoing expenses might include maintaining educational facilities, police and fire departments, roads, bridges, and so on.

In this chapter, we'll walk you through the elements of the city budget: taxes, expenses, and bonds. We'll also talk about ordinances—your city's laws.

LOOKING INTO THE BUDGET WINDOW

At the top of the City window, the month and year are displayed. (This is not the actual month and year, but the month and year in your game.) In the regular course of events, a Budget window will appear on screen every January.

WHAT'S IN THE BUDGET WINDOW

In the Budget window, you can control city income rates and certain aspects of spending, including:

- Property taxes
- Bonds (issuance and payments)
- Police department funding
- Fire department funding
- Health and welfare funding
- Education funding
- Transit authority funding

Glen Cove 2297 Budget September 2297		2297 To Date Expense	2297 Year End Estimate		
Property Taxes	%7	453	600		?
City Ordinances		-111	-147		?
Bond Payments		0	0		?
Police Department	%100	-30	-55		?
Fire Department	%100	-30	-55		?
Health & Welfare	%100	-15	-27		?
Education	%100	-18	-25		?
Transit Authority	%100	-12	-16		?
Year to Date Total$		$236			
Estimated End of Year$			$275		
Current Treasury$			$117,454		
End of Year Treasury$			$117,729		

You can also pass ordinances (city laws) in the Budget window and get helpful advice from specialized advisors. For more basic how-to advice on the Budget window, turn to Chapter 3. Here, we'll talk strategies and specific techniques.

AVOID THE ANNUAL BUDGET REVIEW WITH AUTO-BUDGET

You can use SimCity 2000's Auto-Budget feature to avoid divvying things up every year. Select Options ➤ Auto-Budget to turn on Auto-Budget, and SimCity 2000 will renew the budget every year without bothering you. A word of caution: the Auto-Budget feature does not exercise any kind of judgment but simply maintains the current budget numbers. You should still keep track of how much you are taking in and spending so you won't run your city into debt or financial ruin. You can see the Budget window any old time, even if you have Auto-Budget turned on, by clicking the Budget window tool (the one with the dollar-sign icon) in the City toolbar or by pulling down Windows in the menu bar and then selecting Budget.

Getting the Lowdown from Your Advisors

You can find out more about public opinion and different aspects of your city by consulting the advisors. To summon an advisor, click on the question-mark icon at the far right of the line for the topic that interests you.

For example, clicking on the question-mark icon on the right side of the Education line will call up the Education Advisor. In Figure 7.1, the Advisor cheerily suggests the need for more grade schools.

If you reduce funding to a dangerous level in any given area, the advisor for that area might issue a stern warning, again as shown in Figure 7.1.

The advisors will also sometimes convey the wishes of your Sims for additional services or suggest ways you can boost your popularity.

FIGURE 7.1   *The Education Advisor says we need more grade schools, while the Transportation Advisor is alarmed at cuts in spending.*

Setting Budget Items in the Books

You can click on the Books icon for any of the Budget window's line items to see the history of funding for that area and its projected budget for the rest of the year. In some cases (police and fire protection, for example), when you click on the Books icon, you'll get only that information; but in other cases, you'll also be able to make changes to the funding levels. For example, when you click on the Books icon next to

Transit Authority, a window will appear like the one shown in Figure 7.2.

In this window you can see the history of spending and funding for the Transit Authority. (Actual amounts in this type of window are shown in blue, while projected amounts are shown in red.) You can also set funding levels for the upcoming maintenance needs of different aspects of transportation. You may, for example, decide to cut funding to this or other city services as an emergency cost-saving measure.

> **WARNING**
>
> **Setting funding levels here will affect maintenance but not your ability to build items. If you set Tunnels to 0, for example, you can still merrily build (and pay for building) all the tunnels you like; they'll just crumble almost immediately after you build them because their maintenance is underfunded. That means you wasted your money in building the things.**

Month	Road	Hwy.	Brdg.	Rail	Sub.	Tunnel	Total
Jan	0	0	0	0	0	0	0
Feb	-1	0	0	0	0	0	-1
Mar	-1	0	0	0	0	0	-2
Apr	-2	0	0	0	0	0	-4
May	-1	0	0	0	0	0	-5
Jun	-1	0	0	0	0	0	-6
Jul	-2	0	0	0	0	0	-8
Aug	-1	0	0	0	0	0	-9
Sep	-1	0	0	0	0	0	-10
Oct	-2	0	0	0	0	0	-12
Nov	-1	0	0	0	0	0	-13
Dec	-1	0	0	0	0	0	-14

Road 100% Hiway 100% Bridge 100%

Rail 100% Subway 100% Tunnel 100%

Done

FIGURE 7.2   *Click on the Transit Authority Books icon to see this budget area's history of funding and to change funding levels.*

ESTABLISHING TAX RATES: INCOME FOR YOUR CITY

As we keep saying, all this great stuff you can do in SimCity 2000 costs SimMoney. You start with a set amount of money at the beginning of the game, but if you don't have an income, that money will dwindle away in

no time flat. Establishing an income in SimCity 2000 is an essential part of the game. To do it, you can *tax* or you can *borrow*.

There are two general ways to maximize your tax base in SimCity 2000:

- By raising or lowering the tax rate and by maximizing land values, you can control the income generated by the property tax, which taxes *all* zoned and developed land in the city.

- By raising or lowering the tax rate for individual types of industries, you can more specifically control the income generated by areas zoned Industrial. (This way you can also encourage—or discourage—the development of specific types of industries.)

QUICK CASH WITH CASS

There is an undocumented way to come up with some quick cash: Just type **cass** at any time during a simulation, and you'll be awarded an instant cash bonus of $250. (Game designer Will Wright's daughter's name is Cassidy.)

You can even do this more than once in a simulation. *Watch out,* though—what you're doing is actually embezzling, and if you type **cass** more than once a month (or more than three times), your city will self-destruct by fire as a result of your greed.

You can also raise funds through income and sales taxes and through the issuance of bonds.

RAISING INCOME THROUGH PROPERTY TAXES

Because most of your income in SimCity 2000 will come from property taxes, let's take a look at their ins and outs and how they're affected by land values.

GET THOSE LAND VALUES UP AND KEEP THEM THERE

Keep in mind that taxing occurs on a percentage basis, and that your major source of income is from property taxes. You'll get greater income taxing land that is worth $150,000 at 7% (you'd get $10,500) than you will taxing land that is worth $75,000 at 10% (you'd get $7,500). Always remember:

- If your land values are high, you can tax at a lower percentage and still get more income.

Following this guideline has an additional advantage: Sims are happy when they pay lower taxes and happier still when they get more for their buck. High land values mean not only that the Sims' homes and businesses are worth more but also that city services are better, commerce and industry are strong, employment is high, and crime is low.

The bottom line here is that to provide a good, strong tax base for your city, you want to get land values as high as possible and keep them there.

SETTING GENERAL PROPERTY TAX RATES

The general percentage rate for property taxes is controlled from the first option in the Budget window—you guessed it, *Property Taxes*. When SimCity 2000 starts a new game, it sets the tax rate at 7%. This is a nice, conservative rate that will bring in some revenues but will not alienate the Sims. You can increase the tax rate by clicking on the up arrow or decrease the rate by clicking on the down arrow (they're both next to the text box containing the percentage).

If you increase the tax rate too much, the Sims will show their displeasure by moving their homes and businesses out of town. We've found that Sims reach the limit of their tolerance at about 9%. You'd think, following the logic of this, that setting the tax rate to 0% would be a big boon to your city, but it's not. When you lower the tax rate substantially

> **W A R N I N G**
>
> **The fastest way to kill off your city is to raise taxes to 20% and cut city services. If you do this, Sims will move out in droves.**

and a lot of Sims move in, they tend to be somewhat transient and unstable, and bring with them exceptional crime rates. And lowering the tax rate too far while trying to keep up services is obviously a recipe for bankruptcy. Only if you have a pile of money at your disposal—oh, say, a million bucks or so—can you turn the tax rate down to just about nothing, keep services up, and let the city live off its savings for a while.

So—generally speaking, the safety zone for property taxation seems to be between 6% and 9%. However, with some quick double-clicking, you might pull a taxation trick to rake in some extra cash without alarming the citizenry.

TIP

Try this: Keeping in mind that taxes are collected retroactively for the entire year in December of that year, jack up the Property Tax rate in December to 20% (the highest possible percentage). Then, immediately after the taxes are collected, change the rate in January back to 7%. You'll collect some nice extra income without giving the Sims a chance to notice or react.

SETTING TAX RATES FOR SPECIFIC TYPES OF PROPERTY

NOTE

You can also control the tax rate industry-by-industry. See the section of this chapter titled "Industry Taxes" for more information.

In addition to the general Property Tax rate, you can set tax rates for specific kinds of property. You might set a single rate for all three types of property in the Budget window (as described earlier) or delve further into the tax-rate structure and set different rates for residential, industrial, and commercial properties.

To set different rates for different properties, open the Budget window, then click on the Books icon at the rightmost end of the Property Tax line. A window will appear showing the history of taxation this year for each type of zoned property. At the bottom of the window are three buttons. To raise the tax rate for one of the three types of

Month	Residents		Commerce		Industry		Total
Jan	7%	27	7%	5	7%	18	50
Feb	7%	27	7%	5	7%	19	101
Mar	7%	28	7%	6	7%	19	154
Apr	7%	29	7%	5	7%	19	207
May	7%	28	7%	5	7%	19	259
Jun	7%	29	7%	6	7%	18	312
Jul	7%	28	7%	5	7%	18	363
Aug	7%	29	7%	5	7%	18	415
Sep	7%	29	7%	6	7%	18	468
Oct	7%	28	7%	5	7%	18	519
Nov	7%	29	7%	6	7%	18	572
Dec	7%	28	7%	5	7%	18	623

Res% 7%   Com% 7%   Ind% 7%   Done

zoned property, click on its up-arrow button. (Each time you click, the tax rate jumps 1%.) To lower the tax rate, click on the down-arrow button.

The tax rate for each type of zoned property is set by default to 7%. To encourage the building of residential areas (to increase your population, for example), you could lower the Residential rate to 5% or 6%. If you simultaneously raised the Industrial rate to 8% or 9%, you would discourage industry somewhat, which would lessen pollution. You would also maintain your overall Property Tax rate at 7%, implying that you would not lose revenues. You can see that this is so by closing the Property Tax Books window (click the Done button or OK) after you've adjusted specific property tax rates. In the Budget window, you'll see how your changes to specific tax rates affected the overall Property Tax rate.

INDUSTRY TAXES

In addition to setting the Property Tax rate for all zoned land, you can set tax rates for individual types of industries. This has the double advantage of allowing you to control revenue and encourage or discourage development of certain industries.

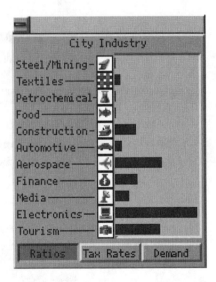

For example, if the agenda for your city includes environmental safeguards, you can reduce the tax rate on clean industries while taxing polluting industries more. If you want to encourage city growth, you can check for those industries that are in demand and lower their tax rates to encourage them to move in and set up business in your area.

 To set tax rates individually on specific types of industries, select Windows ➤ Industries or select the Industry Window tool on the City toolbar. In either case, the City Industry window will appear.

Industrial Ratios

When it first appears, the City Industry window shows Ratios—the percentage of each type of industry that makes up the total amount of industry in your city.

There are two other bar graphs available in the City Industry window:

- Tax Rates
- Demand

To switch between them, click on the buttons that appear at the bottom of the window.

Changing Industrial Tax Rates

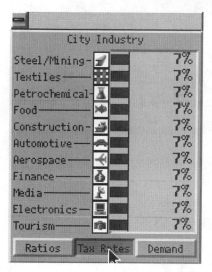

The Industrial Tax Rates graph appears as a series of horizontal blue bars, each representing the tax rate for a specific industry (aerospace, petrochemical, food, tourism, etc.). The default for the industrial tax rate is 7% straight across the board. You can raise or lower the rate by clicking on the blue bar in the graph for the particular industry you want to regulate and dragging to the left (to lower the tax rate) or to the right (to raise it).

You can set the tax rate as low as 0% or as high as 20%, but beware of the consequences: setting an industry's tax rate to 20% will chase that industry right out of your city. In some cases this may be a *good* thing. If reducing pollution is your goal, for example, you might want to place a particularly high tax on industries that produce more pollution.

Industries that produce heavy pollution include:

- Steel/Mining
- Textile
- Petrochemical
- Automotive

Industries that produce less pollution include:

- Food
- Electronics
- Tourism

Viewing Industrial Demand

Before you start fiddling with the industrial tax rates, you might want to get some intelligence. To find out what is in demand at any given time, open the City Industry window and click on the Demand button at the bottom of the window. A bar graph will appear showing you the relative rates of demand for each of the industries that exist in SimCity 2000.

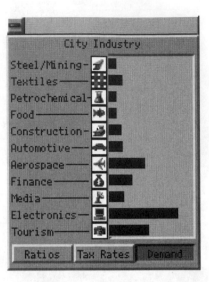

Some of what creates demand for an industry is obvious: If you have a city that relies heavily on transportation by car, for example, the automotive industry is likely to be in demand. But external factors come into play here. There may be an economic or industrial trend you aren't immediately aware of that affects the need for a given industry. The timeline factors into this, too, in the sense that heavier industry is more likely to be in demand earlier in the 20th century (just as it was in real life), while electronics will be more in demand later in the 20th century.

The Demand bar graph is a handy tool for determining the needs of your city, allowing you to make choices that have long- and short-range impact on development.

BORROWING INCOME THROUGH ISSUING BONDS

Let's say you've developed a beautiful, burgeoning city. Now the newspaper's announcing the upcoming death of your power plant, and you realize your city's perfect in every respect except this: you spent all its money.

You can, if you really, really want to, borrow the cash by issuing a bond (or *bonds*, if you're a real credit hound).

A bond is essentially a loan from your Sims—they buy shares in the bond, and the city pays them back *with interest* over time. It's the interest that's going to kill you.

The SimCity 2000 program figures an interest rate based on prime rate plus 1%, plus an additional percentage based on your city's current value and credit rating. Value and credit rating are based on land values and the general economic vigor of your city, as well as external economic factors over which you have no control (like SimNation's economic health). A good credit rating, high land values, and generally favorable economy means you will be able to borrow at a low interest rate (5%, for example). Obviously, issuing a bond is less advisable the higher the interest rate is. This is one of those things in SimCity 2000 that's just like life: if you really *need* to borrow, you probably can't afford to.

You should only consider issuing a bond to finance a part of your city that will *generate* tax revenue in the future—a small airport, maybe—or to get over what is really and truly a *temporary* economic hurdle.

As a rule of thumb, we discourage issuing bonds. It's just the kind of thing that can lure you into a downward economic spiral that will bankrupt and eventually kill off your city.

THE CLASSIC "FUND" TRICK, FOILED

In SimCity Classic, a famous undocumented trick was to type **fund** anytime you were playing the game. The program would then issue you a large sum of money to use as you wished with no obligations. In SimCity 2000 there's a twist to this trick: When you type **fund**, a window will appear offering you a *bond* at 25% interest! (This is a bad deal.)

Month	Bond$	Rate%	Cost$	Total$
Jan	0	0.0%	0	0
Feb	0	0.0%	0	0
Mar	0	0.0%	0	0
Apr	0	0.0%	0	0
May	0	0.0%	0	0
Jun	0	0.0%	0	0
Jul	0	0.0%	0	0
Aug	0	0.0%	0	0
Sep	0	0.0%	0	0
Oct	0	0.0%	0	0
Nov	0	0.0%	0	0
Dec	0	0.0%	0	0

| Show Bonds | Issue Bond | Repay Bond | Done |

If you've decided to disregard our warnings about the evils of borrowing, you can issue a bond from the Budget window. Click on the Books icon next to the Bond Payments line, and the Bond Payments window will appear.

In this window, you can review all the bonds you have issued in the past along with your payment history, and if it seems wise, you can issue a bond.

Four columns of numbers are displayed:

Bond$ The total amount of your city's current debt (up to the current month)

Rate%   The interest rate being charged this month

Cost$ The amount of interest you must pay that month for the bonds

Total$ The cost of interest for the year to date

A number of buttons appear along the bottom of the Bond Books window. These buttons allow you to:

- Show a summary of your current bonds and the cost of issuing a new bond
- Issue a new bond
- Repay current bonds
- Close the Bond Books window (by clicking the Done button or OK)

To issue a new bond, click on the Issue Bond button at the bottom of the window. Another window will appear in which you'll be notified of the current interest rate and asked if you wish to issue the bond at that rate.

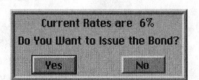

Click on Yes if you must; a whopping $10,000 will be added to the total funds listed in the top of your City window. Click on No if you want to back out of the deal.

You can see your city's credit rating, along with other helpful info that will help you decide whether the bond is worthwhile, by clicking on the Show

WARNING

Because you must repay the bond with interest, it's going to be a big drain on your future tax revenue. This is only worthwhile if the bond is financing something that will generate more tax revenue than it drains away.

```
Loan Rating:   AAA         Outstanding Bonds
Total Bonds:   $0
Bank Rate%:    5%
Next Bond%:    6%

City Value: $52,645,000
```

Bonds button at the bottom of the Bond Payments window. AAA is the best; F is the worst. This credit rating is based on the value of your city, which is also shown in the window.

Summarized in the Show Bonds window, you'll see:

Loan Rating	Your city's credit rating
Total Bonds	The total dollar value of all your city's outstanding bonds
Bank Rate%	The current prime interest rate in SimNation
Next Bond%	The interest rate you will have to pay on your *next* bond
Outstanding Bonds	The total dollar amount of all of your city's currently outstanding bonds (not shown in the Bonds window because our city didn't have any)
City Value	The current dollar value of your city

To close this window, click anywhere within it.

If you have some bonds outstanding, but you've made it through your fiscal crisis and found your way to prosperity again, you might want to consider repaying one or more bonds to get that interest off your back. To repay a bond, click on the Repay Bond button at the bottom of the Bond Payments window. In the Repay Bond window that appears, you'll get information on the interest rate of the oldest outstanding bond. To repay it, click Yes. The outstanding amount of the bond will be deducted from the total funds listed at the top of the City window, and the Repay Bond dialog box will close.

> **NOTE**
>
> If you're a SimCity 2000 for DOS user, you can pad your coffers using one of a number of cheat programs that modify the program's data file. Look in CompuServe's Sybex and Gamers forums for these programs.

"STEALING" INCOME AND REWARDS

In version 1 for the Mac, you can get quick cash—and plenty of it—by typing **porntipsguzzardo** anytime in the game. You'll get half a mil, along with all the known rewards, including *arcologies*—large self-contained utopian communities holding thousands of Sims each. (Arcologies, discussed in Chapter 14, usually aren't available to you until you've reached a population of 120,000 in the 21st century, but *hey*, you can get them in 19*50* this way.) This trick will also prevent the military from building up a base in your city.

Once you've typed **porntipsguzzardo**, you can type **ardo** any time, and you'll get another half million.

Just to prove once more that everything's easier with the Mac, you won't get punished for your grand larceny when you type **porntipsguzzardo** the way you did for your petty larceny when you typed **cass**.

BUDGETING YOUR CITY'S EXPENSES

Although it's not glamorous, budgeting for your city's expenses is a major part of your challenge as SimMayor. Don't neglect your city's finances; the Budget window is a treasure chest of tools for controlling your city's growth and maximizing your ability to achieve the goals you've set.

Take some time to play around with budget settings. You might want to save your city before you experiment, then run the simulation with different settings to see what the effects are on growth and development.

We've found, for example, that setting the tax rate for electronics to 4% in the late 20th century is a big boon to urban growth, and that discouraging the steel industry at that same time with a high tax rate seems to have no ill effect on the economy but prevents some pollution.

> **NOTE**
>
> The default funding level for city services is 100%. This does not represent 100% of the total funding pie, but 100% of that service's *slice* of the pie.

To help you along in setting the budget, the following sections contain specific information on the costs of maintaining your city's infrastructure.

Month	Police	Fund	Cost	Total
Jan	1	100%	-8	-8
Feb	1	100%	-8	-16
Mar	1	100%	-9	-25
Apr	1	100%	-8	-33
May	1	100%	-8	-41
Jun	1	100%	-9	-50
Jul	1	100%	-8	-58
Aug	1	100%	-8	-66
Sep	1	100%	-9	-75
Oct	1	100%	-8	-83
Nov	1	100%	-8	-91
Dec	1	100%	-9	-100

POLICE

In the Police Department line of the Budget window, you can set the funding level for your city's police. Maintaining a high funding level for police will keep crime down.

Funding for one police station is $100 per year; that amount × the number of police stations you have in your city will be deducted from your total cash in the annual budget review every January.

To see a detailing of the year's past and projected funding, click on the Books icon in the Police Department line. To close the funding detail window, click anywhere within it.

FIRE

In the Fire Department Budget window line, you can specify the funding percentage for your city's fire departments. Maintaining a high level of funding here will help prevent fires and allow you to respond to emergencies.

Funding for one fire station costs $100 per year; that amount × the number of fire stations you have in your city will be deducted from your total cash every January.

HEALTH & WELFARE

You can set the funding percentage for your city's hospitals in the Health & Welfare Budget window line. Maintaining a high funding level

for Health & Welfare will help keep the Sims in your city healthy, and if you fund this area at 100% for several decades, you'll see a rise in life expectancy among your Sims.

One hospital costs $50 per year to fund; that amount × the number of hospitals you have in your city will be deducted from your total cash every January.

EDUCATION

The funding you set in the Education line of the Budget window will be distributed among the schools and colleges in your city. If you don't adequately fund schools and colleges here, your Sims will not receive the kinds of education that allow for the development of technology or enterprise. You can set the percentage of funding for schools and colleges independently of each other (see below).

One school costs $25 per year to fund; that amount × the number of schools you have in your city will be deducted from your total cash in the annual budget review that occurs every January. One college costs $100 per year to fund; that amount × the number of colleges you have in your city will be deducted in the same manner.

To see a detailing of the year's past and projected funding, and to set the specific levels of funding for schools and colleges, click on the Books icon in the Education line. In the bottom of the detail window that appears, you'll see up- and down-arrow buttons for Schools and for Colleges. To raise or lower funding levels, click on the up- and down-arrow buttons.

> **N O T E**
>
> Although libraries and museums are part of the educational infrastructure of your city, you don't set a budget for these items. The Education budget affects only schools and colleges. Placing libraries and museums around your city will help to raise the overall educational level of your Sims, however—for more on libraries and museums, see Chapter 12.

Month	School	%	Cost	College	%	Cost	Total
Jan	2	100%	-4	1	100%	-8	-$12
Feb	2	100%	-4	1	100%	-8	-$24
Mar	2	100%	-4	1	100%	-9	-$37
Apr	2	100%	-4	1	100%	-8	-$49
May	2	100%	-4	1	100%	-8	-$61
Jun	2	100%	-5	1	100%	-9	-$75
Jul	2	100%	-4	1	100%	-8	-$87
Aug	2	100%	-4	1	100%	-8	-$99
Sep	2	100%	-4	1	100%	-9	-$112
Oct	2	100%	-4	1	100%	-8	-$124
Nov	2	100%	-4	1	100%	-8	-$136
Dec	2	100%	-5	1	100%	-9	-$150

Schools **100%** Colleges **100%** **Done**

To close the funding detail window, click on the Done button or OK.

TRANSIT AUTHORITY

The funding level you set in the Transit Authority Budget window line will be distributed to maintain your transportation system:

Month	Road	Hwy.	Brdg.	Rail	Sub.	Tunnel	Total
Jan	-31	-8	-1	0	-16	0	-56
Feb	-32	-9	-1	-1	-16	0	-115
Mar	-32	-9	-1	0	-16	0	-173
Apr	-31	-8	-1	-1	-16	0	-230
May	-32	-9	-2	0	-17	0	-290
Jun	-32	-9	-1	-1	-16	0	-349
Jul	-31	-8	-1	0	-16	0	-405
Aug	-32	-9	-1	-1	-16	0	-464
Sep	-32	-9	-1	0	-17	0	-523
Oct	-31	-8	-2	-1	-16	0	-581
Nov	-32	-9	-1	0	-16	0	-639
Dec	-32	-9	-1	-1	-16	0	-698

Road 100% Hiway 100% Bridge 100%
Rail 100% Subway 100% Tunnel 100%

Done

- Roads
- Rails
- Highways
- Subways
- Bridges
- Tunnels

If you don't adequately fund a given part of your transportation system, you'll see it fall into disrepair and crumble; that will adversely affect commerce and commuting in your city.

You can set levels for each of these parts independently of the others in the same way you did for schools and colleges.

ESTABLISHING ORDINANCES: LAWS FOR YOUR CITY

In the City Ordinances line of the Budget window, you can pass city laws. This gives you specific controls: you can make your city a nuclear-free zone, pass laws discouraging smoking or automobiles, or raise small amounts of additional revenue through fines and special taxes. By carefully picking the ordinances you pass, you can encourage your SimCitizens to "do the right thing," or at least whatever *you* think is the right thing.

In the City Ordinances line of the Budget window you can see the total current estimated cost for all the city ordinances you have passed.

The actual cost of city ordinances varies and is not known beforehand, just like in real life. To pass or revoke ordinances from the Budget window, click on the Books icon in the City Ordinances line. The window that appears will list all the available ordinances.

To pass an ordinance, click on the selection box next to its name. When an ordinance has been passed, a check mark will show up in the box. You can revoke a passed ordinance by clicking on the selection box again—the check mark will go away.

Some of the ordinances—adding a sales tax, for example—will generate revenue for your city. Others will cost your city money to implement and maintain, but will (you hope) pay for themselves in other ways. Free clinics, for example, aren't free to you, but will benefit your Sims' health and quality of life, attract Sims, raise property values.... Get the picture?

> **NOTE**
>
> You can also display the City Ordinances window by selecting Windows ➤ Ordinances from the menu bar.

Finance			Safety & Health		
1% Sales Tax	✓	239	Volunteer Fire Dept.		
1% Income Tax			Public Smoking Ban		
Legalized Gambling			Free Clinics		
Parking Fines	✓	334	Junior Sports		

Education			Promotional		
Pro-Reading Campaign	✓	-111	Tourist Advertising	✓	-239
Anti-Drug Campaign			Business Advertising	✓	-494
CPR Training			City Beautification	✓	-167
Neighborhood Watch	✓	-222	Annual Carnival		

Other			Estimated Annual Cost	
Energy Conservation			Finance	573
Nuclear Free Zone			Safety & Health	0
Homeless Shelters			Education	-334
Pollution Controls	✓	-494	Promotional	-900
			Other	-494

Done		YTD Total$	-94	EST Total$	-1154

Finance

In the Finance section of the City Ordinances window you get to pass ordinances that raise money. *These are the only ordinances in the City Ordinances window that net your treasury money yet cost your city nothing to implement.* They may, however, have hidden costs, as noted earlier in this chapter.

> **NOTE**
>
> After you pass any of the ordinances, you can see the *estimated* income from that ordinance reflected in the total shown at the bottom of the City Ordinances window.

1% Sales Tax   Passing this ordinance will place a 1% sales tax on all items sold in the city, which will bring some revenues into your treasury, but which will also slightly discourage commerce.

1% Income Tax   Pass this ordinance, and 1% of the income of each of your Sims will go into the city treasury. This can increase your coffers but slightly discourage Sims from moving into town.

Legalized Gambling   Pass this one, and legalized gambling may bring extra money into the city. The estimated income to the city will be reflected in the total shown at the bottom of the City Ordinances window. But watch out: legalized gambling brings higher crime rates with it, meaning that you'll have to pay for extra police services.

Parking Fines   If you pass this ordinance, your city treasury will receive a small additional income from parking fines. Your Sims will also be slightly discouraged from driving. If your agenda for the city includes encouraging public transit, this can help; however, it will slightly inhibit commercial growth, as Sims are more inclined to run errands in their cars than on the subway or bus.

Safety & Health

The ordinances included in Safety & Health can help to create the high quality of life your Sims always want. This, in many cases, will benefit property values in your city.

Volunteer Fire Dept.   If you pass this ordinance, your Sims will help out with fire protection. Activating the volunteer fire department *will not* give you any additional forces to send to a disaster, and it's not much help in a large city. But in a small, new city, having a volunteer fire department can be an alternative to maintaining an expensive professional fire department and will reduce the already slight chance of fire breaking out.

Public Smoking Ban Passing this ordinance can help increase the health level and life expectancy of your Sims by lowering the number of smokers and the amount of second-hand smoke exposure.

Free Clinics Pass this ordinance to give your Sims access to the health system, and you'll increase the overall health level in your city. Remember, though, that free clinics are free to the Sims—*not* to your budget.

Junior Sports Pass this one, and eventually there will be an increase in the health of SimYouth in your city.

Education The city ordinances grouped under Education all address societal issues (literacy, drugs, health, safety) in an educational way.

Pro-Reading Campaign
Stamp out SimIlliteracy: pass this ordinance to encourage your Sims to read, and the educational level of your Sims will rise *slightly* over time.

Anti-Drug Campaign Pass this one, and you'll take a step toward stopping your Sims—especially SimTeenagers—from using drugs, which will reduce the crime rate in your city.

CPR Training If you pass this ordinance, your Sims will become prepared to help each other if one of them is having a heart attack. This will increase the health level in your city.

> **N O T E**
>
> **Implementing the Education ordinances (except the Pro-Reading Campaign) will not increase the general smartness or educational level of your population. Your Sims' educational level is most affected by the presence of schools, colleges, and libraries in your city. See Chapter 12 for more information on the SimEducational system.**

> **W A R N I N G**
>
> **If things are going really well, your City Council may pass entitlement ordinances you don't want, without checking with you. (This happens only when you're playing with disasters enabled.) Therefore, you should review the City Ordinances window from time to time to make sure no one is passing laws behind your back. Or, to avoid the problem altogether, toggle on No Disasters in the Disasters menu.**

Neighborhood Watch   Pass this ordinance, and your Sims will learn how to reduce crime in their own residential neighborhoods through vigilance (*not* vigilantism).

Promotional

The ordinances that appear in the Promotional section allow you to spend money promoting and publicizing your city. This can encourage Sims, Sim-Businesses, and even SimTourists to come to your city and can help to increase your city's value, improve the economy, and generally make your city a better place to live and work.

> **TIP**
>
> If you're going to advertise for tourists, you'd better have something for them to do or see in your city—parks, museums, a zoo, and a stadium are good choices. An annual carnival (described in an upcoming section) is a good idea, too. You might lower the tax rate for tourism in the City Industry window and provide a natural recreation area (trees and water) just outside of town.

Tourist Advertising   Pass this ordinance, and you'll launch a campaign of advertising outside your city to attract visitors to your city. This will benefit commerce and the tourism industry.

Business Advertising   Pass this one, and you'll launch an advertising campaign to attract businesses into your city, which will benefit industry and commerce.

> **TIP**
>
> To support your business-advertising dollar, provide adequate amounts of land zoned industrial and commercial, then lower taxes on the specific types of industries you want to attract.

City Beautification   Pass this ordinance to encourage beautification projects and spend city money on keeping the streets clean. A clean city increases residential desirability and raises land values.

> **NOTE**
>
> The splendor, cost, and benefit of your annual carnival will vary from year to year depending on the size of your city.

Annual Carnival   Pass this ordinance to sponsor a yearly carnival. This will make your city a more enjoyable place for the Sims and will attract tourists from other cities, promoting commerce.

Other

In the Other section of the City Ordinances Books window you can pass or revoke a hodgepodge of ordinances that affect the broad societal issues of pollution, conservation, and poverty.

Energy Conservation   Pass this ordinance to control the amount of electricity used in your city—by adding insulation to homes and water heaters, for example. It takes a few years for this ordinance's benefits to take effect, but when your conservation program is in full swing, your power plants will be able to provide juice to 15% more buildings. If you pass this ordinance, you might want to keep an eye on its cost, which rises quickly from year to year. That cost, however, can be offset by the benefits of added power production.

> **TIP**
>
> If your power plants are running at 100% or more of their capacity, Energy Conservation may be a worthwhile temporary alternative to building a new power plant.

Nuclear Free Zone   Pass this ordinance, and nuclear power plants will vanish from your choices of power plants. Your city (at absolutely no direct expense) will seem like a safer place to many Sims. This can be a small advantage to residential desirability, but will slightly discourage industry.

> **NOTE**
>
> When your city population reaches 60,000, the military will ask if they can build a base near your city. If you say yes, they build what they like where they want to build it. Making your city a nuclear-free zone will in no way inhibit the military from basing missile silos or nuclear weapons near your city.

Homeless Shelters   Passing the Homeless Shelters ordinance will provide the less fortunate Sims in your city with places to live. This will increase the number of residents in your city and will make it possible for those Sims to get jobs, increasing the available work force and slightly raising land values.

Pollution Controls Pass this ordinance to compel industry to reduce the pollution it creates in your city. This will somewhat discourage industry, but may make the Sims living in your city happier. Again (as with Energy Conservation), this ordinance can quickly rise in cost over time. You might want to monitor its financial drain.

Estimated Annual Cost In the Estimated Annual Cost section, which appears in the bottom-right corner of the City Ordinances window, you can see the expected income or cost from each of the ordinances you have passed, grouped by their type. Income is displayed as a positive number, while expenses are displayed prefixed with a - (minus sign). Only the ordinances in the Finance section of the City Ordinances windows generate income for your city—all of the other ordinances drain income to provide for the cost of implementation and maintenance.

> ### N O T E
> Don't just blindly pass ordinances and forget about them. You should monitor their continued cost, which will change from year to year, and make the adjustments you deem wise.

Along the very bottom of the City Ordinances window you can see two numbers, labeled:

- YTD Total$
- EST Total$

The first—YTD Total$—shows the actual cost of all city ordinances so far this year. The second—EST Total$—shows the total *projected* cost of all ordinances for the entire year. (In both of these totals, income from ordinances is figured in and the cost of other ordinances is deducted.)

When you are finished with the City Ordinances window, click on the Done button or OK (at the bottom of the window) to close it. You'll find yourself back in the Budget window.

 **146** The City Budget and Ordinances

THE NEW AND IMPROVED "FUND" TRICK FOR PCS

If you're using the DOS version, at any time in the game type **fund,** and when the dialog box appears asking if you want to issue a bond at 25%, click on Yes to issue the bond. Type **fund** again and click on Yes to issue a second bond at 25%. Now open the Budget window and, in the Bonds books, issue another bond at whatever the interest rate appears to be. Wait until January, and as the year changes, you'll find you have millions of dollars. In fact, you'll have millions more the next year! (You can pay off the first two 25% bonds quickly and easily with the profits from this trick. Watch out if you start the cheat early in a year when you're nearly broke, though; that 25% interest rate eats up your cash fast.)

BIG BUCKS FOR WINDOWS USERS

If you're using the Windows version, you can get plenty of cash and all the rewards with none of the usual effort. Any time in the game, just click on the toolbar's title bar, then type **buddamus**. The first time you do this, you'll get $500,000 and all the rewards. Every time you do it again, you'll get another $500,000.

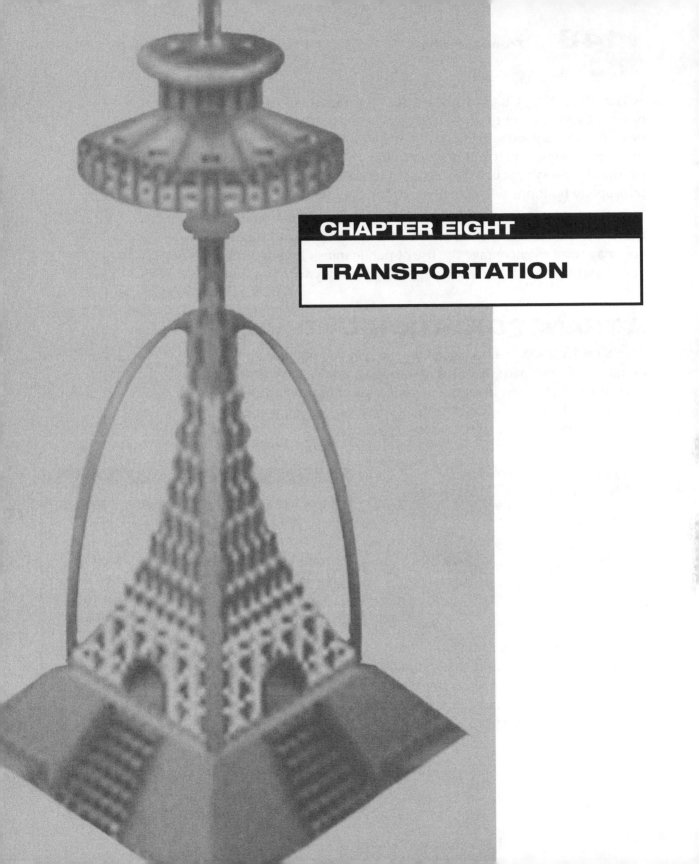

CHAPTER EIGHT
TRANSPORTATION

THE SIMS IN YOUR CITY rely on the transportation system you build—it allows them to move freely, going to and fro in their daily business. Without a good and effective transportation system your city might not survive long, and it will never develop. In addition, a properly built transportation system can help reduce pollution in your city, while an improperly built one will actually generate pollution.

As is usual in SimCity 2000, you get to set the agenda in building a transit system. You may want to rely heavily on roads and highways, or you may want to encourage the use of public transit by providing plenty of rail and subway stations and peppering your city with bus depots.

A TRANSPORTATION OVERVIEW

In SimCity 2000, the transportation system you build is composed of as many different parts as you wish—as long as you stay within the constraints of what's been invented in your SimCivilization at the time you're building. In building your transportation system, you can draw from the following transit methods:

Transit Method	Year Invented
Roads	1900
Trains	1900
Subways	1910
Buses	1920
Highways	1930

Each of these types of transportation has its own set of advantages and disadvantages, which we'll cover in this chapter, along with some strategies for setting up a sound transit system.

> **N O T E**
>
> Airports and seaports in SimCity 2000 are not considered part of your city transportation system. Their function—which is not to move Sims and goods around within the city but to move travelers and goods *in* and *out* of the city—does relate to the commercial and industrial development of your city, however. Airports and seaports are covered in Chapter 10.

HOW SIMCITY 2000 SIMULATES TRAFFIC

SimCity 2000 uses a mathematical method to estimate the number of trips between locations in the city. For every building in your city, the simulator generates a number of "trips." Each of these trips assumes travel through the SimCity to a type of zone different from the one containing the building where the trip originated.

Each trip results in either success or failure. A successful trip is one in which the Sim makes it from the original building (which must be within three tiles of transportation) to the destination building (which must be right next to transportation).

If the Sim is unable to make it to the destination building, the trip is a failure. If too many failure trips occur, the Sims will start to complain about the state of your transportation system.

When a Sim on a "trip" encounters some form of public transit, there's a 50/50 chance that the Sim will take public transit the rest of the way instead of driving. If the Sim takes public transit in one trip and the trip is not completed, the Sim will not bother to take public transit in the next trip. Thus, if you're going to have any public transit at all, you should have a complete and properly constructed system.

Your city will develop into a really big metropolis only with a well-designed transit system that includes public transit.

CONSIDERATIONS IN LOCATING TRANSIT

As you lay out your city, remember that Sims will walk no more than three tiles in any direction to get access to transportation. They will walk to a road and drive from there, or they will walk up to three tiles to a rail or subway station where they can board the train or the subway. You'll find more on this in Chapter 6.

As you're laying down transit lines, try to plan a couple of steps ahead, thinking as you go about where one sort of transportation will link with another. For example, when you're laying down roads or other transit lines near water, think about if and how you're going to cross the water, and where.

If you're planning to use public transit, place bus depots and subway stations near busy intersections to take some of the heat off the road system.

CONSIDERATIONS IN USING PRIVATE TRANSIT

Private transit means, in a nutshell, *cars*. Sims love to drive. To give your Sims the mobility they want, you'll have to build roads and even highways.

Roads are pretty much required for a successful city in SimCity 2000. There are, however, two drawbacks to crisscrossing your city with asphalt:

> **N O T E**
>
> In SimCity Classic there was a built-in bias toward rail transit—you could, in fact, build a city with no roads at all. This is not true in SimCity 2000, where every Sim wants to be king of the road. Try to build a city with no roads, and you'll wait a very long time to see any development take place.

- Sims love to drive so much that roads will fill to capacity and become inadequate.
- A lot of cars means a lot of pollution.

If you let the Sims drive around as much as they want, you'll soon find the need for roads exceeding the capacity of your road system. (You'll know this is happening because the message "Citizens Demand Road and Rails" will appear in the Info box or status bar.) Building more roads will not fix this situation—Sims in cars will just crowd the new roads. Besides, roads take up valuable space in a densely crowded city— space that could be devoted instead to zoned areas that will increase the overall value of your city and raise your tax base.

Cars create pollution, and, as you know from reading earlier sections of this book, pollution decreases residential desirability and begins the nasty downward spiral toward city failure.

So here's your private-transit paradox: Sims love to drive and want to drive everywhere, but they hate the effects of their own collective obsession with cars.

CONSIDERATIONS IN USING PUBLIC TRANSIT

Public transit in SimCity 2000 means *trains*, *subways*, and *buses*—all of which are administered by the city and designed to carry a lot of Sims together to their most frequented destinations. Both trains and subways require you to build special transit routes—train tracks or subway tunnels—while buses run on the same roads and highways that your Sims use for automobiles.

The major advantage in providing public transit is that a lot of Sims can then move around your city without causing pollution. The big trick here, though, is to get them to use the public transit you provide. (More on this in upcoming sections.)

KEEPING AN EYE ON THE TRANSIT AUTHORITY BUDGET

WARNING
SimCity 2000's Mac version 1 includes a bug that, at times and without warning, will cause your transportation budget to skyrocket and bankrupt your city. If this happens to you, your only recourse is to restore the game from a saved city and continue from before the fiscal accident.

The Transit Authority's budget is visible in the Budget window and shows you the total expected cost for the year. By clicking on the Transit Authority's Books icon, you can have a detailed look at how much each form of transportation is costing you. See Chapter 7 for more information about budgeting.

TYPES OF TRANSPORTATION

Each form of transportation has its own set of advantages and disadvantages, as described in the following sections.

ROADS

Roads are the most expedient mode of transportation available in Sim-City 2000, especially at the beginning of a game.

Cost: Roads cost $10 per tile. Roads on hilly land cost the same as roads on flat land. (Bridges and tunnels are built and charged separately from roads.)

Advantages: Roads are the easiest and cheapest form of transportation available in SimCity 2000. You'll never have a problem getting your Sims to use the roads you build.

Disadvantages: Sims will, however, complain at length about the adverse effects of their own driving: crowded roads and pollution. As your city grows these problems will get worse, yet you'll have an increasingly tough time getting your Sims to use public transit instead of driving.

Planning for Roads

You can place roads on either flat land or hills. If you encounter a hill, you can build a tunnel, or you can allow your road to go up the slope at what the program considers to be the best angle and route. (See "Tunnels" later in this chapter for more info.) On some steep hillsides, ramps and gradations may appear in order to smooth the road's way, in fact.

> **TIP**
>
> **Avoid placing roads (and rail lines) diagonally. It's a waste.**

If, as you are placing a road, you run into water, you will be presented with the option to build any of several types of bridges. (Bridges are discussed later in this chapter.)

Placing a Road

To place a road, select the Road tool from the City toolbar, then select Road from the menu that appears. Click and drag along the route you want your road to take. As you move the pointer, you'll see an outline (shadow) of the road appear along the route you're indicating, and you'll see the mounting cost of the road displayed.

INVESTIGATING ROAD AND TRANSPORTATION USAGE

The first method for finding out the current state of any part of your road system is the most obvious: SimCity 2000 animates the road with moving cars, showing you at a glance how much usage the road is getting.

For a citywide overview of the traffic, you can click on the Map tool in the City toolbar, then select Roads ➤ Traffic. A map showing density will appear.

You can get a more exact picture of any part of your transportation system by using the Query tool. Click on the Query tool in the City toolbar, then click on the object you want to investigate. An info box will appear showing you, among other things, the number of cars per minute on a particular road (actually, the tile on which you've clicked), passengers per day on your citywide bus system, and more.

If you're happy with this, let go of the mouse button and the road will appear. If you want to bail out, hold down Shift and then let up the mouse button.

Bridges

When you're laying down a road and you come to any kind of water, a

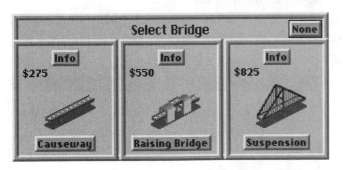

dialog box will appear offering you the option to build one of as many as three types of bridges. (The number and type of bridges you're offered depend on the width of the water.) Each type of bridge has its own set of advantages and disadvantages. The cost of a bridge depends on the width of the waterway you wish to cross.

Causeway

Causeways—low-lying bridges that are really just roads on pilings—offer the simplest, least expensive way for roads to cross water in SimCity 2000. Their main drawback is that ships cannot pass underneath them. In floods or hurricanes, you may also find that causeways can be washed away pretty easily. But then, they're not expensive to replace, either.

If you're building a crossing over a lake or the edge of a bay, a causeway can be your best choice. If you're building a crossing over a river or the mouth of a bay, where ships will need to pass underneath, use one of the other two types of bridges instead.

> **N O T E**
>
> You can rename your transportation systems, just as you can many other items in the game. Click with the Query tool on a rail depot, for example, just as you would to find out the ridership. In the Query window that appears, you'll see a text box containing the generic name "SimRail System." Type a new name into the field and click the Rename button. The new name will appear in the text box next time you use the Query tool on a rail depot.

Raising Bridge

A raising bridge—one that can be mechanically raised and then lowered—is more expensive to build than a causeway, but it allows ships to pass underneath. Raising bridges are also less expensive to build than suspension bridges—the other option that allows ships to pass underneath. Suitable locations for raising bridges include narrow passages across rivers, isthmuses, or the smaller mouths of bays.

Suspension Bridge

Suspension bridges—engineering marvels that use suspended cables to support a long, graceful roadway—are expensive, but they allow ships to pass underneath. Suitable locations for suspension bridges include broad rivers and the wide mouths of bays.

Tunnels

You don't *have* to run your roads up hill and down dale—you can instead blast a tunnel right through the hill to get to the other side. This has the advantage of

> **N O T E**
>
> You can't build tunnels under water. If you want cars to cross water, you have to use a bridge.

WHEN BRIDGES GO AWRY

So you're laying down your road, you get to the edge of water, you decide to build a bridge, and you do everything just right. Then, fwomp! the bridge appears—but it's heading off at a 90° angle from where you wanted it to go!

What happened?

Well, SimEngineers and SimContractors seem to be in cahoots to build bridges along the route of least resistance. ...Hey, you got to the other side, *right*?

You can exercise some control over the direction a bridge is built—but it takes some work. Use the Bulldozer ➤ Raise Terrain tool to raise land a bit around the tile from which you want your bridge to originate, making it inconvenient for SimEngineers and SimContractors to go any other way. Then do the same on the opposite shore. In both cases, make it so water touches only the side of the specific tile you want your bridge to extend from or reach.

Once the bridge is in place, you can carefully lower the terrain back to where it was, if you want, using the Bulldozer ➤ Lower Terrain tool.

That ought to do it.

leaving the hillside open for other development (although most other development will ultimately involve laying down a road anyway). Tunnels are not cheap, though. They cost $150 per tile to build. Then, once they're built, each tunnel racks up an additional cost per year for maintenance. Tunnel maintenance is paid via the Transit Authority's line and books in the Budget window (see Chapter 7).

RAILS

Rail systems consist of the rail lines themselves and rail stations.

Cost: Railway tracks cost $25 per tile. Rail depots, which take up four tiles, cost $500 each.

Advantages: The chief advantage of using rails in your transit system is their greater capacity to carry Sims and SimStuff without polluting your city.

Disadvantages: Rail lines alone (not counting the stations) are more costly than roads. Access to rails is not broad and does not run the length of the rail line. You must provide rail depots (at $500 a pop) in addition to the rail lines so your Sims can get on and off the trains.

> **T I P**
>
> Rails don't just carry Sims around the city—they also carry freight. Placing rails and train depots in industrial areas will help those areas develop. Keep in mind when you place a rail depot in an industrial area that the usual rules apply: access is made available to an area three tiles in any direction of the access point; the *station*, not the rail line, is the access point.

Because Sims can get on and off the train only within three tiles of a rail depot, they're probably going to drive to the train anyway.

Planning for Rails

When you start a new city, you probably won't want to include rails at first, because of their cost.

If you plan to use rails as part of your overall transit system, try to leave transit corridors open as you lay out the city so you can later fill them with tracks. Remember, also, to leave room for rail depots. Always remember that it is only the *depot* that is the actual access to your rail line.

Building a Rail System

Rail systems consist mainly of tracks and stations. (They can also include rail bridges, which are discussed later in this section.) Trains, obviously, run along the

> **N O T E**
>
> Let's say a Sim, driving along from place A to place B, encounters a rail depot. If the rail line goes to where the Sim is going, there is a 50/50 chance the Sim will park, get on the train, and go via public transit instead of driving. Of course, if you want to encourage public transit, that's not a bad percentage. To increase the chances your rail system will be used, include a lot of rail depots and make the tracks go everywhere.

tracks, and rail depots (stations) are where Sims get on and off the trains. You need to include both to build a rail system your Sims will use.

First, Lay the Tracks
To lay the tracks for your rail system, select the Rails ➤ Rail tool on the City toolbar. In the City window, click and drag the tracks along the route you wish them to take.

Then, Place a Rail Depot
To place a rail depot, select the Rails ➤ Rail Depot tool on the City toolbar. In the City window, point and click wherever you want a rail depot to exist. Be sure to place it correctly—they aren't cheap.

> ### N O T E
>
> **The trains that appear on the track are only animations; they have nothing to do with the effectiveness of your rail line. If you build a complete rail line and trains appear on it, and then you build a separate, complete rail line across town on which no trains appear, not to worry. Your rail line is effective as long as it's hooked up correctly—even if you never see a train on the tracks.**

You'll have to provide power to your rail depot (it will flash the by-now-familiar red and then yellow bolt to indicate it is un-powered at first). To do so, select the Power ➤ Power Lines tool and click and drag power lines from the nearest powered place (structure) to the rail depot. When the depot has power, it will stop flashing. Assuming you put down rails first, a train will soon run up and down the line.

Crossing Water with Your Rail System

You have two options if you want your rail system to cross a waterway:

- Use a rail bridge
- Run the rail line through a subway tunnel under the water

Running your rail line across a rail bridge is a relatively simple matter. When you're laying down track and you reach water, a dialog box will appear offering you the option to build a rail bridge and telling you what it's going to cost. (The cost varies based on how long the bridge will be.)

If you want to go ahead, click on the Rail Bridge button. If you don't want to, click on None and your track will end at the water's edge.

To run your rail line through a subway tunnel, connect your rail lines to your underwater subway lines with a sub <—> rail station. See "Connecting Rails and Subways" for details on how to do this.

SUBWAYS

Subways, which are invented early in the 20th century, provide your Sims with a quick way to move around the city without pumping pollution into the air and without taking up valuable aboveground land. Be careful, though, as subways can have a high price associated with them. Subway systems, like rail systems, include both the line itself and stations that allow your Sims to get on and off the subway line.

> ### WARNING
>
> SimEngineers and SimContractors are in cahoots over building bridges—they build them along the route of least resistance, which is probably not what you had in mind. See "When Bridges Go Awry" earlier in this chapter to find out how to get some control over this.

> ### TIP
>
> You can also build sub <—> rail links to integrate your aboveground and underground rail systems. These are discussed in an upcoming section of this chapter. And, while you cannot run a subway line as a direct connection to a neighboring city, you can run a subway from your city almost to the edge of the map, then build a sub <—> rail link to make the final connection to your neighbor.

Cost: Subway tubes themselves cost $100 per tile. Each subway station costs an additional $250.

Advantages: Subways have a number of distinct advantages over roads and rails. Like a rail system, a subway system can transport large numbers of Sims (but not freight) without the pollution or congestion associated with roads. Unlike rail systems, however, subway systems take up little surface space—really just a single tile here and there for the subway station—so they are easier to add to existing cities and can be used to relieve traffic problems.

Disadvantages: The major disadvantage of building a subway system is the cost. At $100 per tile for the underground subway line, and $250 per (aboveground) station, the cost adds up fast.

Planning for Subways

Subways require little early planning because they take up so little surface space. You need only make room aboveground in your existing city for the single-tile subway stations. The rest of the system is constructed underground, where it fits neatly in among the pipeways that carry your city's water supply. Figure 8.1 shows a subway system sharing the underground of a city with pipelines.

Subway stations look a little different aboveground than below.

Aboveground, the subway station will look like this.

Underground, the same subway station looks like this.

Building a Subway System

> **TIP**
>
> You can exercise your right of eminent domain by quickly bulldozing the building on a corner where you wish to place a subway station. You can do this using the Bulldozer ➤ Demolish/Clear tool on the City toolbar, or you can use a shortcut on the PC: hold down the Ctrl key while you click on the tile you want to clear. (Ctrl-clicking is a shortcut for bulldozing.) Be sure to put subway stations where you want them—you can't bulldoze them away later.

Subway systems consist of the underground lines and aboveground stations. (The subway lines, which are actually tunnel-like tubes, can go under water as easily as under ground.) Subway trains run through the underground tubes, and the Sims get on and off at the aboveground subway stations. For a viable subway system, you need both lines and stations.

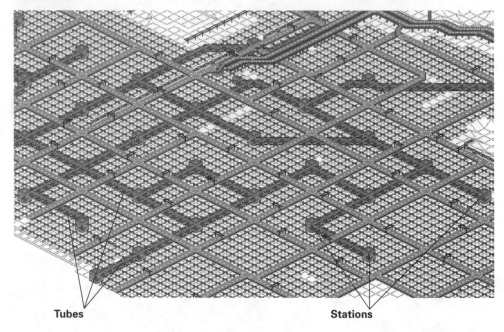

Tubes   **Stations**

FIGURE 8.1 *This subway system consists of subway lines (big tubes) and stations (vertical boxes) coexisting peacefully underground with water pipes.*

First, Build a Subway Station

To add a subway system to your city, start by picking out likely locations for subway stations. Existing intersections that show plenty of car traffic suggest themselves as the best locations. Place subway stations strategically throughout the dense areas of your city—the more stations you have, the greater your chances of attracting a large ridership.

Then, Build the Subway Lines

Having placed subway stations around your city, now build the subway tunnels to connect your stations. Select Rail ➤ Subway from the City toolbar. The underground view of your city will

> **TIP**
>
> To get rid of unwanted underground pipes and subway tubes, you must be in the underground view of your city. Click on the Bulldozer tool and select Demolish/Clear, then click on the pipe or tube one section (tile) at a time.

TIP

If you link your aboveground rail system and your underground subway system (as described in an upcoming section), you can run your aboveground trains under waterways via a subway tube. This will avoid the presence of unsightly rail bridges in your fair city.

appear, showing mainly the pipelines that carry your city's water supply. Here and there—wherever you placed them—you'll also see vertical gray boxes, which are the subway stations. Click and drag from one station to another along the route you wish your subway line to take; a green tube (the subway's underground line) will appear, connecting the stations.

When you're finished, click on the Show Underground tool icon on the City toolbar to revert to the aboveground view of your city.

Crossing Water with Your Subway System

Crossing a waterway with your subway line is really easy. When you're placing the underground line and you reach water, just keep going. There is no additional cost for this.

BUSES

Buses are a part of the public transit system that allows more Sims to use your existing road system. Buses run on the roads and highways, and all you have to do to provide buses is place four-tile bus depots at strategic locations.

Cost: Each bus depot costs $250. A maintenance cost of $25 per bus depot is added each year to the cost of roads that's paid out of the Transit Authority line in the Budget window.

Advantages: The biggest advantages in using buses are that they are easy to add to your city and Sims don't mind riding them very much. You'll have a lot less trouble getting your Sims to use buses as a mode of public transportation than subways or trains.

CONNECTING RAILS AND SUBWAYS

You can connect your aboveground train system with your subway using a special rail-to-subway connection. The Sub <—> Rail tool places an above-to-below-ground link to the subway tubes so surface trains can enter and exit the subterranean system. This can be a great advantage in that it lets you share the resource of underground tubes and save valuable land on the surface for other types of development than rail lines. It also lets you run your trains underwater in a cheap and easy way.

To make one of these connections, you must have a rail line placed aboveground with subway tunnels underneath it. You must also have a cleared space aboveground for the sub <—> rail station. Select Rails ➤ Sub <—> Rail from the City toolbar. Then point and click where you want to place the linking station.

Note that you won't automatically see the underground view; to be sure you're linking correctly, you'll want first to have clicked on the Show Underground map a couple of times to check that both the aboveground rail line and the underground subway line are correctly placed for a successful connection. When you point-and-click the linking station into place, you'll want to be in the aboveground view of your city.

This is another time when you might want to exercise your right of eminent domain by bulldozing away an existing building to make room for the linking station. If you do this, you can rationalize the destruction by thinking that in the long run, you'll provide a lot of space for other buildings. (You saved that space by not using it for train tracks.)

Disadvantages: Buses don't have a lot of disadvantages. Unlike trains and subways, they produce pollution, but compared to the pollution produced by cars, it's nothing.

Planning for Buses

Buses run on existing roads, so you don't have to do much advanced planning for them. You will have to place bus depots around your city, and each bus depot will take up four tiles. Bus depots, to work to their best advantage, should be placed in the busy sections of your city. You can either plan ahead and leave blank spaces of four tiles each at strategic locations for bus depots, or you can exercise eminent domain by bulldozing away existing buildings to make way for bus depots.

Building a Bus Depot

To build a bus depot, you will first need to locate a good place. Look for intersections that show a lot of car traffic—this means that many Sims are already in the area. Select the Roads ➤ Bus Depot tool from the City toolbar. Then simply point and click where you want the bus depot to appear.

> **N O T E**
>
> Buses are the easiest form of public transit to get your Sims to use. Adding a bus system is cheaper than adding a subway system and uses much less land than adding a rail system.

HIGHWAYS

Highways are, of course, just big roads that can handle the traffic of many more cars than regular roads. Highways (Figure 8.2) are raised on pilings above your city, so they can pass over roads, rails, and power lines. You cannot, however, construct a highway over buildings. (Nor can you place these structures under the highway once it's built.)

If you want to build a highway where buildings already exist, you'll have to bulldoze those buildings away.

Cost: Highways cost $100 per stretch. Each stretch is two tiles long and two tiles wide. After building the highway itself, you will have to add on ramps to allow your Sims to get on and off the highway. On ramps cost $25 a piece.

FIGURE 8.2   *A highway system crossing a small city*

Advantages: Highways allow many more cars to move around your city than do roads. Sims just love to drive, and they will love to use the highways you build. Highways can also cross over roads, rails, and power lines, so you can get quite a complex mix going in a small area.

Disadvantages: Building highways means you're allowing more cars; more cars, as we've said before, means more pollution. Also, Sims can get on and off highways only at on ramps, so you will need to place on ramps near areas of your city that have heavy traffic—not easy in a densely congested city.

Planning for Highways

Highways take up a lot of land in your city. When you decide to build a highway, either you will have planned ahead, allowing the room for it

(what foresight you must have!) or you will need to free up land by bulldozing structures to make room for both the highway itself and its on ramps.

Highways can go up and down hills and can cross water. (When a highway crosses water, it builds its own highway-type bridge, as described in an upcoming section.)

Building a Highway and On Ramps

To build a highway, select the Roads ➤ Highway tool in the City toolbar. Click and drag the highway into place just as you would a road. Note that highways are *two tiles wide* and that each section of highway is *two tiles long*. Note also that you must allow room for on ramps at strategic locations.

On ramps are necessary between roads and highways to provide access to the highway. To place an on ramp, you will need an empty tile right next to both a highway and the road to which it will connect, as depicted in Figure 8.3.

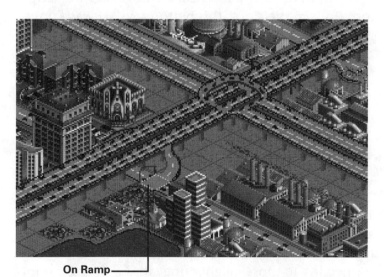

On Ramp

FIGURE 8.3 *The on ramp must be on a tile that is next to both a road and the highway, to connect them.*

Select the Roads ➤ Onramp tool in the City toolbar. Point and click at the place you've chosen for the on ramp.

Crossing Water with Highways

When you're laying down a highway and you reach water, one of two things will happen:

- If the water isn't terribly wide, the highway will just cross it.

- If the water is wide, a dialog box will appear, offering you the chance to build a reinforced bridge for your highway and telling you what it's going to cost. (The cost varies based on how long the bridge will be.)

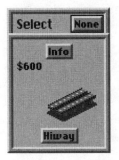

If you want to go ahead, click on the Highway button. (In some versions, this button says "Hiway" on it instead of "Highway.") If you don't want to do this, click on None and your highway will end abruptly at the water's edge.

CONNECTING TO YOUR NEIGHBORS

While this might not be immediately apparent, your city does not exist in total isolation. It is part of SimNation, and it has neighboring Sim-Cities. (To get a glimpse of these cities, click the Neighbors tool icon in the City toolbar.) Connecting to those neighboring cities is very good for business of all sorts.

To connect to neighboring SimCities, you can simply run a road, highway, or rail line from your city to the edge of the land-mass in any direction. (By this we do not mean to run the road, highway, or rail line into water—stick to the land.) A dialog box will appear offering—at a cost of $1,000 for a road or highway, or $1,500 for a rail line—to make a connection to your neighbors in that direction (Figure 8.4).

You'll have to weigh the expense of a connection against the high value to commerce and industry of trading with those neighbors.

If you select Yes to build a connection, a sign will appear at the end of the road, highway, or rail line to mark the connection. (You'll never see

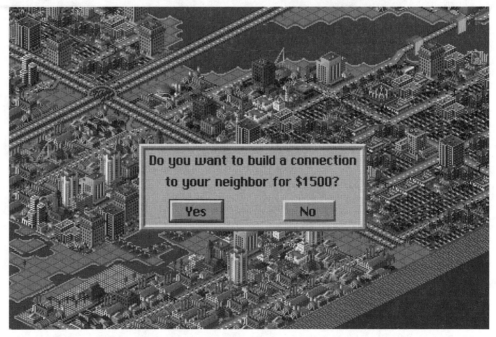

FIGURE 8.4 *Connecting to neighboring cities can be a big boon to your city's commerce and industry.*

any other actual evidence of the good of your connection. The evidence is folded into the economic well-being of your city and your Sims.) If you select No, the road, highway, or rail line will simply end at the apparent edge of the land.

From time to time in a simulation you Sims may demand connections. (You'll see a message saying so in the Info box or status bar.) You don't *have* to make the connection then—it's up to you when to do what—but you might consider the Sims' demand an important indicator.

This business of connections to your neighbors can be a reminder that your SimCity is part of a bigger simulated world whose economic factors can affect your city's economy. This, of course, provides one of the elements of randomness that make SimCity 2000 challenging.

> **TIP**
>
> There is little point in having two road, highway, or rail connections to any one neighbor. All the good you'll get out of this deal can be accomplished with one connection per neighbor. Build rail connections to your neighbors early in the game when industry needs a boost; rail connections support industry. Build road connections to your neighbors later, when commerce needs a boost.

CHAPTER NINE

YOUR CITY'S
WATERWORKS

WHEN YOU START A NEW CITY, the landmass you're building on will include some bodies of water—maybe some lakes, a river, even an ocean coastline. And, as you've seen before when we showed you the Show Underground tool in Chapter 4 and the subway system in Chapter 8, the subterranean view of your developing city is a rich web of pipelines wanting to be connected to a water supply so fresh water can be had by your Sims.

This business of being able to see under your city (and of having to provide your city with water) is a new feature in SimCity 2000, one that lends extra depth (pun intended) to the simulation.

In this chapter, we'll cover pumping, piping, and treating water to make a constant supply of fresh water available to your Sims.

WATER BASICS

Your city can survive—and even grow—without a water system. But it will never develop fully; to make its population really boom, every city in SimCity 2000 needs water.

You need some very basic information to get started on a water system:

- You need to know if you're working with fresh or salt water.
- You need to look around aboveground and underground to see where pumps or plants can go and to get a look at the pipe systems.

To investigate these matters, use the Query tool and the Show Underground tool.

Finding Out Whether That's Fresh Water or Salt Water

The first thing you need to know is whether your major source of water is fresh (lakes, a river, etc.) or salt water (the ocean or a saltwater bay). This may be immediately obvious, but if it's not, use the Query tool from the City toolbar to click on the water. The info box that appears will tell you just what kind of water it is.

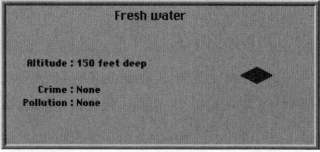

You need to handle salt water a little differently than fresh water, but more on that in a minute.

Looking Underground

Click on the Show Underground tool in the City toolbar to switch back and forth between the aboveground view of your city and the underground view. (For more about the Query tool and the Show Underground tool, see Chapter 4.

PUMPING WATER TO YOUR CITY

The Sims will build pipes in grids under the buildings they've built in the areas you've zoned. When you click on the Show Underground tool you can see these grids of underground pipes. If the pipes appear gray, they are not carrying water. If they appear blue, they are carrying water. Your goal is to provide water to your city, primarily by pumping the water out of the water source and making connections among the grids of pipelines so everything's running blue.

ABOUT WATER PUMPS

In 1900, and for the early part of the 20th century, you'll find pumps to be your only option for managing water. Water pumps pump fresh water efficiently. If you have a source of fresh water like a river or lake, and if you don't let it get polluted, you can get by just fine with water pumps indefinitely. All you have to do is add more pumps and more connecting pipes as your city grows. Water pumps cost $100 each. Each pump will provide water to at least 17–38 tiles, depending on where the pump is placed and how much it rains.

CHOOSING LOCATIONS FOR YOUR PUMPS

Pumps can be placed on the edge of a body of water (a river, lake, or oceanfront) or on land, where they will act as wells. Pumps are less efficient, however, in pumping salt water or acting as wells, so if you have a choice (say, if your city is located near a river that dumps into the

ocean), you might want to place your
pumps near the freshwater source rather
than the saltwater source or on land.
Water pumps placed on a freshwater
source will pump twice as much as those
placed on a saltwater source or land.

The amount of water a pump pumps is
also proportional to the number of water
tiles adjacent to the pump. The more
water tiles touching the land tile your
water pump is on, the more water the
pump will pump. (See Figure 9.1.) You can
add 12 tiles to the number of tiles supported by each pump for every water tile
that touches the tile holding the pump.

TIP

You can maximize pump output by placing
the pump on a tile of land that is touching
two or more tiles of water. Long jetties
sticking out into the water, or even islands
will do the trick. If you don't see such an
outcropping or island conveniently located on
the map, you can create one. Just select the
Bulldozer – Raise Terrain tool from the City
toolbar, and click one water tile after another
until a long jetty is in place, or click once
where you want an island to appear. Then put
your pumps on the jetty or island.

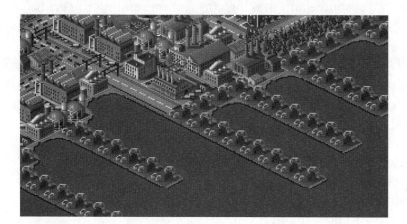

FIGURE 9.1 *Build yourself a little jetty or two (or even more) and place your pumps there to maximize pump efficiency.*

PLACING PUMPS

To place a water pump, select the Water ➤ Water Pump tool from the
City toolbar and point and click where you want the water pump to
appear. (You can do this as many times as you want.) When the pumps

appear, they'll be flashing the alternating
yellow and red bolts to indicate that they
need power. Select the Power ➤ Power
Lines tool from the City toolbar and then
point and click a single power line or click
and drag a stretch of power lines into place to connect the pumps to the
nearest powered area.

The pumps and power lines to them will stop flashing when everything's juiced up. From the aboveground view you can see at the moment, it may look then like your job is finished, but it's not.

PIPING WATER TO YOUR CITY

As you've zoned areas and your Sims have built in those areas, part of
what they've been building is grid after grid of underground piping. You
will have to connect those underground pipeline grids to the pumps and
to each other. Pipes cost $3 per tile.

PLACING PIPELINES

To place pipes to connect up your city's water supply, select the Water
➤ Pipes tool from the City toolbar. *Your aboveground view of the city will be
replaced by an underground view.* Figure 9.2 shows the aboveground view
of a city with water pumps in place and the view that appears after selecting Water ➤ Pipes.

Note on your screen that the city's pipes are gray and that the heavier
pipes representing your water pumps are running blue with water. Click
and drag to connect the nearest gray pipes to the heavier blue ones. You'll
see the gray pipes turn blue. You'll also notice, however, that not all the
gray pipes turned blue—the pipeline grid
under your city is interrupted by roads
and undeveloped areas. You must now
connect each piece of the grid that is gray
(no water running through it) to each
piece that is blue (water running through

it). If the distance is short—if, for example, you have to cross a road—you can just point and click a section of pipe into place. If the distance is longer, you'll have to click and drag.

> ### N O T E
>
> To get rid of unwanted pipes, you must be in the underground view of your city. Click on the Bulldozer tool, select Demolish/Clear, and click on each section (tile) you want gone.

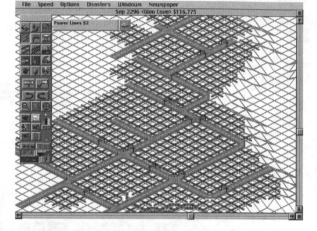

FIGURE 9.2 *Before and after selecting Water ➤ Pipes*

HOW'S YOUR WATER PRESSURE?

Once in a while, large or small sections of the pipe grid will first run blue, then for a moment gray, and then perhaps back to blue (or perhaps not). This means that your water pressure is dropping—the water's not pumping hard enough or fast enough, and there's just plain not enough water in the system to push itself around everywhere it needs to go.

There are a number of potential solutions to this problem; the simplest and most obvious one is to build more water pumps. (This is actually your *only* option early in the 20th century, when water pumps and pipes are all you've got to work with.) You can also—if you're working with salt water and if desalinization has been invented—plop into place a desalinization plant or two. It may also be that the long, hot summers are taxing your water system to the hilt and you need to put in some nifty water towers. Read on in this chapter for more info on maximizing water output.

DESALINIZATION: MAKING SALT WATER USABLE

After the invention of desalinization is announced in the newspaper, desalinization plants become a more efficient alternative to water pumps for cities on the edge of the ocean. Basically, desalinization plants remove the salt from salt water. They can provide twice as much water as an ordinary water pump placed next to one tile of fresh water, or, in other words, four times as much water as a water pump placed next to one tile of ocean water. Desalinization plants cost $1,000 each.

CHOOSING A LOCATION FOR YOUR DESALINIZATION PLANT

Desalinization plants take up four tiles each, so make sure you're allowing enough room for them. You can minimize the power lines and pipes you need to place to get your desalinization plants going by bunching a group of them together.

PLACING A DESALINIZATION PLANT

To put a desalinization plant into place, select the Water ➤ Desalinization Plant tool from the City toolbar and point and click where you want the plant to appear. (You can point and click into place as many plants as you want.) Connect the desalinization plants to the nearest powered area in the usual way.

The desalinization plants and the power lines to them will stop flashing when everything's got juice, but you still need to place connecting underground pipes as described earlier in this chapter.

Water Treatment

When water treatment plants are invented (close to the middle of the 20th century), you'll read about it in the newspaper. Treatment plants treat waste water, reducing pollution. They cost $500 each.

Treatment plants need not be placed near a water source—you can put them anywhere.

PLACING A WATER TREATMENT PLANT

To place a treatment plant, select the
Water ➤ Treatment tool from the City
toolbar and point and click where you
want the plant to appear. (You can point
and click into place a bunch of plants if
you want, but they're not cheap.) Connect the treatment plants to the nearest
powered area, and they'll stop flashing to show that they're juiced up.

> **N O T E**
>
> You can connect water treatment plants to
> the rest of your system with pipes, but you
> don't have to.

INVESTIGATING THE OUTPUT OF PARTS OF YOUR WATER SYSTEM

To see just how efficient any part of your water system is, select the
Query tool from the City toolbar and click on any item in your water system. You'll see info boxes like those shown in Figure 9.3.

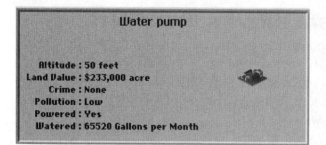
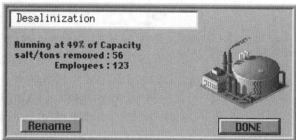

FIGURE 9.3   *Use the Query tool to find out about your water system's efficiency.*

HANDLING WATER SHORTAGES

From time to time you'll see a message in the Info box or status bar indicating that a water shortage is occurring. Water shortages are not as
great a disaster as floods can be, but they do stunt your city's growth by
inhibiting population density.

WHAT CAUSES WATER SHORTAGES

Water may run short because you have no water pumps, not enough water pumps, or plenty of pumps but not enough connecting pipes underground. (That "not enough pipes" thing often happens if you've been expanding your city for a while without any regard to providing the newly developed areas with water.)

Water shortages can also happen because of a long dry spell or because you've had the good (or bad, depending on your perspective) luck to build your city in an arid climate.

WHERE THE WATER GOES

Water is first pumped to the center of your city, and from there outward. SimCity 2000 models the water this way to avoid having to calculate the water pressure from numerous pumps throughout the city.

You can sometimes see the effects of this when, despite the number of pumps you place, water will flow to the center of the city before it flows to the building right next door.

The Weather Indicator

At the rightmost end of the Info box that appears (usually at the top) of your City window, a little box shows the current weather conditions.

In SimCity, it's usually sunny in the summer and rainy or worse in the winter. But depending on the climate in which your city is built, you'll

find that there may be a little more sun or rain than normal. When something really dramatic is occurring, you'll see that announced in the Info box or status bar.

Of course if it doesn't rain or snow for a while, or if you're in the middle of a desert, you're going to run short of water.

STORING WATER IN TOWERS TO DEAL WITH WATER SHORTAGES

To deal with potential water shortages, place water towers here and there around your city. Water towers cost $250 each. To place a water tower, select the Water ➤ Water Tower tool from the City toolbar and then just point and click where you want the water tower to appear. You must connect your water tower to the pipeline system and provide it with power.

Water towers are filled with water only when there is a surplus. Each tower holds as much as 40,000 gallons of water when it is filled. You may find it more productive to add four water pumps than to use four tiles for a single water tower.

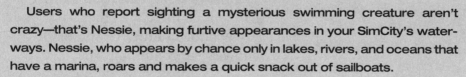

WHAT'S THAT SWIMMING IN MY CITY?

Users who report sighting a mysterious swimming creature aren't crazy—that's Nessie, making furtive appearances in your SimCity's waterways. Nessie, who appears by chance only in lakes, rivers, and oceans that have a marina, roars and makes a quick snack out of sailboats.

CHAPTER TEN

PORTS: ON THE WATER AND IN THE AIR

IN MOST OF THE MAJOR cities of the world—New York, London, Paris—ports were the starting points of urban development. Originally, *sea*ports were the commercial hub of the city, the point of contact that allowed for communication with the world outside the city, and the core of the city's industrial area.

Ports today (the most important ones are now *air*ports) are equally necessary for commerce and industry. (Communications occur more through a worldwide electronic web, however, and less through ports.)

In this chapter, we'll look at ports—what makes them important in SimCity 2000, and how to make the most of them.

WHY YOU WANT PORTS IN YOUR CITY

The bottom line here is that ports are good for business. They allow the city's produced goods to be traded and sold elsewhere, and they allow ships and planes to carry business and tourist travelers to and from your city.

A seaport becomes important to your city's growth when the city's population reaches 10,000; an airport becomes important at a population of 15,000. If you haven't yet built a seaport or airport and industry or commerce begins to feel the lack, a message will appear in the Info box or status bar telling you that there is demand for one or the other type of port.

Seaports, which in SimCity 2000 are available in 1900, provide more of a boost to industry. Air travel technology gets invented later and is announced in the newspaper. When it *does* become available, having an airport will provide a boost to commerce.

The actual size of the port—as long as it meets the minimum size for a port to develop—doesn't really matter at first. The simulator just checks to see whether the port exists. Ports are pretty big polluters, so you might want to place them far from residential areas.

SEAPORTS

You will have the option to build a seaport from the beginning of a simulation (they're available early, in 1900). Seaports consist of docks, warehouses, and auxiliary buildings. When the seaport is fully functional, you'll see ships come sailing in, dock occasionally, and drift around nearby before sailing off again.

SELECTING A LOCATION FOR YOUR SEAPORT

The most obvious necessity for a seaport's best location is…well, the

ocean. This is not the incredibly simple matter it seems at first—sometimes in SimCity 2000 what looks like the ocean turns out to be a big river.

To determine whether that big watery area you see is actually an ocean or a river, you can use the Query tool on it—or hold down Shift and click—to see its info box.

There are a few other matters you might consider in selecting a location for your seaport.

Think through, for example, how the seaport will fit into the overall layout of your city. Keep in mind that seaports are busy, smelly, *industrial* areas with cranes and dusty warehouses and stacks of goods from overseas. They're not those nifty new residential/tourist versions with trendy loft housing and a boardwalk. Sims won't want to live near your city's port.

> **N O T E**
>
> **If you build a seaport correctly (meaning that it's big enough and has power) and only warehouses appear, you may have built it on a river that has no ocean access. Another possibility is that the water isn't deep enough for a pier. Piers can develop only over water at least 150 feet deep.**

This can get a bit tricky, because seaports must be placed by the oceanfront—the same area that would make for some very valuable residential property.

One way to deal with this is to bunch your seaport together with water pumps, desalinization plants, and (further inland) an industrial area in space you've decided to sacrifice to these purposes.

BUILDING A SEAPORT

To build a seaport, select the Ports ➤ Seaport tool from the City toolbar. Click and drag on the area of land where you want to place the seaport, just as you would do to zone an industrial, residential, or commercial area. As you drag, the mounting cost of the seaport will appear on screen just as it does when you zone areas. Seaports cost $150 per tile.

> **N O T E**
>
> **If you change your mind while you're click-and-dragging your seaport—or any other structure—into place, just hold down Shift and release the mouse button.**

Seaports can be either square or rectangular. The larger they are, the more docks should appear. Larger seaports are not necessarily a big boon to your city, however. Having one with just a couple of docks will do fine in many cases.

You will have to provide the seaport with power before it will develop; to do this, run power lines from the nearest powered area. Select the Power ➤ Power Lines tool from the City toolbar and point and click one stretch of power line or click and drag a long stretch of power lines into place.

Soon after the power lines stop flashing, warehouses, docks, and auxiliary buildings should appear. It will take a little while after that for the

first ship to arrive, but if the seaport is there for it to visit, your ship will eventually come in.

SPECIAL PORTS: WHEN THE MILITARY LANDS IN YOUR CITY

When the population of your city reaches 60,000, the SimNation military will indicate its interest in building a base in your city. It'll do this by announcing the offer in a dialog box.

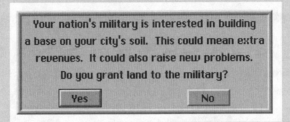

If you say no, it'll simply go away. If you say yes, it will build the base of its choosing in the location of its choosing.

The SimNation military might decide, for example, that yours is a fine city in which to place an air base, an army base, a navy base, or missile silos.

Believe it or not, having missile silos in your city has little effect on your city. (Apparently missile silos don't require a lot of personnel, so you won't have a lot of soldiers, sailors, or marines tramping around in town causing trouble.)

The advantages to your city's having a military base will show up as a boost in the local economy and more jobs. You will also have the military as a handy resource to combat disasters of all sorts (which will be completely unnecessary if you have turned on No Disasters). The disadvantage to having a military base is a higher crime rate, especially near the base.

AIRPORTS

The technology of air travel is not available in 1900, but it becomes available soon thereafter. The news of its development will be a banner headline in your city's newspaper. Airports consist of lighted runways, an air traffic control tower, hangars, and auxiliary buildings.

When the airport is fully functional, you'll see planes arrive and depart. Eventually you'll also see traffic helicopters taking off, flying around the city, and landing.

HELICOPTER FLAMBÉ

You can give the traffic helicopter pilot a big surprise. Select the Centering tool from the City toolbar, center on the helicopter, and click once. (Make sure you have a fire department handy.)

SELECTING A LOCATION FOR YOUR AIRPORT

Find a place for your airport that is out of town but not too far out of town (this can be tricky). Plan ahead here as much as possible—you want to allow room for your airport to expand, and for the *growth of your city* as well.

Nobody wants to live next to an airport or under the planes' approach lanes. If residential areas of your city are creeping out too close to your airport, you'll find they have lower land values. This, as you know by now, will lower your tax base, making developing your city and budgeting harder for you.

> **WARNING**
>
> **For the sake of all that's good, *keep your airport far away from your nuclear power plant.***

Unless you want to watch a lot of spectacular aerial fireworks culminating in your city burning down, build your airport away from hills, tall buildings, and *arcos* (if you have them—see Chapter 14). In fact, if you find that tiles you've zoned for an airport and provided with power still aren't developing runways, look around for stuff that's tall—the approach lanes may be blocked.

BUILDING AN AIRPORT

To build an airport (once this becomes an option), select the Ports ➤ Airport tool from the City toolbar. Click and drag on the area of land where you want to place the airport, just as you would do to zone an industrial, residential, or commercial area. As you drag, the mounting cost of the airport will appear on screen just as it does when you zone areas. Airports cost a big $250 per tile.

Airports can be either square or rectangular. The smallest airport you can build must be 1×5 tiles to allow for a runway. Larger airports may have more runways, but if you build an airport too big for your city, only part of it will develop into an airport; the rest will lie dormant. (Don't build a big airport just for fun; it's expensive and it won't be an advantage to your city.)

> **NOTE**
>
> **We have heard rumors that some airports develop interesting auxiliary buildings in them, like bed and breakfast inns.**

You will have to provide the airport with power before it will develop. To give your airport juice, run power lines from the nearest powered area. Select the Power ➤ Power Lines tool from the City toolbar and point and click or click and drag a long stretch of power lines into place.

Soon you should see runways, hangars, an air traffic control tower, and auxiliary buildings appear. Planes will come and go, casting their shadows across the land, and eventually a little blue helicopter will buzz about.

YOU SAY YOUR AIRPORT WON'T DEVELOP?

Sometimes if you simply provide power to the nearest corner of your airport and wait, nothing develops. This seems odd, because usually that's all you have to do to provide power to zoned areas and seaports, but there you go. We've found that it's important to provide juice to certain key tiles in your airport area, and that crisscrossing your airport with power lines often speeds up development.

Meanwhile, if your airport just doesn't seem to be getting off the ground, there are a few other possibilities. It may be that you've zoned an area too small. Make sure you've provided an area at least 2×5 tiles in size; 2×6 is better yet. Make sure, too, that you haven't made the classic bloopers in locating your airport: Is it too close to a tall structure or hills? Is it located on a hillside?

Finally, here's a detail of location that can get you turned around quickly: Believe it or not, the north/south, east/west orientation makes a difference in some cases. If you've tried everything else and your airport isn't developing, trash it and zone an area turned in a different direction. For example, if your 2×6 area was oriented north/south, get rid of it and zone one that's 6×2 instead—one that's oriented east/west. That ought to do it.

CHAPTER ELEVEN

PROTECTING YOUR SIMS WITH CITY SERVICES

AS MAYOR OF YOUR OWN SimCity, you are responsible for providing the basic services that support the safety and well-being of your SimCitizens. In SimCity 2000, this means that you are the provider of:

- Police stations
- Fire stations
- Hospitals
- Prisons

You must build enough of these city service facilities—in strategic locations—to satisfy the needs of your citizens.

Clearly, each type of facility has a different purpose and price, and each can best be used in a different way.

POLICE PROTECTION

Police stations are needed throughout your city to combat crime wherever it occurs. The presence of police stations also allows you to dispatch police units in response to riots and other problems as they pop up. The number of police stations you need will depend on a number of factors, including:

- City size
- Land values
- Unemployment level

REVIEWING YOUR CITY'S CRIME RATE

SimCity 2000 gives you a number of tools with which to measure your city's crime rate. The easiest method is just to listen to complaints from your Sims, which will appear in the Info box or status bar and/or in the newspaper. (Read the newspaper—it's full of helpful

> **T I P**
>
> **Crime is a bigger problem in areas zoned Industrial than in areas zoned Commercial or Residential. Pay close attention to crime levels in the industrial sections of your city, as well as in any residential sections that are _near_ industrial areas. Areas zoned Commercial often have higher crime rates than areas zoned Residential. The lowest crime rates occur in areas zoned Residential with higher land values—that means residential sections that do not border industrial or even commercial areas, and that have land-value–raising features like trees, water, parks, and schools nearby.**

information and it's very entertaining.) You can also use the Graphs and Maps windows to display information about the current and historical state of crime in your city. For detailed information on using the Maps and Graphs windows, turn to Chapter 3.

Listen to the Sims

The most fundamental measures of your crime rate come from the police chief, one of the advisors who can appear at your bidding in the Budget window; and your Sims themselves, who speak out through their movements, the Info box/status bar, and the newspapers.

You can check in with the police chief by clicking on the advisor icon (the one with the question mark on it) in the Police line of the Budget window. (See Chapter 3 for more on this.) When the police chief advises you to increase police protection, take him seriously if you want to avoid higher crime rates and lower land values.

When crime becomes a serious problem, your Sims will complain

> **TIP**
>
> **Don't think you are doing splendidly when the police chief reports that your crime rate is comparable to the national average. What you want to hear is that crime is *low*—that's what inspires higher land values.**

about it through the Info box/status bar and the newspaper. Again, you should take them seriously. If things get really out of hand, they will simply move away from the troubled area. If the whole city is troubled, and you let the trouble go on, you'll see mass migration by your Sims, leaving large residential areas abandoned.

Check the Graphs and Maps Windows

You can further gauge the level of crime in your city with SimCity 2000's Graphs and Maps windows. From the Graphs window you can see the crime rate over the past 1, 10, or 100 years. This allows you to spot trends over time. To display the Graphs window, select Window ➤ Graphs or click on the Graphs tool on the City toolbar.

When the Graphs window appears, you have to drag it to where you can see it. Click on the Graphs tool, then hold down the mouse button while you drag the window away from the toolbar.

With the Graphs window displayed, you can select the Crime button by clicking on it, and de-select any other graphs currently displayed in the window by clicking on their buttons. (For more detailed how-to info on using the Graphs and Maps windows, turn to Chapter 3.)

By turning on other graphs, you can see patterns in how the crime rate has moved in relation to various other rates (such as unemployment and the rise or fall of property values) in your city.

You can also use the Maps window to display various types of information about your city's police protection and crime rate.

  To display the Maps window, select Windows ➤ Maps or click on the Maps tool icon on the City toolbar. To make the Maps window visible, you have to drag the window away from the toolbar a bit.

The first map that appears will be the last one that was displayed. You can switch the Maps window display from one type of map to another by selecting among the icons along the left side of

  the window. Hold down the mouse button with the pointer on the Crime icon to see a list of maps that relate to police power and crime, including:

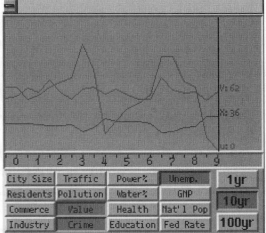

Crime Rate	Shows the crime rate throughout your city
Police Power	Shows the strength of the police department throughout your city
Police Depts.	Shows the location of every police station in your city

A quick look at Figure 11.1 will show you that the Police Power and Police Depts. maps are very similar. Police power radiates into an area of your city from a police station. Compare the maps, and you'll see that a police station is at the center of every area of police power.

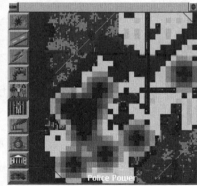

FIGURE 11.1 *Take a look at the Crime Rate, Police Power, and Police Depts. maps to get a clear picture of crime areas in your city.*

BUILDING A POLICE STATION

To build a police station, select the City Services ➤ Police tool from the City toolbar and point and click the police station into place wherever you want it. Police stations take up four tiles, so make sure you have enough space. The police station, after you place it, will flash with the alternating yellow and red bolt that indicates the need for power. Provide power as described in Chapters 1 and 5.

A police station costs $500 to build and $100 per year to maintain. You can review funding of your citywide police department in the Budget window (see Chapters 3 and 7).

THE PRORATED COSTS OF MAINTAINING CITY SERVICES

The simulator prorates the maintenance cost of whatever you build in the first year of that item's existence. So, for example, if you build a police station—which adds $100 per year to the police department's budget—in the *middle* of the year, that year the police department expenditure will increase by only $50. In the second year, you'll have to pay the full $100 maintenance fee. The same principle holds true for other services that have annual maintenance charges.

FIRE PROTECTION

With fire stations in your city, you'll be able to send firefighters all over the city to fight a variety of fires, including those started by:

- Plane crashes
- Power plant accidents
- The monster
- Rioters

You'll also need firefighters on hand in the Oakland scenario, included with SimCity 2000, to deal with the ever-popular Oakland Hills Fire Storm.

When fire protection power is getting low, you'll hear about it from the Sims via either the Info box or status bar, or the newspaper. You can also check in with the fire chief any time by clicking on the advisor icon (the one with the question mark on it) in the Fire Department line of the Budget window. (See Chapters 3 and 7 for more on this.)

> **TIP**
>
> You actually won't *need* fire stations if you're playing with No Disasters toggled on.

LOOKING AT YOUR CURRENT FIRE-FIGHTING STATUS

You can use the Maps window to find out information about the fire preparedness of your city just as you used it to find out about the level of police protection available.

To display the Maps window, select Windows ➤ Maps or click on the Maps tool icon on the City toolbar. To view the Maps window, you'll have to drag it away from the City toolbar a bit.

Which map appears first will depend on which map was viewed last. You can switch the Maps window display from one type of map to another by choosing from among the icons along the left side of the window. Hold down the mouse button with the pointer on the City Services icon to see a list of maps that relate to fire protection, including:

- Fire Power
- Fire Dept.

These two maps (see Figure 11.2) will look somewhat similar. The Fire Dept. map will show you the locations of all the fire stations in your city and the Fire Power map will illustrate the fire-fighting power throughout your city. It's probably not surprising that a fire station is located in the center of each area of fire protection.

> **NOTE**
>
> **Consult the Fire Dept. and Fire Power maps before you place new fire stations in your city. Then you can distribute fire stations evenly throughout your city.**

BUILDING A FIRE STATION

To build a fire station, select the City Services ➤ Fire Station tool on the City toolbar. Point and click the fire station into place wherever you want it. Fire stations take up four tiles, so make sure you have enough room. The fire station, after you place it, will flash with the alternating yellow and red bolt that indicates the need for power. Connect the fire station to the nearest power source in the usual way.

SENDING OUT THE POLICE, FIRE FIGHTERS, AND EVEN THE MILITARY

When disaster strikes—even mini-disaster—you'll want to send out the right personnel to deal with it. Make sure an arsenal of disaster-fighting personnel is at your disposal, including some combination of police, fire, and military units.

When disaster strikes your city, the Emergency tool (the one with the emergency light icon) in the City toolbar will become active. (You can tell this has happened because the icon, which is dimmed most of the time, will become undimmed.) Click on this icon, and a menu will appear listing the types of disaster-fighting units at your disposal.

Which types of units appear in the menu's list will depend on which types of services you've made available. You make police and fire protection available by building their stations; you make military units available by saying Yes to the government's offer of a military base (see Chapter 10). If you haven't built any police or fire stations, and you do not have a military base, you will still have *something* with which to fight disasters—the SimNational government has provided you with the SimNational Guard, which will show up as the Military choice on the menu.

Click on the menu choice that represents the type of unit you want to dispatch, then click on the place in the City window to which you want to dispatch the unit. (You can't dispatch your disaster-fighting units *into* the tile that contains the disaster—they can't fight the thing from within—you have to dispatch them to a tile *next* to the disaster. You can click more than once to dispatch more than one unit. You can also click around in various places to move the units once you've dispatched them.

For more on fighting disasters, see Chapter 15.

A fire station costs $500 to build and $100 per year to maintain. You can review the total funding level of your entire fire department in the Budget window (see Chapters 3 and 7).

N O T E

Don't send police to fight fires or firefighters to quash riots. It just doesn't work. You can, however, send the military (if it's available) to deal with either of these problems.

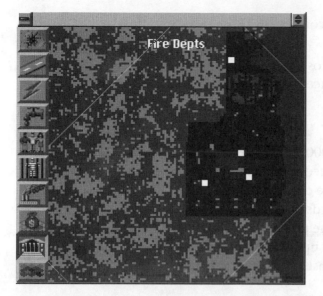 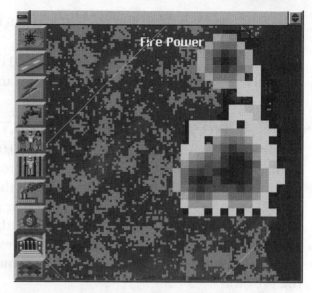

FIGURE 11.2 *The Fire Depts. map and the Fire Power map; together, these maps will tell you where the fire stations are and how fire-fighting power is distributed through your city.*

PRISONS

 You may feel the need to provide a prison in your city to house some of your less-desirable Sims. Adding a prison to your city will help reduce crime, especially when your police department is being overworked.

Prisons emit pollution and lower nearby land values. You want to place them in less-desirable locations—the kinds of locations that wouldn't be more profitably used for industrial, commercial, or residential areas. Remember, for example, that no Sim will want to live near a prison. Putting a prison next to a residential area can lower the land value by more than 20%. Place prisons—if you must have them—inland and at a good distance from the main area of your city.

NOTE

Interestingly enough, Sims never ask for prisons the way they ask for other things. Some users believe that if your city has gotten into enough trouble to need a prison, you have work to do at a more fundamental level, and building a prison is like putting a Band-Aid on an artery wound.

BUILDING A PRISON

To build a prison, select the City Services ➤ Prison tool on the City toolbar. Point and click the prison into place where you want it. After you place it, you can connect it to the nearest power source.

Prisons are 16 tiles square in size (4×4) and cost big time—$3,000—to build. There is, however, no annual maintenance cost.

THE SIMPAROLE BOARD AT WORK

Prisons in SimCity 2000 can hold up to 10,000 inmates each. Every year, 25% percent of the prisoners will be paroled to make room for new prisoners. This can be a significant factor in the crime rate—if 25% of 10,000 prisoners (2,500 prisoners, in other words) are paroled, and if more than 2,500 new prisoners are added to the prison population the next year, the prison overflows and crime goes up (presumably because some prisoners never received sentences, because there was no room in the prison).

Clearly, the best way to handle this issue is to keep crime down and provide adequate police protection in the first place.

HOSPITALS

The presence of hospitals in your city will increase the overall healthiness and the life expectancy of your Sims. A healthy Sim is a Sim with a long, productive life to look forward to. A healthy, productive Sim is one who will put more into the city's economy (through an active work life) than he or she takes out (through being a burden and drain on the system).

Healthy Sims, it follows, are good for industry, commerce, and the general economy.

The number of hospitals your city requires will depend on the city's size (you'll need more as the city grows). One hospital serves the needs of as many as 25,000 Sims. Within the hospital walls, the number of doctors available will depend on population and funding levels, while the number of patients will depend on population and number of beds. (Sims without health insurance don't get beds—they languish on gurneys in the halls.)

TIP

Don't put hospitals on land that could be more valuable if used for another purpose. The waterfront, for example, can become very valuable if zoned as a residential area.

You'll know when you need to add hospitals because the Health advisor in the Budget window will tell you so when you check in, and because messages will appear in the Info box or status bar saying your Sims demand that you build them a hospital.

Where you put the hospitals isn't of very great significance—you can cluster them together or spread them throughout your city. The Sims care about the number, not the locations.

As you add new hospitals, the general health of your Sims should increase. (Keeping pollution in check will help, too.) Click on the Graphs ➤ Health tool in the City toolbar. A graph will appear showing the health level of your Sims. You can view changes in the health level over a 1-, 10-, and 100-year period by clicking on the buttons for that time span at the bottom of the graph. (The graph actually shows the life expectancy of laborers in your city.) Adding hospitals and reducing pollution will improve these statistics.

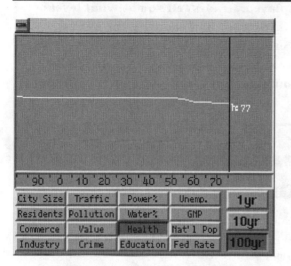

TIP

It is economically important to keep your Sims healthy, vigorous, and *productive*. Raising the health level and life expectancy of your Sims will ease the burden of education, too—educating Sims is an investment on the part of your SimCity, and if that investment is wasted on Sims who die before they're aged, more and more Sims have to be educated to take their places in the work force.

BUILDING A HOSPITAL

To build a hospital, select the City Services ➤ Hospital tool on the City toolbar. Point and click the hospital into place where you want it. After you build it, you can connect your hospital to the nearest power source.

A hospital is 9 square tiles in size (3×3). Each hospital costs $500 to build and $50 per year to maintain. You can

review the total funding level of your hospital (Health & Welfare) system in the Budget window (see Chapters 3 and 7).

INVESTIGATING CITY SERVICES

To find out about any of the police stations, fire stations, hospitals, or prisons in your city services system, select the Query tool from the City toolbar and click on the item, or hold down Shift and then click on the item.

TIP

In the info boxes that appear when you query various items, "grades" will be displayed. Grades tell you at what level of efficiency and capacity the item is performing. You can usually increase grades by raising the funding level (if you are funding at less than 100%) or by building more of the same type of item.

RENAMING YOUR CITY SERVICE STRUCTURES

You can rename city services in honor of yourself, SimSports figures, SimMilitary heroes, or just about anybody or anything you want. In the info window that appears when you use the Query tool on an item, just type a new name into the text box and then click on the Rename button. The new name will appear in the text box the next time you use the Query tool on the item.

CHAPTER TWELVE

EDUCATION AND ITS PLACE IN A SIMCITY

IN REAL LIFE, MANY PROSPECTIVE buyers of residential real estate are persuaded by the agent's description of the neighborhoods' wonderful schools. In SimCity 2000, the Sims are persuaded to move into your city in just the same way, but in this case, the educational system is not described in glowing words, but rather in the form of a number—the *Education Quotient*, or EQ.

WHAT'S IMPORTANT ABOUT THE EQ

Your Sims pride themselves on having a high EQ. They will be more inclined to move into and raise their children in a city with a high EQ. In addition, a high EQ will make it more likely that your city will develop high-tech industries (electronics and the like).

A low EQ will discourage pride and development among your Sims. If they get miserable enough about the way things are going, they will grumble about the lack of educational opportunity in the newspaper (which, because of growing illiteracy, they actually won't be able to *read*). And if things continue to get worse, you will be faced with a higher unemployment rate and perhaps even rioting.

> **NOTE**
>
> The Sims who move into your city when it's new are educated elsewhere before they arrive. (The EQ of those Sims will be approximately 85.) This means you don't have to build schools right away, but you should do it fairly soon, for the sake of the new Sims' children. If you don't build schools, education in your city will be based only on the lore one generation tells the next. The first generation of Sims to be born in your new city will then have only 20% the EQ their parents had, and the next will have 20% the EQ *their* parents had.

WHAT AFFECTS THE EQ

The EQ of your Sims is affected by a number of factors, most notably the presence of schools, colleges, museums, and libraries in your city. Each school (grades K through 12 are included) covers the educational

needs of Sims between the ages of 5 and 15 for a population of up to 15,000 Sims. If you have only schools in your city and if those schools are fully funded in the Budget window, your city's EQ will reach 90 over a period of years.

Each college (these are four-year colleges) covers the educational needs of Sims in the 15–25 age group for a population of up to 50,000 Sims. If you have colleges in your city and if your schools are funded well enough (in the Budget window) to fully prepare students for a higher education, your city's EQ can reach 140 over time.

Your Sims' EQ will diminish once they've graduated from college unless you provide them with further intellectual stimulation in the form of libraries and museums. This does not mean, however, that the presence of libraries and museums raises the EQ of only older Sims—the benefits affect all age groups. Note that museums are somewhat more effective than libraries.

NOTE

You will notice a slight shift in EQ in the year after you place schools. The full impact won't be felt, however, until 10–15 years later, when the SimStudents who attend those new schools graduate and enter the work force.

TIP

Turning on the Pro-Reading Campaign city ordinance will also help to increase your city's EQ. To maximize your Sims' EQ as they come of age, provide your city with one fully funded school per 15,000 Sims and with one fully funded college per 50,000 Sims.

VIEWING AND INTERPRETING THE EQ

 To see the EQ for your city, you can either click on the Population window icon in the City toolbar, or pull down Windows ➤ Population from the menu bar. Deselect the Population and Health buttons, and select the Education button by clicking on it. A graph will appear.

Here's what the numbers mean when you look at the Education Quotient of your city:

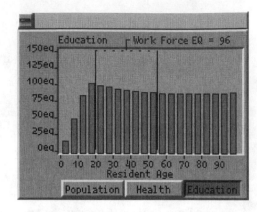

EQ	Level of Education Indicated
0	Brain dead
90	High school education
100	SimNational average
140	Four-year college graduate

You can also check development of the EQ in your city over a 1-year, 10-year, or 100-year span of time. Click on the Graphs tool icon in the City toolbar. When the Graphs window appears, deselect any other buttons that appear depressed and select the education button. You can select any of the three time spans available by clicking on one of those buttons. (Using the Population and Graphs windows is covered in more detail in Chapter 3.)

EDUCATION LEVEL AND AGES

As you add more schools and colleges to your city, the younger Sims will attend the schools and can therefore become more educated than the older Sims. The EQ as it appears in the graph will rise first for the young Sims. Later, as the more educated Sims age, the level of their education will show up as a rising EQ in older age groups.

BUILDING SCHOOLS, COLLEGES, LIBRARIES, AND MUSEUMS

Building schools, colleges, libraries, and museums is about the same. Apply the principles described in the sections that follow when placing any of these items.

READING YOUR EDUCATIONAL SERVICES' GRADE REPORTS

Each of the educational services we discuss in this chapter has a grade associated with it (as do a lot of other items in SimCity 2000). To see the grade, click on the Query tool in the City toolbar, then click on the school or other institution you want to investigate. The grade will appear in the window that tells you about whatever you clicked on.

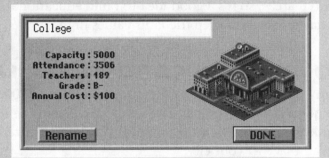

The grade is affected by two basic factors: the number of those items in the city as compared to your population, and the funding level for the citywide system of those items. You can increase the grade either by building more of that type of item or by increasing the funding level in the Budget window.

WHERE TO BUILD EDUCATIONAL FACILITIES

In a sense, it doesn't matter where in your city you place educational institutions. The simulator just checks to see whether or not you have each type of facility, not where they're located. That means that you don't have to place learning centers anywhere in particular to get their statistical benefits to the EQ. (In fact, you don't even have to provide learning centers with power or transportation access.)

You could stick the schools and colleges in your city on remote islands, in dried-up corners of the landmass, or even in the middle of a zone full of factories if you really wanted to.

However, there are other factors to consider. One, of course, is your own sense of aesthetics. Another is the effect the presence of schools has on land values. The simulator does take into consideration the proximity of learning centers to residential areas when calculating land values for those residential areas, so it's a good idea to build educational facilities near residential property to keep the land values high.

HOW TO BUILD EDUCATIONAL FACILITIES

To build any of the institutions of learning in SimCity 2000, select the Education tool on the City toolbar. Click and hold down the mouse pointer on this tool, and a menu will appear listing the educational institutions you can place in your city:

Facility	Size (in tiles)	Cost to Build	Annual Cost to Maintain
School	3×3	$ 250	$12
College	4×4	1,000	12
Library	2×2	500	0
Museum	3×3	1,000	0

Point and click the educational institution of your choice into place wherever you want it to appear. You'll see the usual power bolt flashing red alternating with yellow that indicates the building is unpowered; you can connect the building to the nearest power source, and when juice is

flowing the flashing will soon stop. To provide power, select the Power ➤ Power Lines tool on the City toolbar. Point and click a single power line into place if the power source is nearby, or click and drag a length of power lines if the power source is farther away.

CHECKING UP ON YOUR EDUCATIONAL SYSTEM

You can click on the Query tool in the city toolbar and then on any item of your educational system (or just Shift-click on the item) to see important information about the citywide system of that type of item.

N O T E

To tell you how many students are attending and other such stuff, some buildings—schools included—*microsimulate*. You can have only 150 microsimulations in a city. For more on microsimualtions, check out the boxed text titled (appropriately) "Microsimulations: Citywide Statistics vs. Individual Statistics" in Chapter 1.

CHAPTER THIRTEEN

WHAT SIMS DO ON THE WEEKENDS: PARKS AND RECREATION

ALL WORK AND NO PLAY makes Sims a dull species. Your Sims are going to want to cool out at the end of a long, productive week, and your city will be a happier, wealthier place if you provide them with pleasant recreational facilities and open, airy spaces to use. The presence of open spaces, parks, and recreational facilities will benefit your entire city.

OPEN SPACES AND PARKS

At first glance, open spaces—those places in the landmass that contain "only" trees or water—may seem like nothing more than raw material for the SimDevelopers. Not so—the presence of open spaces in or near your city will increase land values. In fact, one tile in your city that contains nothing but trees will increase the value of nearby land as much as one tile that contains a neatly manicured small park. Big parks, however, increase land values twice as much as small parks.

> **WARNING**
>
> The only downside to having a lot of trees in your city is that they're flammable and can allow fires to spread very quickly.

Parks and open spaces have the most impact on areas zoned Residential and Commercial, but their presence also increases the success of the tourism industry in your city. It stands to reason, then, that you want to place parks in or near residential areas. You might also consider providing your city with one or more greenbelts—areas with tiles containing only trees, or combinations of trees and ponds or lakes, as shown in Figure 13.1.

CREATING OPEN SPACES

Creating open spaces in your city is often just a matter of letting some open space go undeveloped. You can, however, add trees and/or water to your city using the Landscape tool on the City toolbar. Select Landscape ➤ Trees or Landscape ➤ Water, and then point and click or click and drag to paint trees or water on any undeveloped tiles in your city. Be careful when you're painting water into place, though—if you click

> **NOTE**
>
> It's easier (and costs nothing) to add trees and water to your landscape *before* you start to build your city. Turn to Chapter 22 to find out about using the Terrain toolbar to create or modify the landmass as you like it.

FIGURE 13.1 *A greenbelt like this can buffer residential areas from less-appealing areas.*

away recklessly, you can easily cause trouble for yourself by accidentally creating a big lake where you meant a small pond to appear.

Creating trees and water in an existing city is not cheap—trees cost $3 per tree, and water costs $100 per tile.

CREATING PARKS

While the SimCity 2000 program does not require a certain park-to-resident ratio, some land-use planners have suggested four acres of parkland per 1,000 residents. To figure your park-to-population ratio, first pause the game. Then click on the Neighbors Window tool in the City toolbar to find out your city's population. Jot down that number. Now use the Query tool on a big park to find out the total park acreage for your city. Do you have four acres of park land per 1,000 residents?

> **TIP**
>
> Parks, like open spaces, can be used as a buffer between zones. Parks raise land values in the four-tile area around them. They can be placed at the center of a 9×9 residential or commercial area to maximize contact to the zoned tiles in that area, or they can be scattered throughout the city to increase land value over a greater area.

There are two types of parks in SimCity 2000:

Small parks, which are just one tile in size and cost $20 each.

Big parks, which are 3×3 tiles in size and cost $150 each.

While at first blush parks may seem like an expendable luxury, you should consider their real value. Placing one small park next to land valued at $88,000 soon can raise the value of that land to $99,000. At 7% (the standard property tax rate), that means an increase in annual tax revenue from that property of $770—your *first* return on the onetime $20 investment of building the park.

> ### N O T E
>
> **Parks do not need to be provided with power. They also don't transmit power, and they look ugly covered with power lines anyway, so don't put a park where you're going to have to string power lines later.**

To place a park in your city, select Recreation ➤ Small Park or Recreation ➤ Big Park from the City toolbar. Then point and click the park into place where you want it to appear.

RECREATIONAL FACILITIES

Providing recreational facilities in your city will allow your Sims to enjoy specific leisure activities. Recreational facilities, which are used by SimResidents more than SimTourists, can be a big boon to residential growth in your city (and they sure don't hurt tourism, either).

Three types of recreational facilities are available:

- Zoo
- Stadium
- Marina

IT'S WHAT'S NEXT DOOR THAT COUNTS

To give you a clear idea of the value of parks, let's look at an example. Say you have a nice office building in a commercial area. The office building is worth $96,000. (You know this because you used the Query tool on the building.) Next door there are other office buildings. If you demolish/clear those buildings next door and leave rubble in their place, your nice office building's value will drop to $30,000. If you dezone and leave blank the area where the rubble was, the nice office building's value will jump to $86,000. If you build a big park where the blank tiles were, the nice office building's value will go to a big $165,000 almost right away.

These numbers are not the same for every simulation, but they're pretty typical, and the same effects occur in other type of zones depending on what you place next to buildings. Wield your Query tool often to get an idea of the impact of your actions on the value of individual properties—it'll give you broader insight into the whole game.

CREATING A ZOO

To create a zoo, select Recreation ➤ Zoo from the City toolbar, then point and click the zoo into place. (When you do this, you'll hear the roar of the elephant, which we have heard is actually the recorded roar of a Maxis employee.) Zoos do blink with the yellow and red bolts that indicate they want to be connected to power, and they do transmit electricity.

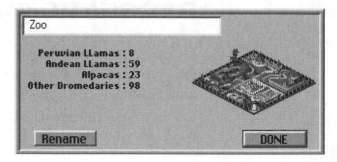

Zoos take up 3×3 tiles and cost $3,000 each.

HAVE YOU HEARD THE ONE ABOUT...

If you're using a Mac, type **joke** anytime while playing the game and you'll get a sampling of Maxis-style humor.

CREATING A STADIUM

To create a stadium in your city, select Recreation ➤ Stadium from the City toolbar, then point and click the stadium into place. Each stadium uses 5×5 tiles and costs $5,000.

A dialog box will appear in which you'll be asked to select the type of team you want from a list of available sports. The dialog box looks different depending on which version of the game you have (see Figure 13.2). If you have either the DOS or Mac version, simply click on the check box for the type of sport you want. If you have the Windows version, click on the down-arrow button to reveal a drop-down list of sports, then select the one you want by clicking on it.

In either case, you'll see a text box with a suggested name for your team. You can make up your own name if you want and type it into the text box. Or you can accept the suggested name by doing nothing. Click on the Done button or OK when you're finished.

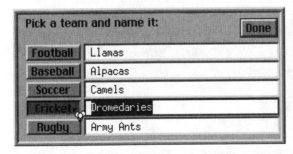
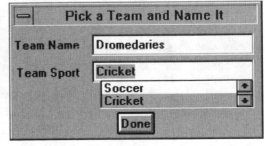

FIGURE 13.2 *On the left you see the "Pick a team" dialog box as it appears in the DOS and Mac versions. On the right you see it as it appears in the Windows version.*

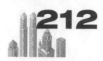

A big, shiny stadium will now grace your city.

To provide your stadium with power, select Power ➤ Power Lines from the City toolbar, then point and click a single line or click and drag a length of lines into place to connect your stadium to the nearest powered area.

To find out how your team's doing at any given moment, Shift-click on your stadium (or select the Query tool from the City toolbar and then click on the stadium).

NOTE

If you notice that your team's losing a lot, you may wonder what gives. Is it bad coaching? Well, the answer is that this is one of the "random" elements built into SimCity 2000, like the weather and the SimNational economy.

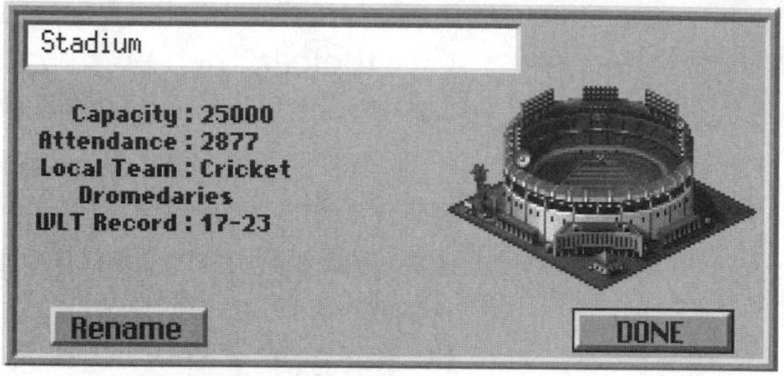

NOT IN MY BACKYARD

While a stadium in your city will be a boon to overall residential development, it can drive land values in its immediate vicinity down a good 20% right away. After you build a stadium next to an $88,000-an-acre property, the neighboring property may soon be worth as little as $66,000 an acre. This adds a first-year loss in annual tax revenues of $1,540 for that building to the $5,000 cost of building the stadium. This is not to say you should not build a stadium—the boost to your overall city value is incalculable. Instead, just be sure to build it somewhere where it won't lay waste to high property values.

Similarly, a zoo in your city will attract tourism and give your Sims something fun to do on weekends, which keeps them happy. But there seems to be no good place within your city to put the zoo. Try placing it next to a residential area, and you can watch nearby land values drop like they've been tied to a concrete block and dropped in a lake.

Having a stadium or zoo will benefit your city as a whole; just keep it away from the Sims' backyards, offices, and shops.

CREATING A MARINA

When you select Recreation ➤ Marina from the City toolbar, then point and click on a water tile, a marina will appear. You can provide your marina with power in the usual way.

Marinas cost $1,000 and take up 3×3 tiles—those tiles, however, do not have to be land tiles. You can place your marina just about anywhere, as long as at least one land tile and even just one water tile are among the tiles under the marina.

Soon after you place your marina, a little boat will start to sail around nearby. (See Figure 13.3.)

By the way, if you're curious about the total acreage of your city devoted to recreation and parks, use the Query tool on City Hall and click the Analysis button.

BUILDING A LANDLOCKED MARINA

Want a marina but don't have any suitable waterfront available right now? Here's a neat trick: Place a marina far from the nearest real water by first selecting Landscape ➤ Water, then clicking once to place just *one drop of water* on a tile of land anywhere on your landmass. Place your marina to cover that tile, and there you have it—a landlocked marina!

FIGURE 13.3   *This marina is home to a happy little sailboat.*

CHAPTER FOURTEEN

THE PERKS OF POWER: REAPING YOUR REWARDS

NOTE

When you click on the Rewards icon on the City toolbar, a menu will appear noting the currently available rewards. You don't have to use or accept a reward when it appears on the menu—you can let it sit there until you want to put it into place, or you can let it sit there forever.

AS SIMMAYOR, YOU GET REWARDS. These rewards, which are tied to the size of your city's population, are sometimes designed to stroke your ego, sometimes to remind the citizenry of your good work. Sometimes, too, they are rewards to your city rather than to you, but hey, aren't you happy when your city's happy?

REWARDS THAT ACKNOWLEDGE YOUR STATURE IN THE CITY

The first group of rewards that appear can serve as reminders to you and your Sims that you're doing a great job as mayor.

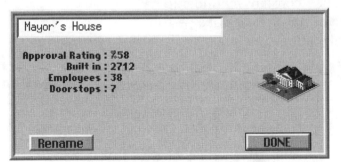

Mayor's House

The mayor's house becomes available when your population reaches 2,000. The mayor's house is all splendor and luxury. You can put it wherever you want—many users favor prominent locations that provide panoramic views of the city or scenic wonders.

City Hall

City Hall, which appears as an option when your population reaches 10,000, is an acknowledgment that you now have more complex administrative needs. In SimCity 2000, City Hall is not just a reward—it's actually a good tool to have at your disposal—use the Query tool to click on City Hall, then click the Analysis button, and you'll find out some helpful information (Figure 14.1).

LAND USE		ACRES		% of CITY
Transportation	–	2196	– %	27
Power	–	174	– %	2
Water	–	114	– %	1
Residential	–	2629	– %	33
Commercial	–	928	– %	11
Industrial	–	1468	– %	18
Ports/Airports	–	58	– %	0
Education	–	109	– %	1
Health/Safety	–	142	– %	1
Recreation	–	71	– %	0
Arcologies	–	0	– %	0

FIGURE 14.1 *City Hall is a working reward.*

Statue

The presence of a statue in your city will be a constant reminder to your Sims and to yourself that you, the mayor, are one heck of a person. The statue option appears when your population reaches 30,000.

Llama Dome

The llama dome is a really fascinating thing that seems to serve as both an on-going wedding chapel and a bungee-jumping launch pad. Oddly, the number of weddings that take place in any given llama dome equals the number of bungee jumps...h-m-mm.

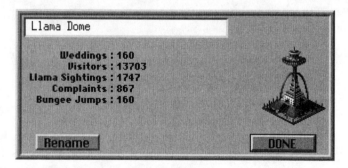

The llama dome becomes available when your population reaches 90,000. In the Australian version of SimCity 2000, the llama dome is replaced by the Sydney Opera House.

N O T E

Will Wright says, "The llama is a quadraped."

REWARDS THAT ACKNOWLEDGE YOUR CITY'S STATURE IN SIMNATION

When your city reaches a population of 60,000, it will be offered a military base. The military bases, while not strictly rewards, are an acknowledgment of your city's lofty stature in SimNation. The offer will come in the form of a dialog box message rather than a menu option under the Rewards icon. Military bases, which have advantages and disadvantages for your city, are covered in Chapter 10.

REWARDS THAT ACKNOWLEDGE YOUR CITY'S PROGRESS

When your city reaches a population of 120,000, and if the year is past 2000, the first of four types of *arcologies* appears on the menu under the Rewards tool icon. Arcologies are self-contained communities that are housed within one large building and that attempt to separate the harsh realities of urban living from the surrounding natural landscape.

THE INSIDE SCOOP ON ARCOLOGIES

Arcos contain about 50,000 Sims each, and, although they are "self-contained," they need some services (schools, colleges, police), and they are adversely affected by pollution in the city. They also create both pollution and crime, so it's important to monitor these conditions.

One way you can tell how things are going is to look at the maps for the area a given "arco" occupies to check on crime and pollution. Another way to check on an individual arco is to use the Query tool to look at the arco's grade. You can improve the grade by providing the appropriate amount of services nearby and by keeping pollution down. The actual population in the arco will go up if the grade goes up. On the

> **TIP**
>
> To make the best of arco technology and keep pollution to a minimum, buffer your arcos with greenbelts—parks and open spaces with trees.

other hand, the arco might become over-crowded, in which case the grade, once it has gone up, can decline.

In reality, arcologies are an option that lets SimCity 2000's developers give you the opportunity to build a megalopolis. In the 1.0 versions of SimCity 2000 for DOS and the Mac, the maximum number of arcos you could have was 140. In versions 1.1 and later (including the Windows version) the limitation no longer existed, and it became possible using arcos to build a city with a population of more than nine million Sims.

TIP

In Chapter 15 we describe a cool trick called the Magic Eraser, which lets you "erase" part or all of a building. The partially erased building keeps functioning, and you can even build something else overlapping it. You can use this trick to great advantage by wiping out part of an arcology and building another one overlapping the first one. (The partially erased arcology's population will remain as part of your city's total population even though the arcology itself is pretty much gone.)

"ARCOLOGY" IS LIKE "ARK"

Arcology, a term that may have been invented by visionary architect Paolo Soleri, is meant to describe a city in a building- -a self-suffcient community combining architecture and ecology. The term also appears in Niven and Pournelle's novel, *Oath of Fealty,* and in David Brin's *Earth,* but that's not the real news.

Soleri is actually building one of these things. *Arcosanti,* the realization of Soleri's vision, is under construction just 70 miles outside of Phoenix. Funding for the project comes mainly from the sale of bells manufactured using local soil. You can tour the place for a $5 donation; you can even rent a room at a pretty reasonable rate and spend the night. Dining is available at Arcosanti's cafe and bakery. Call 602-632-7135 for more information.

If you want to find out more about Soleri and his arcologies but you'd rather stay home in the comfort of your armchair, check out his book, *Arcology: The City in the Image of Man* (Massachusetts Institute of Technology Press, 1969).

THE TYPES OF ARCOLOGIES

You'll find these arcos appearing as your population grows:

Arco	Year It Appears	Cost	Population
Plymouth Arco	2000	$100,000	55,000
Forest Arco	2050	120,000	30,000
Darco (De-Urbanized Arcological Construct)	2100	150,000	45,000
Launch Arco	2150	200,000	65,000

There really aren't a lot of rules about where you place arcos—because they're essentially self-contained, you can put one next to just about anything else. They don't float, though, so forget placing them in the middle of a body of water. And you should pay attention to their needs for services and buffering from pollution. Figure 14.2 shows arcos in city settings; Figure 14.3 shows the various arcos available.

FIGURE 14.2 *Arcos in "action"*

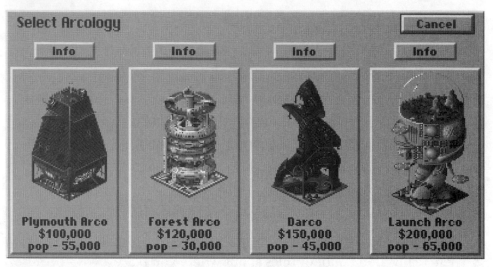

FIGURE 14.3   *Here you see one each of all the arcos available.*

THE LAUNCH ARCO SECRET

Users frequently want to know how to make their launch arcos launch. The big secret here is that in the DOS and Mac versions *launch arcos don't launch*. At least they don't take off in any kind of animated sequence. Pity, isn't it? In the Windows version, they do take off, but you have to have 350 of them for this to happen.

BUILDING AN ARCOLOGY

To build an arco (when any is available), select Rewards ➤ Arcologies from the City toolbar. A window will appear listing all of the arcos currently available. (You can find out more information about each of the arcos by clicking the Info buttons [Figure 14.3] above their names.) Click on the one you want, then point and click it into place in your city. Arcos don't need much to "operate," but they do need power. Juice them up as described in Chapters 1 and 4.

THE GIANT CHOCOLATE BUNNY

In SimCity 2000 for Windows you'll find the Easter egg that gets you the giant chocolate bunny. When you type the right cheat word (read on for that secret to be revealed), a new item appears on the menu bar—the Debug menu. What's this *debug* business? Well, while they're developing any given version of SimCity 2000, the programmers need the ability to control the game in various ways so they can test the program. For their own convenience, they keep some options—more money, all the rewards, various disasters—on a drop-down menu they can use whenever they want. This allows them to "debug" the program more easily.

In the usual course of events, they take out the Debug menu just before they send the game to be manufactured. (It has outlived its usefulness to the programmers at this point.) But when they sent the *Windows* version off, they took out the Debug menu as usual, *and they added a cheat word that would bring it back!*

To invoke the Debug menu, type **oigevald**. Debug will appear as an option on the menu bar. Click on it, and you can choose from these yummy possibilities:

Click on This	To Get This
Show Version Info	A description of the version of SimCity 2000 you're running
More Money	A big $500,000 added to your treasury at the start of the next month
Add All Gifts	All the Rewards (and as many of each of them as you want) without having to earn them by building up your population
Add All Inventions	All the inventions *today* without the inconvenience of waiting 'til they're invented
Melt Down	A meltdown, if you have a nuclear power plant
Microwave	A microwave "oops," if you have a microwave power plant
Volcano	A volcano in or near your city
Fire Storm	A fire storm in or near your city
Mass Riots	Sims rioting all over your city
Major Flood	A major flood in or near your city
Toxic Spill	A toxic spill in or near your city

continued

One catch, however—some of these choices work only if you have in place the elements necessary for the event to occur. For example, you'll have enough money to build whatever you want anytime, and you'll have arcologies listed as a reward, but if you have no population to move into them, the arcos might not appear. And you can take the action to trigger riots before you've even built a city, but if you have no Sims, there will be no rioters to hoist signs and so there will be no riots.

On the other hand, a lot of things will be available to you that weren't before—you can click on More Money more than once a month, and the next month you'll get oodles of cash (click three times and you'll get $150,000 the next month, click four times...). You can plaster the town with llama domes, statues, city halls, and all the mayor's houses you'll ever want. (You can put one in the city, one in the country, one on a lake....)

CHAPTER FIFTEEN

WHEN DISASTER STRIKES

IN THE COURSE OF REAL-LIFE events, random disasters strike even the most successfully managed cities. In SimCity 2000, disaster can take many forms—from the more localized to the widespread—and you need to be prepared to deal with disaster if it strikes. You must take steps to avoid preventable disasters, build an appropriate number of services to deal with the results of disaster when it occurs, and know how to use those services to their best advantage when they're needed.

AVOIDING DISASTERS

The simplest method for avoiding disaster has been discussed before in this book: just turn off disasters (Disasters ➤ No Disasters). Then you won't be bothered—even if a plane crashes, it won't set part of your city on fire.

If you prefer the challenge of managing a city where anything can happen, leave No Disasters turned off. Plane crashes, then, can have either minor or tragic results, and all kinds of other disasters (described in this chapter) can occur without warning.

In general, you will probably want to run your city so that events like plane crashes, riots, meltdowns, and serious pollution won't happen. Throughout this book we have advised you on ways to avoid those unpleasant circumstances as you build your city. In this chapter, we'll present each disaster—and the best ways to avoid it.

CAUSING DISASTERS

If you get bored or impatient at some point in a game, and you want to destroy your city or just experiment with any specific disaster, pull down the Disasters menu and toggle on any disaster in the list. It will occur immediately.

> **TIP**
>
> **Save your city to disk before you do this, and you can go back and play the same events out in a different way or with a different disaster to hone your disaster-fighting skills.**

WHO YOU GONNA CALL?

When disasters do strike, you may have any combination of services at your disposal, depending on what you've placed in your city. You can use

- Fire fighters to deal with fires resulting from any kind of disaster
- Police to quash riots
- Military to deal with just about anything

The number of fire-fighter or police units you have available depends on the number of fire and police stations you've built in your city and the power of your fire and police coverage, as determined by the strategic placement of those stations and the level of funding provided in the Budget window.

> **NOTE**
>
> If you have no fire or police stations in your city and you haven't built a military base, one unit of the SimNational Guard will be sent to your city when disaster strikes. (This will show up as the Military option on the menu under the Emergency tool icon.)

You have no control over the number of military units available to respond to disasters; it depends on the size of your base—which is controlled by the SimNational government—and how many units the military is willing to spring.

SEEING DISASTER AS IT HAPPENS

You'll know when disaster strikes your city—whatever you're doing, the screen will shift suddenly to the scene of the disaster, and you'll see the terrible event taking place (assuming you have Auto-Goto toggled on). You'll also be informed by a message in the Info box/status bar.

> **TIP**
>
> Pause the simulator as soon as a disaster starts so you'll have more time to prepare. With the simulator paused, you can get an overview of the situation and come up with a response plan. (Some people—fussy diehards, really—consider this a little sneaky.)

If you don't want your view to be shifted automatically to the scene of striking disaster, pull down the Options menu and toggle off Auto-Goto. We don't really recommend this, though, because disaster can become fairly widespread before you notice any problem. If you do toggle off Auto-Goto, you'll see the message telling you there's a disaster in the Info box or status bar (if you happen to look at it) and you can then quickly jump your view of the City window to the location of the disaster by:

- In the DOS and Mac versions, clicking on the arrow that appears at the far right end of the Info box, if you have one, just before the Weather icon.

- In the Windows verion, clicking on the GoTo button in the bottom-right corner (on the status bar).

CAPTAIN HERO SAVES THE DAY

Look! Up in the air! Fighting off disaster when all else was unavailable! It's Captain Hero, come to save the day.

Captain Hero, a tiny, flying, pink-clad superhero, shows up—sometimes without being called forth—just when you thought all was lost. Captain Hero's appearance is as sudden and unpredictable as disaster is random, though—he/she/it may never arrive or may show up at any time to save your city from doom. (Actually, there's a 25% chance Captain Hero will appear if a disaster occurs and you have no police or fire stations. Captain Hero will never show up if you have a military base.)

Don't count on Captain Hero, just be grateful if you see a pink flash buzzing around your screen when disaster strikes.

DISPATCHING HELP

After reading through the rest of this chapter, you'll get specific ideas for fighting each type of potential disaster. Let's just say that disaster has now struck; you must respond. What to do? Start by clicking and holding on the Emergency tool icon on the City toolbar.

A menu will appear. This is a list of *all* the currently available services for fighting the disaster—it's up to you to judge which to use. Select the type of unit you need from the list. The

name of that service will appear in the Info box/status bar. Move the mouse pointer to the disaster's location and click response units into place.

You cannot send the response units to the tiles that actually hold the disaster. You must click the response units into place in *neighboring* tiles.

Your best bet in most cases is to surround the area where the disaster has occurred with response units. More detailed instructions follow.

FIGHTING AND PREVENTING SPECIFIC DISASTERS

Most disasters in SimCity 2000 can be fought, and many can be prevented. Let's go over each type of potential disaster, telling you how to combat it and, wherever possible, how to *prevent* it from occurring in the first place.

PLANE CRASH

A plane crash will involve an airliner tumbling from the sky into whatever's below, causing a localized explosion and a fire, which can be really disastrous if the plane crashes into the city itself.

Preventing Plane Crashes

Plane crashes are sometimes random events, but more often they are preventable (Figure 15.1). To control preventable plane crashes, build your airport far away from tall buildings, hills, and anything else the planes might crash into. See Chapter 10 for more on where to build airports to prevent crashes.

FIGURE 15.1 *Many planes will crash and burn if you build your airport next to a tall structure or hill.*

Dealing with Plane Crashes

When a plane crashes, it will explode and start a fire. Your main goal should be to put out the fire quickly before it spreads and becomes a bigger problem. Before the plane actually hits the ground, anticipate the falling plane's crash site and surround the area with firefighter units as quickly as possible. If the fire becomes large, you'll have to resort to more drastic measures (see the following section).

FIRE

Fires can sometimes break out around your city—they can be caused by industrial accidents, arson, carelessness on the part of some Sim, or they can come in the aftermath of a riot, plane crash, or a meltdown. The advice in this section is equally applicable regardless of how a fire was started.

Preventing Fires

The best way to *fight* fires, as we are told in countless real-life televised public-service announcements, is to *prevent* them. Don't let your citizens get so unhappy they riot, don't build your airport in a location that's bound to cause plane crashes, and whatever you do, *don't build your airport next door to a nuclear power plant.*

Fighting Fires

Try to put out a fire before it spreads—things can get out of hand really fast, especially if you're running the simulator at the Llama or Cheetah speeds. Select Emergency ➤ Firefighters from the City toolbar, and position the fire fighters in a line between the fire and the rest of your city, or, if the fire is small enough, in a circle around the fire. If you need more help, you can always select Emergency ➤ Military from the City toolbar and dispatch military units in the same way.

> **TIP**
>
> When a fire starts—especially a large one—you might want to first pause the simulation. This will give you a chance to position your response units before the fire spreads.

If the fire spreads, or if it starts out too large for the number of fire fighters and military units you have available, you might want to use the Bulldoze ➤ Demolish/Clear tool to create a firebreak (a line of rubble). Fire will not spread to tiles that hold rubble. Again, if you use this method, you can either create the firebreak in the form of a line between the fire and other structures or in a circle around the fire.

Another, more risky method of responding to a small fire is to quickly build a fire station directly on top of the tiles that are on fire. This method works only if you can cover the entire fire with a single fire station, and it's not cheap—Fire Stations cost $500—but it can be effective. Be careful, though: if the fire is larger and you build a fire station *in* it rather than on top of it, the fire station will fry in no time.

Battling a Fire Storm

A fire storm—a huge fire raging out of control—can destroy your entire city. A fire storm is, believe us, a big risk if a little dinky fire isn't stamped out immediately. You can't really hope to stop a big fire storm with a few units of firefighters and military.

If a fire storm starts in an undeveloped part of your landmass, you can use the Water tool to build a waterway that will act as a firebreak between the fire and your city. Be forewarned, however, that creating a waterway of this size is very expensive. You may be better off letting a fire storm in an undeveloped area just burn itself out. You may also find that creating a firebreak of rubble does the trick.

If a fire storm occurs in your city, pull out all the stops to contain and fight the blaze. First, pause the simulation. Place firefighters and military units where they're needed most—you probably won't have enough of them to put out the whole fire—and then use Bulldozer ➤ Demolish/Clear to create a firebreak of rubble wherever needed to stop the blaze from spreading further (see Figure 15.2). When all the pieces of your fire-fighting strategy are in place, turn the simulation speed back to Turtle or Llama and hope for the best. (You may have to move some of the response units and create more of a firebreak to further battle the fire.)

FIGURE 15.2 *This fire storm may be stopped by the fire-fighting units and the firebreak.*

MELTDOWN

If a meltdown occurs at your nuclear power plant, you'll have a very serious problem. Actually, you'll have *two* problems: first, there will be a lot of big fires; second, there will be widespread areas of radioactivity.

Preventing Meltdowns

Meltdowns are random events in SimCity 2000; to prevent one, you have only two choices:

- Don't use a nuclear power plant
- Use a nuclear power plant, but toggle on No Disasters

If you choose to use a nuclear power plant and keep disasters enabled, build your nuke far from your city and far from the airport. This won't prevent a meltdown, but it may partially protect your city from devastating fire and radiation if a meltdown occurs. If you choose to use a nuclear power plant and toggle on No Disasters, you can put the power plant wherever you like.

Managing the Effects of a Meltdown

If a meltdown does occur, you'll first have to isolate and put out the fires. That's just like putting out a lot of any other type of fire—see the section titled "Fire" earlier in this chapter. But you'll still have to deal with the radioactivity. This will be very inconvenient, because there are likely to be a *lot* of radioactive tiles. Can you clean it up? Well, no. After a meltdown, all of the tiles marked with radioactive signs will simply be out of play for the rest of the game (see Figure 15.3).

The bottom line when a meltdown occurs is that it's likely to destroy most of your city. You'll also be out a nuclear power plant, which might cause a lot of trouble in the form of power shortages and the cost of replacing the power plant.

But the real trouble is the length of time (forever, in SimTime) that the radiation will hang around. You probably won't be able to convince new Sims that yours is an attractive city to move into as long as it's glowing with a bunch of radiation symbols.

MICROWAVE OOPS

If you use a microwave power plant, from time to time the microwave beam from your satellite will miss the microwave plant and hit a nearby

FIGURE 15.3 *Not only is our nuclear power plant gone, we have to deal with all this radioactivity.*

structure instead. The structure will burst into flame. (Accidents happen, right?)

Avoiding Microwave Accidents

To avoid microwave accidents, you can either avoid using a microwave power plant, or toggle on No Disasters. If you choose to use a microwave power plant and you want to include the challenge of possible random disasters as part of your SimCity 2000 experience, build your microwave power plant as far from the city and ancillary structures (airports, etc.) as possible.

Handling the Effects of a Microwave Accident

A microwave accident is going to make itself felt, like so many other of life's little problems, as a fire (Figure 15.4). You need to isolate and put

out the fire as quickly as possible before it turns into a bigger mess. See the section titled "Fire" earlier in this chapter for more information.

FIGURE 15.4 *Sometimes the beam relaying solar energy from the satellite to your microwave power plant will miss and hit the neighborhood instead, causing a fire.*

POLLUTION

Pollution exists in every city that has industry—in SimNation, that's every city. It only becomes a disaster when it's so thick it forms a noxious cloud that hovers above and moves around your city (Figure 15.5). You'll know that pollution has reached a disastrous level when the cloud appears and a message in the Info box or status bar tells you so.

Preventing Pollution

There is actually quite a lot you can do to prevent pollution from becoming disastrous. First, keep in mind that pollution is not going to be a tremendous problem in the early 20th century—the economy is heavily reliant on industry, the city just won't be that big, and there will still be

FIGURE 15.5 *A cloud of pollution threatens this city.*

open spaces around it. Pollution gets to be a bigger problem as your city grows, especially if you continue to depend on dirty sources of power, like coal, and if you continue to rely on heavy industry even as the economy gradually shifts from industrial to commercial.

Remember that you can control the density and environmental impact of industry in your city not just through zoning (light or dense) but also through taxation. You can encourage cleaner industries and discourage dirtier ones by shifting the rate of taxation on individual types of industries. (See Chapter 7.) You can also pass the Pollution Controls ordinance in the Budget window's Ordinances books. (See Chapters 3 and 8.)

> **TIP**
>
> **Adding one water treatment plant will reduce pollution 10–15%. Build one treatment plant per 20,000 Sims in your city to keep pollution down.**

To monitor the level and location of pollution in your city as it grows, check the Maps window frequently, as described in Chapters 3 and 4.

Curing Pollution

If pollution gets out of control and the telltale noxious clouds appear, you can combat it by sending police, fire fighters, and/or military units to the tiles over which the cloud of pollution is hovering. (Fire fighters actually seem to do the best job.)

This, however, is a short-term cure. You should also address the cause of pollution. To prevent a recurrence of clouds of pollution, follow the guidelines in "Preventing Pollution," the previous section.

WASH POLLUTION AWAY THE MAGIC ERASER WAY

So you've got a problem with a building that's throwing off scads of pollution? You can't bring yourself to get rid of this building because it's important—like, maybe it's a *power plant?* Using the magic eraser trick, you can wipe part of the building out of view, reducing its polluting output, *yet it will keep functioning!*

To use the magic eraser:

1. Select Landscape ➤ Trees from the toolbar.
2. Point and click at the landmass and keep holding down the mouse button. A couple of trees might appear, but keep the faith and go to step 3.
3. Press and hold down the Shift key (keep holding down the mouse button) and pass the cursor across whatever you want to make disappear.

Abracadabra! The magic eraser does its trick. (If you do this to a power plant, note that the more of the plant you erase, the lower the plant's output of power will fall.)

MONSTER

The monster is a many-legged thing with a blinking eye and a seemingly evil manner. The monster may emit beams that cause fires, or may cause mini-tornados, or may plant wind power plants in your city!

Preventing Monster Attacks

The monster seems quite evil and may seem to appear randomly—until you realize that it is seeking and attacking industries and power plants that cause high levels of pollution. It stands to reason that to prevent monster attacks, you should prevent pollution, as described in "Preventing Pollution," earlier in this chapter.

Getting Rid of the Monster

There is nothing much you can do to get rid of the monster itself, so forget that. (On rare occasions, Captain Hero will show up and drive the monster away, but that's a random event.)

The monster may start fires; if so, don't bother fighting the monster (that's futile); simply concentrate on putting out the fires. If the monster causes tornados, all you can do is clean up the damage. If the monster places wind power plants, consider it a warning and just deal with your pollution problem.

In any case, once the monster's gone and the fires (if any) are out, your real job is to clean up the damage. This includes, but is not limited to, replacing the polluting industries and power plants the monster went after with cleaner ones.

RIOT

Riots are the result of extreme unhappiness among your Sims. When a riot takes place, you'll see the rioting Sims marching about in a group, carrying picket signs. They will soon start fires to get your attention.

Preventing Riots

Preventing riots is a matter of keeping the Sims happy. They will become unhappy enough to riot mainly over matters of money: unemployment or low funding levels that undermine the effectiveness of city services. Keep your Sims employed and healthy and give them things to do on the weekends, and they'll be happy. Let them get unhappy, and they'll riot.

Quashing Riots

If a riot occurs, send out some combination of the police and military units right away. If you don't get the cops (and military, if necessary) there quickly, the rioters will set fires. Then you'll have to send out the cops, the military, *and* the fire fighters, and you'll have a real time of it. The rioters will move quickly, setting more fires, splitting into two, even three groups, each setting even *more* fires, and you'll have to track them all with the cops at the same time you try to put out the fires with the fire fighters.

Dealing with Mass Riots

Mass riots are larger riots that take place in many places in your city at once; you can respond to mass riots using the same combination of police, military, and fire fighters you use for smaller riots. (Try building water around the rioters!) If a mass riot occurs, give yourself a break: *pause the simulator right away* so you can position your disaster-response units strategically before things get way out of hand (Figure 15.6).

FIGURE 15.6 *A mass riot can be quite a handful.*

FLOOD

Floods are random events that you can't really prevent. Floods can, however, be somewhat *anticipated*—if you keep your eye on the Weather icon. Floods often follow hurricanes. They start at the edge of a body of water (a river or oceanfront) and spread inland.

Stopping Floods

When the floodwaters rise, one option is to send some combination of fire fighters and military to contain the flood before it gets too big and widespread. Position the units between the floodwaters and your city in the hope that they can repel the flood and turn the water back. Note however, that stopping a flood is no easy matter—it can just sweep around your fire fighters and military units.

A far better option (albeit an expensive one) is to use the Bulldozer ➤ Raise terrain tool to raise a levee into place to contain the flood (Figure 15.7). When you do this, be careful not to raise tiles that contain flood-water—the flood will then rise with the levee, spill over, and continue into the city.

When you build the levee, you may have to sacrifice some buildings. Don't stop to demolish/clear the buildings; just raise the ground and they'll blow up. (The flood would have destroyed them anyway.)

FIGURE 15.7   *Build a levee to hold back the flood before it rises too much.*

Eventually the flood will go down of its own accord, and you'll be left with rubble in the damaged areas. You can then clean up and rebuild.

Dealing with Major Floods

Major floods—those that are not confined to a single area—can be truly devastating. When a major flood occurs, it will (just like a more localized one) start at existing water and, as it rises, move inland. You can dispatch firefighters and military units to try to prevent the floodwaters from destroying parts of your city, but you probably won't have enough units to protect the whole place.

In this case, the levee technique described in the preceding section is your best bet, but even using that method you may find yourself one step behind the rising waters.

It's important then to save what is most important to your city (your power plant, for example, or expensive items like the airport) and quickly rebuild after the flood recedes.

TOXIC SPILL

As industry flourishes in your city, it can depend increasingly on toxic chemicals, chemicals that will occasionally spill and cause trouble. While toxic spills are not on the Disasters menu, they can still occur in play (but only when Disasters is toggled on). Use the techniques described in the Pollution section to deal with a toxic spill.

HURRICANE

The threat of a hurricane will be foreshadowed in the Info box or status bar, and its arrival will be shown in the Weather icon. You are really in for it when the hurricane sweeps through your city—you'll have to deal with high winds and flooding simultaneously. The high winds can destroy buildings throughout your city, while the floods will do damage only closer to large bodies of water.

Coping with a Hurricane

You can't do much about the high winds during the hurricane except ride them out. You can respond to the flooding using the techniques described earlier in the "Flood" section. When the hurricane is over and the floodwaters have gone down, you can rebuild those parts of your city destroyed by either the wind or the flood.

VOLCANO

Your Sims can be having a peaceful day, minding their business, when the earth begins to rise, a cone-shaped peak forms, and ashes spew forth—it's a volcanic eruption right in your Sims' backyard (Figure 15.8). There is absolutely nothing you can do to prevent a volcano (hah!) and nothing you can do to contain the damage. Note that "volcano" is not an option on the Disasters menu—it will occur only at random (and only if Disasters is toggled *on*).

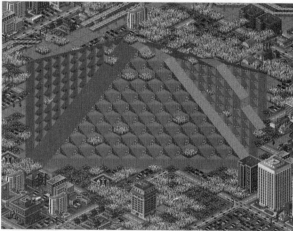

FIGURE 15.8   *The sudden appearance of a volcano can really ruin your day.*

Coming to Grips with a Volcano

The volcano will rise, the volcano will erupt, and fires will break out. While all this is happening, the mouse pointer on your screen will turn into an hourglass, and you will be unable to do anything to manage the eruption or its effects. When the eruption is over, you can try to put out the fires (see the "Fire" section earlier in this chapter). There isn't much else you can do 'til things settle down completely and all the fires are out. Then you can rebuild damaged areas of your city, this time zoning *around* the new mountain you've been provided with.

AN OUNCE OF PREVENTION...

If there is a general message to be heard in this discussion of potential disasters, it might be that your best bet in dealing with disasters is to prevent those that are preventable through careful and wise management of your city and its resources. Only a few of the disasters in SimCity 2000 are truly random—the rest are the result of some mounting problem in your city. Make yours a nice city, where the Sims are happy and pollution is kept to a minimum, and all you'll have to worry about is a sudden flood, or hurricane, or volcano. How likely is that to occur?

PART THREE

WINNING THE MODEL SCENARIOS

CHAPTER SIXTEEN

ABOUT WINNING
THE SCENARIOS

WINNING THE MODEL SCENARIOS IS a test of your city-management abilities *and* your skills in using the program's features. In some of the scenarios you will have to first respond to a disaster and then rebuild the city to a certain size within an allotted time. In others, you just need to get your city to the right size within a certain period of time. If you accomplish these tasks, you'll be given the key to the city. If you fail, you'll be removed from office.

JOY! RAPTURE! DIVINITY! You have completed all necessary objectives for this scenario. You are awarded the key to the city and are asked to continue in your role as community leader.

Winning a scenario is often a matter of creative disaster management combined with "creative" budget management. (Okay, so there can be some minor trickery involved here and there. It's a *game*.) To give yourself a leg up on the skills you need to win the scenarios, go back and take a look at Chapter 7 for budget info and Chapter 15 for disaster-control advice.

NOTE

Maxis puts out an add on package of scenarios that includes (among other gems) explosions, volcanoes, and riots. You can win those scenarios using the skills you've learned throughout this book and employing strategies like those we describe in Chapters 17–21.

STARTING THE SCENARIOS

To start the scenarios, you can either click on the Scenarios button in SimCity 2000's first screen or select File ➤ Load Scenario from the menu bar while you are playing a game. A window will appear (Figure 16.1) with a short description of each scenario's problem (and your goal) displayed. Double-click on the scenario you wish to play.

TIP

The first step in winning many scenarios is to pause the simulator. To *quickly* pause during any of the scenarios, press Alt-P on the DOS PC, Ctrl-P on the Windows PC, or ⌘-P on the Mac. During a disaster, SimCity 2000 responds much more quickly to Alt-P, Ctrl-P, or ⌘-P than it will if you select Speed ➤ Pause from the menu bar.

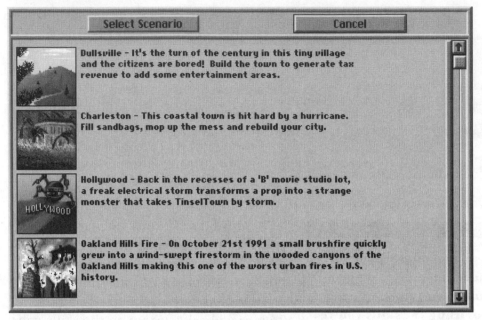

FIGURE 16.1 *Double-click on the scenario you want to play.*

AVOIDING ADDITIONAL DISASTERS

The last thing you want is another disaster happening while you play out a scenario. (One's enough.) You can prevent additional disasters from occurring by selecting Disasters ➤ No Disasters from the menu bar immediately when the scenario begins. A bonus to doing this is that you can then reduce your Fire Dept. funding level in the Budget window to 0% without danger. This will make more money available for use in winning the scenario.

CHAPTER SEVENTEEN

HURRICANE IN CHARLESTON

IN THE CHARLESTON SCENARIO YOU must first respond to a hurricane and then within five years build the city's population up to 45,000 people using only $20,000. Charleston starts with a population of 35,000 before the hurricane. The population will drop to about 30,000 right after the hurricane, so you'll need to attract 15,000 Sims.

Respond to the Hurricane

As soon as you start the Charleston scenario, the hurricane will hit the city. Areas of the city near the coast will be flooded and winds will destroy buildings throughout the city.

When the hurricane leaves your city, pause the simulator by pressing Alt-P, Ctrl-P, or ⌘-P to give yourself a chance to review the damage. Repair and zone new areas of the city before you resume the simulator. This will give new Sims more time to move into your city before your deadline arrives.

> **TIP**
>
> **You can reduce the amount of flooding by building a levee around the coast of your city before the water gets too high. We discuss responding to floods by building levees in Chapter 15.**

Fix the Water System

The flood will usually wipe out most of your water pumps; you'll have to replace them. Adding about 20 new pumps will supply Charleston with enough water. Be sure to attach these pumps to your power system and to place pipes to connect them to the existing underground pipe grids.

Replace the Marina

Charleston's marina will probably be destroyed in the flood. While replacing it will cost you $1,000, the presence of the marina will encourage Sims to move back into the city, so one of the first things you should do is rebuild the marina.

Repair and Rezone the City

With the hurricane past, you must now start rebuilding.

Zone Dense Residential in the waterfront areas destroyed by the flood. Be sure to replace roads and connect new zones to the city's power system by placing power lines to connect the zones to powered areas.

> **TIP**
>
> You can leave the City Population graph on screen to monitor your progress toward your goal of 45,000 inhabitants. To display the City Population graph, click on the Graphs tool in the City toolbar and then toggle on the City Population graph. (There's more on the Graphs tool in Chapter 3.)

After you repair Charleston's waterfront, inspect the rest of the city for damage. Bulldoze tiles that are covered with rubble to make them into zoned but undeveloped tiles. (Zones tend to redevelop faster if you clear rubble from them using the Bulldozer ➤ Demolish/Clear tool.) Also, watch out for tiles that held churches, schools, and other "unzoned" buildings before the hurricane. You'll have to go in and rezone those tiles so the Sims will be able to redevelop the land.

Pay special attention to roads. You should replace roads that have been destroyed, but only if the new road will help your Sims get around in the city—if no zoned tiles are within three tiles of the road, don't bother to replace it.

Remove Extra Roads

Remove the extra roads that are around the city. This is especially true in industrial areas. Every zone should be within three tiles of a single road. You can rezone tiles that once held roads with the same zone as surrounding tiles.

Replace Schools and Hospitals

> **TIP**
>
> A year after the hurricane, check with the Health & Welfare and Education advisors and judge whether to concede to any demands for new hospitals and schools.

Large buildings are especially susceptible to damage by the high winds of a hurricane, and city services like hospitals and schools will not simply start to redevelop (like zoned areas) when they are destroyed. You'll probably find that your city services are damaged or gone. To help build up your population, replace at least one school and one hospital.

Develop Drum Island

You should add an airport to Charleston to speed development. Drum Island, an empty island that already has road access, is a perfect location for your airport. Remove the highway from the island and build a 5×5-tile airport. Add roads and commercial and residential areas to round things out, and bridge the water with power lines to connect the island to the nearest powered area. Figure 17.1 shows a developed Drum Island.

> ### TIP
>
> **Playing with No Disasters toggled off, you can zone only Light Commercial and Light Residential areas around your new Drum Island Airport.**

FIGURE 17.1 *Add an airport and some areas zoned Commercial and Residential to Drum Island to help Charleston recover from the hurricane.*

Let the Simulator Run

You now have all the pieces in place for a booming city. Set the simulator to Cheetah and open up the City Population graph to watch it skyrocket. With the simulator running you can do one last thing to help encourage development: Open the Budget window and lower the tax rate—all the way down to 0% if you want. A low tax rate will encourage development.

> ### TIP
>
> **Don't waste time fiddling with things while the simulator's running, or you'll miss reaching your goal within the allotted time frame. But for fun you can pause the simulation every January, just after taxes are collected, and spend your new money if you want.**

If your city does not have adequate power-generating capacity, it can't grow and you won't meet your population goal. If you start to experience brownouts, add more power plants to the city. Before five years have passed you'll reach your goal, and you should be given the key to the city.

CHAPTER EIGHTEEN

DEVELOPING
DULLSVILLE

THE GOAL IN DULLSVILLE IS to take a sleepy small town of 1,680 people and build it into a city of 20,000—with only $5,000 cash—in five years. By reducing taxes and borrowing a little from your Sims' children, you will have no problem in achieving this goal.

Issue Bonds

To win this scenario, you need to have $5,000 cash at the *end*—it doesn't matter whether the money comes from current or future revenue. Issue two bonds right away so you will have capital to expand Dullsville. If your funds dip below $5,000 while the simulator is running and before you win the scenario, issue an additional bond.

Provide More Power

The single coal power plant in Dullsville just can't produce enough juice to power a larger city. You need to build a second power plant. Build a second coal power plant (Figure 18.1) behind Dullsville Bluff, near the current one. You can extend power lines from your new plant to the old plant so they are all connected to the same power grid, but this is (technically) unnecessary.

Add a Seaport

Adding a seaport encourages trade and industry. This will improve Dullsville's business climate and attract new Sims to the city. Add your seaport along the riverfront—between the city and the power plant. You'll have to extend a road along one side of the seaport and connect the port to power.

Add a Marina

Extend Main Street to reach the coast and then add a marina at the waterfront. (This is all part of the plan to make Dullsville more attractive to new Sims.) Power up the marina by connecting it to your city's power grid. Add Dense Residential zones on both sides of your new Main Street extension to bring expensive housing into Dullsville.

FIGURE 18.1 *Build a power plant behind Dullsville Bluff.*

Give the City Water

When the Dullsville scenario begins, the city has no water system. To encourage growth, add pumps near the water—behind the power plant—to pump water to your growing city. Then connect your water pumps to the city's underground pipelines. (You'll have to place pipes under roads to connect sections of the city to each other.) As the newly zoned areas of your city are developed, remember to add more pipes to connect the new areas to your water system.

Stadium

A stadium will attract more Sims to your city and allow it to grow faster. Add a new stadium along Dullsville's new Main Street, just above the current industrial area of town (Figure 18.2).

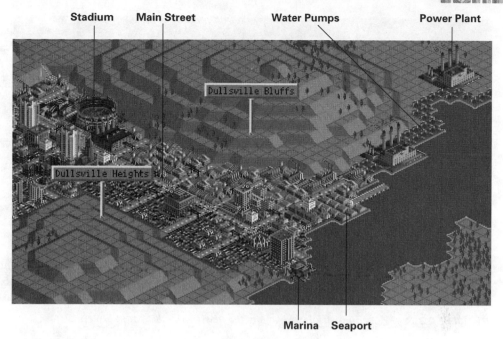

Stadium Main Street Water Pumps Power Plant

Dullsville Bluffs

Dullsville Heights

Marina Seaport

FIGURE 18.2 *You can see that a number of items have been added to help Dullsville grow into a city.*

Zone, Zone, Zone

Now that you have all the infrastructure in place to support a larger Dullsville, start zoning. Extend Main Street away from the river as far as it will go. Zone Dense Industrial areas in 6-tile-wide stretches along one side of Main Street. Place roads to allow Sims access to tiles in the industrial area (Figure 18.3).

Now zone Dense Commercial areas along the other side of the street. The Demand Indicator currently shows little (if any) demand for Commercial, but it will make a buffer zone between the industrial part of Dullsville and the new residential area. Next, zone Dense Residential heading toward the bluffs as far as you can go (Figure 18.4). Having done that, now zone Dense Industrial upward through the flat area.

Build a few new schools and hospitals while you're zoning away. Adding even one hospital and two schools will help Dullsville grow.

FIGURE 18.3   *Zone industrial areas along the newly extended Main Street.*

FIGURE 18.4   *Zone dense industrial areas as close to the bluffs as possible.*

As you zone, remember to connect the newly zoned areas to the city's power grid with power lines. Your power plant should be generating more than enough power for your city because you added a second power plant early in the simulation to support Dullsville's growth. Figure 18.5 shows the newly zoned area of Dullsville after Sims have moved in and built buildings.

Keep zoning until you have only about $7,000 left.

Let the Simulator Run

Once you have created zones for your incoming Sims to inhabit, set the simulator to Cheetah and let it go. You should lower Dullsville's tax rate. You can set it as low as 0% if you want. Check the Population Graph to watch your progress toward a city of 21,000 Sims. If your treasury drops below $5,000 at any time before you win, just take out another bond to keep going.

FIGURE 18.5   *Fill in this shallow valley with new, dense zones—residential, commercial, and industrial.*

CHAPTER NINETEEN

ECONOMIC FAILURE IN FLINT

IN THE FLINT SCENARIO, YOU must guide your city out of an economic slump and build to an *industrial* population of 21,000 in five short years. When the scenario starts, you have an industrial population of only 10,000.

Add an Airport

First, provide Flint with a 5×5-tile airport. You can put the airport in any convenient location. This will encourage new business (commerce) and help build the industrial population.

Remove Excess Roads

Use the Bulldozer ➤ Demolish/Clear tool to remove extra roads. (Excess roads are an unnecessary drain on your budget.) You'll find a lot of extra roads in the residential areas near the edge of the map. Remember that each zoned and developed tile should be within three tiles of a single road, but that having a tile near two roads does you no good—it just wastes land and allows for more pollution (from the extra cars).

Cut Industrial Taxes

To encourage industrial growth in Flint, cut the Industrial Tax rate to 0%. You can do this via the Budget window's Tax books (see Chapter 3).

> **TIP**
>
> Here's a trick you can use to help you see the areas to zone more easily. Click on the Show Zones tool icon, then on the Show Building tool icon, and *again* on Show Zones. In the view of the city that appears, zoned areas that have been built up are shown as solid colors, and areas that are zoned but not yet built up are shown as the dotted patterns you're already familiar with.

Zone

Rezone light residential areas as dense residential areas.

Let the Simulator Run

With all the pieces in place for Flint's full recovery, let the simulator run at the Cheetah setting.

If you find water shortages or brownouts occurring, add new water pumps or power plants to help your city keep growing. As things keep going, watch out for Sims demanding new services and other necessary items and resolve those matters.

Open the Industrial graph in the Graphs window, and you can monitor your rapid progress toward an industrial population of 21,000.

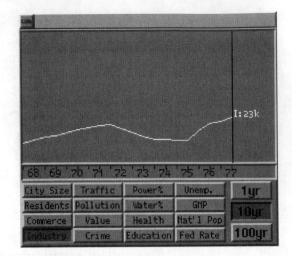

CHAPTER TWENTY

MONSTER ATTACKS HOLLYWOOD

TO WIN THE HOLLYWOOD SCENARIO, you need to battle a blinking, flying monster and then raise the city's population to 100,000 within five years. When the monster begins to destroy it, Hollywood has a city population of 93,500. The population of Hollywood after the monster leaves depends on the amount of damage it does—a random variable because the monster comes and goes as it likes.

> **TIP**
>
> **Forget chasing away the monster. Concentrate on containing and repairing the damage.**

Respond to the Monster's Attack

The Hollywood scenario starts with the city being attacked by a monster. The monster will fly through the air, sending out beams that start fires around the city. As the monster sets fires, isolate them using the Bulldozer ➤ Demolish/Clear tool (discussed in Chapter 15). Once you have isolated the fires, dispatch fire fighters to combat them.

As the monster moves around the city, it may start more fires. You can keep the monster within view in the window by using the scroll bars along the bottom and right side, or, on a PC, by right-clicking on the monster to center the window around it.

> **WARNING**
>
> **Sometimes the monster really blows its stack. It blasts around starting fires faster than any human being (or battalions of SimFire Fighters) can put them out. When that happens, there is almost no way to win the scenario. If you encounter a really *fierce* monster, your best bet is to start the scenario over.**

Pause the Simulator

As soon as the monster leaves Hollywood and you've put out the fires, pause the simulator. This gives you the time you need to plan and implement Hollywood's growth. As you rebuild Hollywood, you may run out of money. Go ahead and issue a few bonds. They don't count against you in this scenario.

Provide a Power Plant

Build a new coal power plant to supplement the existing power system. You'll need the added capacity as the city's population grows to 100,000.

Remove Extra Roads

Hollywood is full of extra roads; remove those that serve no purpose. You will also find many tiles that are serviced by multiple roads, which is unnecessary. Remove all unnecessary roads until each tile is within three tiles of a single road. You should also remove the Hollywood Freeway as it heads out of town, to free up more land for zoning.

Zone

Once you have removed extra roads, start zoning new areas. Zone Dense Residential and Dense Industrial below the Santa Monica Mountains. Also, zone in the area that used to be the Hollywood Freeway. Be sure to add any *necessary* roads as you zone new areas and connect up the power grid.

Let the Simulator Run

With new zones in place around Hollywood, set the speed to Cheetah and watch the simulator do its thing. You can open up the Graph window to monitor your progress as you zoom toward a population of 100,000. If the Sims start complaining about lack of water or about brownouts while the simulator is running, add more water pumps or power plants to satisfy them.

CHAPTER TWENTY-ONE

FIRE STORM IN THE OAKLAND HILLS

IN THIS SCENARIO, YOU MUST first battle a fire storm in the hills of Oakland. Then, with the fire suppressed, you have five years to build the city's population from its prefire level to 50,000.

Stop the Fire

As soon as the scenario starts, pause the simulator (press Alt-P, Ctrl-P, or ⌘-P) to allow time to build a firebreak. Use the Bulldozer ➤ Demolish/Clear tool to level buildings and trees in an area two tiles deep around the fire. Then use the Emergency ➤ Firefighters tool to send in fire fighters. (Send the fire fighters to tiles adjacent to the edges of the fire storm.)

> **NOTE**
>
> **Unlike "normal" fires in SimCity 2000, the Oakland Hills fire is a fire storm. In their ferocity, fire storms can jump the breaks you create with the Bulldozer ➤ Demolish/Clear tool. Carefully watch the fire as the scenario progresses to be sure that it does not spread.**

Now resume the scenario by selecting Turtle from the Speed menu. As the fire diminishes, redeploy the fire fighters as needed so they are always in tiles adjacent to the fire.

Pause the Simulator

After you put out the fire, pause the simulator again. Use this time to create land suitable for high-density development and to zone new areas.

Raise Cash

The technique described here to win the Oakland Hills Fire Storm scenario costs *big bucks*. Issue two bonds from the Budget window's Bonds books now so you will have cash on hand to win the scenario.

Create Flat Land

With the fire out, the remaining problem to overcome is a lack of the flat land that can support high-density development. To fix this, use the Bulldozer ➤ Level Terrain tool to create a patch of flat land at the top of the hill that borders Oakland, along Skyline Drive. In Figure 21.1 you can see how the area around Skyline Drive looks after it has been leveled and zoned.

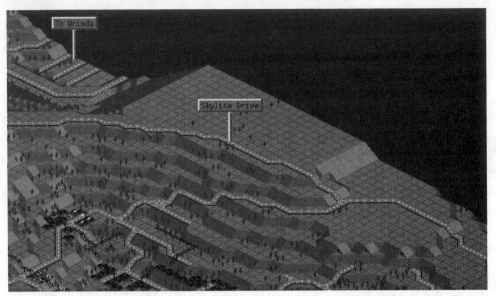

FIGURE 21.1 *Using the Level Terrain tool we were able to create a piece of flat land that supports dense development.*

Zone

Now zone areas for dense residential, commercial, and industrial usage on the terrain you just flattened. Be sure to place roads in an orderly fashion so that every zoned tile is within three tiles of a road. Also, run power lines from powered buildings that are down the hill up to your new development.

Cut Taxes

Cut the Tax Rate to 0% to encourage new development. (Cutting the tax rate also encourages Sims to move into your city.)

Let the Simulator Run

Now, with all the elements in place to attract new Sims to Oakland, switch the speed to Cheetah and let the simulator run. You can display the City Population in the Graphs window to track your progress. At some point your power plant will have to be replaced. If you don't have $5,000 on hand to cover the cost when this happens, you'll have to issue yet another bond.

PART FOUR

ADVANCED SIMCITY 2000

CHAPTER TWENTY-TWO

THE TERRAIN TOOLBAR

BEFORE YOU BUILD YOUR CITY, you have to have a landmass—something the simulator will generate automatically. The landmass will be created of randomly configured elements within a standard mix (25% hills, 10% water, 31% trees, the rest barren, flat land). You can play the landmass you're dealt or modify it, and you can even set up your own mix (percentages of hills, water, and trees).

USING THE TERRAIN TOOLBAR

The Terrain toolbar allows you to control the following aspects of land generation:

- Presence of a river, coast, or both
- Mix (by percentage) of hills, water, and trees
- Level (altitude) of plains, hills, etc.
- Level (altitude) of water surface
- Density of trees on the landmass

To activate the Terrain toolbar, from the opening menu that appears when you start the program, select Edit New Map; or, from any point in the game, pull down the File menu and select Edit New Map. In either case, the Terrain toolbar (Figure 22.1) will appear.

CREATING LAND WITH THE TOOLS IN THE TERRAIN TOOLBAR

The tools that appear in the top part of the Terrain toolbar allow you to set parameters (the mix) for the simulator to work within when it creates a landmass.

Coast and River   Using these two push buttons, you can control whether the next land form that's generated will include a coastline, a river, or a combination of both. If the button looks pressed in, the next new landform you generate will include the feature.

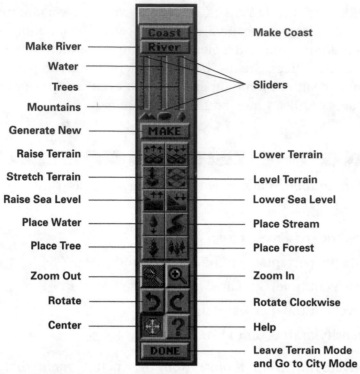

Make Coast

Make River

Water

Trees

Sliders

Mountains

Generate New

Raise Terrain — Lower Terrain

Stretch Terrain — Level Terrain

Raise Sea Level — Lower Sea Level

Place Water — Place Stream

Place Tree — Place Forest

Zoom Out — Zoom In

Rotate — Rotate Clockwise

Center — Help

Leave Terrain Mode and Go to City Mode

FIGURE 22.1 *The Terrain toolbar*

Mountain, Water, and Trees

These are three sliders—bars you can move up and down by clicking and dragging them with the mouse to specify what percentage of the next landmass generated will be hilly, covered by water, or covered by trees.

TIP

If you want a landmass that's utterly without water, you might think just setting the Water slider to zero will do the trick—not so. You also have to make sure the Coast and River buttons aren't selected; otherwise, you'll get a lot of lakes.

Make

When you've set the parameters to your liking, click on the Make button to generate a new landmass based on the specifications you've set.

Creating the Landmass

To create land with the Terrain toolbar:

1. Select whether you want a coastline, a river, or a combination of both. To do this, click on the Coast and River buttons to select what you want and deselect what you don't want. (When one of these buttons looks depressed, it is selected.)

2. Specify the amount of water, hills, and trees you want by clicking and dragging the slider bars for those items up (to indicate a higher percentage) or down (for a lower percentage).

3. Finally, click on the Make button. You'll see a window that tells you the landmass is being generated within the parameters you've specified, and then the landmass will appear in the City window.

If you are satisfied with the landmass that has appeared, you can click the Done button at the bottom of the Terrain toolbar to begin a simulation. If you are not completely happy with the landmass, you can generate a new one (by just clicking the Make button or by setting new parameters and then clicking the Make button), or you can modify it.

MODIFYING LAND WITH THE TOOLS IN THE TERRAIN TOOLBAR

In the sections that follow, we'll cover use of each tool on the Terrain toolbar, describing the ways you can use it to modify an existing landmass—whether it was created using the default parameters or the parameters you specified.

Raise Terrain To raise the terrain anyplace on the map, select the Raise Terrain tool and then point and click or click and drag where you want the land to rise. Every time you point and click, the tile of terrain under the mouse pointer will raise one unit. If you click and drag, the land will rise quickly, following the mouse pointer and forming realistic hilly patterns. If you click on water, the waterbed will eventually rise above sea level and become dry land.

Lower Terrain   To lower any terrain, anywhere, select the Lower Terrain tool and point and click, or click and drag. The Lower Terrain tool lowers the tile under the mouse pointer one unit every time you click. Lowering the terrain on dry land will eventually result in the surface being below sea level, in which case a pond, lake, stream, or river will appear, depending on your clicking technique.

Stretch Terrain   You can stretch terrain up or down using this tool. Click on the Stretch Terrain tool icon, then point and click on a tile in the map. Hold down the mouse pointer and drag the mouse toward the top of the screen to stretch the terrain into a peak. Then, if you like, you can stretch toward the bottom of the map to pull the terrain downward, giving more character to the peak.

> **W A R N I N G**
>
> **The simulator has been known to crash during use of the Stretch Terrain tool. If this happens, you'll have to restart the program.**

Level Terrain   Level Terrain allows you to flatten part of the landmass. Just select this tool and point to a tile that is at the level to which you want to raise or lower adjacent tiles. A little bulldozer appears on the land. Now click and drag the mouse pointer around to make the land level.

Raise Sea Level   Click on this tool to raise the sea level. You'll see water rise one level each time you click the tool. If you keep clicking, eventually water will cover your entire landmass—even if your landmass doesn't include a coastline.

Lower Sea Level   Clicking on this tool lowers the sea level, which exposes more land and reduces the amount of water visible in and around your landmass. Each time you click this tool, water will fall one more level. Keep clicking, and there will eventually be no water whatsoever.

Place Water
Click on this tool and then click wherever in the map you want a bit of water to appear. You can add lakes and streams to your landmass using this tool.

> **TIP**
>
> **This can come in handy for creating waterfall titles on which you can later place hydroelectric power plants.**

Place Stream
Click on this tool and then on your landmass, and a stream will appear. When you place a stream on a hillside using this tool, you will see not only the water as it appears on the hillside, but also water in the valley below the hill.

If you place a stream on flat land near a body of water, the stream will connect with the body of water.

Place Tree
Click on this tool and then on your landmass, and two trees (sometimes one) will appear. Click and drag and many trees will appear. To remove trees, click on this tool, then hold down Shift and click on the trees you want to eliminate.

Place Forest
Click on the Place Forest tool icon and then click and drag, and forests will appear in the wake of your mouse pointer. The more you click and drag over the same areas, the denser the forest will become. To remove the forests, select this tool, hold down Shift, and click on the forests you want to eliminate.

> **NOTE**
>
> **The Zoom Out, Zoom In, Rotate Counter-Clockwise, Rotate Clockwise, Center, and Help tools in the Terrain toolbar work the same as on the City toolbar, covered in Chapter 4.**

CLICK DONE TO MOVE ALONG

When you are finished customizing your landmass, click the Done button at the bottom of the Terrain toolbar. The Terrain toolbar will be replaced on screen by the City toolbar, and the simulator will start the game. To learn how to play SimCity 2000, turn to Chapter 1 of this book.

To create from scratch a SimCity based on a map of your hometown or any other city you choose, turn to Chapter 23.

N O T E

For your urban-development pleasure, Maxis presents an add-on for SimCity 2000 called the Urban Renewal Kit. This handy product gives you even more power in designing your cities. Using the Urban Renewal Kit you can choose what buildings will appear where (rather than letting your Sims make the choice), print copies of your city on paper, and even design and use your own buildings. The Urban Renewal Kit also includes a set of futuristic structures you can use to replace buildings in your existing cities. Versions of the kit are available for DOS, Windows, and the Mac. Check it out.

CHAPTER TWENTY-THREE

CREATING YOUR OWN CITIES

USING THE TERRAIN TOOLBAR SKILLS you learned in Chapter 22 along with a little ingenuity and a map, you can create a SimCity 2000 model of your own hometown or any other city you like. This isn't hard, it's just a matter of following a few easy steps and realizing as you do so that SimCity 2000 (for all its wondrous capabilities) has a few limitations.

> **NOTE**
>
> Check out the games forums on CompuServe and the SimCity 2000 anonymous FTP sites on the Internet, where you can see cities other people have created using the techniques described in this chapter. Chapter 25 talks more about this.

ROME (OR ANY OTHER CITY) IN A DAY

The main thing to consider is the size of the city—in SimCity 2000 you'll be limited to an area of approximately 5×5 miles. In that area, a tile of flat land represents about an acre (that means you can have a city that's fewer than 3,200 acres). A vertical tile (like the bump that appears with one click of Raise Terrain) is about 100 feet of elevation. Keep this in mind as we go along—construction of your land-mass and city must take into account these parameters.

> **NOTE**
>
> You don't have to recreate an entire city. We can't speak for Detroit because we've never been there (California's our home turf), but in the scenario cities, the version of Hollywood that appears is not *all* of Los Angeles or even all of Hollywood, and the version of Oakland is not accurate down to the minor details.

FIRST, GET A MAP

You want a map that shows you the lay of the land, not just the roads. The map you choose should show the elevation; any water (rivers, lakes, coastline); roads and highways; and the locations of important city service buildings like police stations, fire departments, hospitals, schools, and colleges. Topographic maps, available from the US Geological Survey or from map stores like Rand McNally, are a good bet. The US Geological Survey will send you a catalog if you write to them at USGS, Denver, CO 80225; Rand McNally map stores are located in many major American

cities. If you go looking for a map, try to get a 7$\frac{1}{2}$-minute topographic map, as they work out really well.

BLOCK OUT THE TOWN

Map in hand, grab a pencil and mark an area approximately 5 miles × 5 miles. (Your final product could be considerably less, say 1×1 miles or whatever you want, but for now make it 5×5 miles.) Next, break that area down (in pencil on the map) into 64 blocks (8 blocks × 8 blocks), which you'll mark out on your landmass in SimCity 2000 in just a few minutes. Finally, break each of these blocks into 16×16 smaller blocks—each of these represents one tile in SimCity 2000.

Choose from your marked-up map the area you want to create in SimCity 2000. This can be the whole 5×5-mile shebang or just a part of it. Look over that area and identify its key features, remembering all you know about SimCity 2000, so you can pick the features that are both descriptive of your city and possible to create using the program. (You probably can't place every hill and dale exactly as it appears, but you can place *hills* in the general area of your city that's hilly, for example.)

BUILD IT

With your marked-up map and your well-conceived plan, you're ready to start construction.

1. Start SimCity 2000 and, from the opening menu, choose Edit New Map.

2. The City window will appear with the Terrain toolbar in its usual location. Set all three sliders to zero and deselect Coast and River. Click on Make.

3. A landform will appear. It may have some hills and trees; just select the Bulldozer tool and Level Terrain (or whatever else you need) to flatten everything out. You want barren, flat land. (Doesn't everyone?)

4. Now make an 8×8 grid (Figure 23.1) to match the one you marked on your paper map and put trees at the corners to mark the squares. Each square should contain 16×16 tiles.

5. Going along from square to square and using the tools on the Terrain toolbar, raise and lower land to match what you see on your paper map.

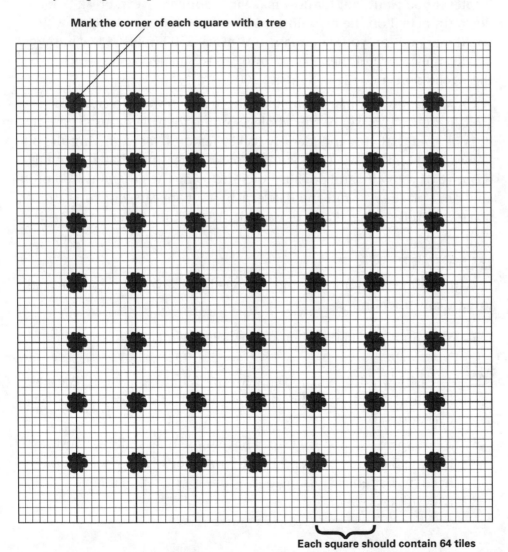

FIGURE 23.1 *You won't be able to "draw" on your landmass; instead, make a tree-studded grid to match the grid on your paper map.*

6. Do the same to recreate other features of the map's landscape (bodies of water in particular). Don't add trees yet, because that will obscure the tree "markers" you have in place and still need.

7. Now switch to the City window by clicking the Done button on the Terrain toolbar. You'll have to name your city and pick an appropriate date and play level. After that, pause the simulator immediately by selecting Speed ➤ Pause.

> **NOTE**
>
> **The rest of the procedure here is going to cost you some SimMoney. Because you can start out with a maximum of $20,000 at the beginning of a simulation and you'll need more to recreate even the smallest of cities, this is a good time to put into practice the "cheating" techniques you'll find throughout this book to get yourself some more money.**

8. Using the City toolbar, add the highways, roads, and city service buildings that make up your city's most obvious urban features. (Forget the smaller stuff; this is a model, not an exact replica.)

9. You'll have to place a power plant in the city you're recreating, even if you don't see one on the paper map. Try to pick a type of plant and a location that seem appropriate to the city's character. Add power lines, water pumps, and pipes to provide these necessities to your city.

10. Mapping out general areas of residential, commercial, and industrial use, zone your city. Add trees, parks, and greenbelts as needed. (Trees are expensive at this point, so make sure you have some big bucks set aside.)

11. Finally, you can sit and admire your handiwork or run the simulator and see how the town survives.

RUN FOR OFFICE

If you run the simulator after building your city, you might want to make adjustments in the city to help it thrive. Maybe you want to take on some of the challenges that face real-life leaders of the city you've modeled yours after. Have a ball. This is your chance to go into politics without putting up the cash for a campaign.

HACKING
SIMCITY 2000
FILES

GOT A YEN FOR SOME big money? A yearning to create and manage custom disasters? In this chapter, we present ways to hack the program for fun (if hex editing is your idea of a good time) and profit (in SimMoney, that is). Tinkering with the SimCity 2000 program files is not for the faint of heart, but it can be rewarding. If you have a little programming experience, you can hack away in the following ways.

CREATING SCENARIOS

You can create your own scenarios whether you have the PC or Mac version of SimCity 2000. It's important to know before we get started here that you cannot create your own scenarios for the PC using your own cities; you have to use existing scenario cities. You can, however, create scenarios for the Mac using cities you've created from scratch, as described in Chapter 23 of this book.

ON THE PC

Want to see a volcano in tinseltown? Mass riots in genteel Charleston?

Using Norton Utilities' Disk Edit program, you can make changes to the existing scenario files, defining the type of disaster you'd like to see and the conditions that must be met to "win" your modified scenario. Disk Edit is a handy utility that allows you to view and make changes to binary files (the SimCity 2000 scenario files, for example). Note that you cannot use a text editor or word processor to edit

these files. *Opening and saving any of the scenario files with a text editor or word processor will make them unusable.*

When you're editing the scenario files, you'll be using hexadecimal numbers. In the hexadecimal system, the decimal numbers 0–9 are represented by the symbols 0–9, and the decimal numbers 10–15 are represented by the symbols A, B, C, D, E, and F.

> **N O T E**
>
> **SimCity 2000 files have the file extension .SC2 and scenario files have the extension .SCN. Scenario files are all located in the SCENARIO subdirectory within your SimCity 2000 directory.**

The data you can change in the scenario file is stored in an area that follows a special marker: the text SCEN (which in hex is 53, 43, 45, and 4E).

In the steps that follow, we'll walk you through changing the Hollywood scenario so that it includes a volcano instead of the monster.

1. Copy the Hollywood scenario file to HVOLCANO.SCN. It is named HOLLYWO&.SCN in SimCity 2000 for DOS and Hollywoo.SCN in SimCity 2000 for Windows. (As we mentioned at the beginning of this chapter, you should modify only *backup copies* of your scenario files.)

2. Start up Disk Edit and load the file HVOLCANO.SCN. Disk Edit should load the file and display a hexadecimal representation of it along the left side of the screen.

3. Now use Disk Edit's Find command to locate the string "SCEN." (This, remember, is the marker at the beginning of the area you can modify in the scenario file.) Figure 24.1 shows the string in our copy of HVOLCANO.SCN.

4. You're ready to start changing the "win" conditions for the scenario. Table 24.1 shows the locations you can change relative to the word "SCEN" in the scenario file.

5. To add the volcano to your new Hollywood scenario, you need to change data in the place that is highlighted in Figure 24.2 to **0B**. (Remember, the old Hollywood scenario is still in existence. We're working on a copy.) Table 24.2 includes the codes for all the disasters.

```
                          Disk Editor
  Object  Edit  Link  View  Info  Tools  Help
0001C0C0:  72 73 20 74 6F 20 77 69 - 6E 20 74 68 69 73 20 73  rs to win this s
0001C0D0:  63 65 6E 61 72 69 6F 2E - 53 43 45 4E 00 00 00 34  cenario.SCEN...4
0001C0E0:  80 00 00 00 00 08 50 34 - 00 3C 00 01 86 A0 00 00  Ç.....P4.<..ãá..
0001C0F0:  00 00 00 00 00 00 00 00 - 00 00 00 00 00 00 00 00  ................
0001C100:  00 00 00 00 00 00 00 00 - 00 00 00 00 00 00 00 00  ................
0001C110:  00 00 00 00 50 49 43 54 - 00 00 10 CA 80 00 00 00  ....PICT....Ç...
0001C120:  41 00 41 00 01 01 01 01 - 01 01 01 01 01 01 01 01  A.A.............
0001C130:  01 01 01 01 01 01 01 01 - 01 01 01 01 01 01 01 01  ................
0001C140:  01 01 01 01 01 01 01 01 - 01 01 01 01 01 01 01 01  ................
0001C150:  01 01 01 01 01 01 01 01 - 01 01 01 01 01 01 01 01  ................
0001C160:  01 01 01 01 01 FF 01 63 - 8D 63 63 63 8D 63 63 63  ..... .cìcccìccc
0001C170:  8D 63 63 63 8D 63 63 63 - 8D 63 63 63 8D 63 63 63  ìcccìcccìcccìccc
0001C180:  8D 01 93 9A 91 01 99 63 - 8D 63 63 63 8D 63 63 63  ì.ôÜæ.ôcìcccìccc
0001C190:  8D 63 63 63 8D 63 63 92 - 99 92 99 97 8D 63 63 63  ìcccìccfiÖfiÖùìccc
0001C1A0:  8D 63 63 63 8D 63 01 FF - 01 8D 63 8D 63 8D 63 8D  ìcccìc. .ìcìcìcì
0001C1B0:  63 8D 63 8D 63 8D 63 8D - 63 8D 63 8D 63 8D 63 8D  cìcìcìcìcìcìcìcì
0001C1C0:  63 8D 8D 99 96 01 93 01 - 01 63 63 8D 63 8D 63 8D  cì ìÖû .ô..ccìcìcì
0001C1D0:  63 8D 63 8D 63 8D 63 8D - 63 96 99 96 9A 97 63 8D  cìcìcìcìcûÖûÜùcì
0001C1E0:  63 8D 63 8D 63 8D 63 8D - 01 FF 01 63 63 63 63 63  cìcìcì. .ccccc
0001C1F0:  63 63 63 63 63 63 63 63 - 63 63 63 63 63 63 63 63  cccccccccccccccc
Cluster 2,601, Sector 21,232
  File                                           Cluster 2,601
    C:\SC2000\SCENARIO\hvolcano.scn         Offset 114,904, hex 1C0D8
```

FIGURE 24.1 *We've searched the file HVOLCANO.SCN for the string "SCEN," and here it is.*

```
                          Disk Editor
  Object  Edit  Link  View  Info  Tools  Help
0001C0C0:  72 73 20 74 6F 20 77 69 - 6E 20 74 68 69 73 20 73  rs to win this s
0001C0D0:  63 65 6E 61 72 69 6F 2E - 53 43 45 4E 00 00 00 34  cenario.SCEN...4
0001C0E0:  80 00 00 00 00 08 50 34 - 00 3C 00 01 86 A0 00 00  Ç.....P4.<..ãá..
0001C0F0:  00 00 00 00 00 00 00 00 - 00 00 00 00 00 00 00 00  ................
0001C100:  00 00 00 00 00 00 00 00 - 00 00 00 00 00 00 00 00  ................
0001C110:  00 00 00 00 50 49 43 54 - 00 00 10 CA 80 00 00 00  ....PICT....Ç...
0001C120:  41 00 41 00 01 01 01 01 - 01 01 01 01 01 01 01 01  A.A.............
0001C130:  01 01 01 01 01 01 01 01 - 01 01 01 01 01 01 01 01  ................
0001C140:  01 01 01 01 01 01 01 01 - 01 01 01 01 01 01 01 01  ................
0001C150:  01 01 01 01 01 01 01 01 - 01 01 01 01 01 01 01 01  ................
0001C160:  01 01 01 01 01 FF 01 63 - 8D 63 63 63 8D 63 63 63  ..... .cìcccìccc
0001C170:  8D 63 63 63 8D 63 63 63 - 8D 63 63 63 8D 63 63 63  ìcccìcccìcccìccc
0001C180:  8D 01 93 9A 91 01 99 63 - 8D 63 63 63 8D 63 63 63  ì.ôÜæ.ôcìcccìccc
0001C190:  8D 63 63 63 8D 63 63 92 - 99 92 99 97 8D 63 63 63  ìcccìccfiÖfiÖùìcec
0001C1A0:  8D 63 63 63 8D 63 01 FF - 01 8D 63 8D 63 8D 63 8D  ìcccìc. .ìcìcìcì
0001C1B0:  63 8D 63 8D 63 8D 63 8D - 63 8D 63 8D 63 8D 63 8D  cìcìcìcìcìcìcìcì
0001C1C0:  63 8D 8D 99 96 01 93 01 - 01 63 63 8D 63 8D 63 8D  cììÖû.ô..ccìcìcì
0001C1D0:  63 8D 63 8D 63 8D 63 8D - 63 96 99 96 9A 97 63 8D  cìcìcìcìcûÖûÜùcì
0001C1E0:  63 8D 63 8D 63 8D 63 8D - 01 FF 01 63 63 63 63 63  cìcìcì. .ccccc
0001C1F0:  63 63 63 63 63 63 63 63 - 63 63 63 63 63 63 63 63  cccccccccccccccc
Cluster 2,601, Sector 21,232
  File                                           Cluster 2,601
    C:\SC2000\SCENARIO\hvolcano.scn         Offset 114,917, hex 1C0E5
```

FIGURE 24.2 *The byte that holds the scenario type is highlighted here.*

TABLE 24.1: *Offsets*

Location Relative to the Word "SCEN" (in decimal)	Size (in bytes)	Description
10	1	Disaster to strike city (See Table 24.2 for a list of disasters)
11	1	X Location of the disaster
12	1	Y Location of the disaster
13	2	Time until the scenario ends
15	4	City population needed to win
19	4	Residential population needed to win
23	4	Commercial population needed to win
27	4	Industrial population needed to win
31	4	Cash needed to win
35	4	Total land value needed to win
39	4	Maximum pollution level allowed
43	4	Maximum crime level allowed
47	4	Maximum traffic level allowed

Once you've made the modifications to the scenario file, you'll need to save it to disk. With the Norton Disk Editor, you can use the command Edit ➤ Write Changes to save your changes to disk. Remember, for SimCity 2000 to find the scenario, it must be located in the SCENARIO subdirectory in the SimCity 2000 directory.

There now. Wasn't that easy? Next time you start SimCity 2000, your new scenario will be available.

TABLE 24.2: *Disaster types*

Number (in hex)	Type of Disaster
01	Fire
02	Flood
03	Riot
04	Pollution
05	Air crash
06	Earthquake
07	Tornado
08	Monster
09	Nuclear meltdown
0A	Microwave oops
0B	Volcano
0C	Firestorm
0D	Mass riot
0E	Flood
0F	Chemical spill
10	Hurricane

ON THE MAC

To create a scenario on the Mac, you need a piece of software from Apple called ResEdit. If you are a true and experienced Mac hacker, you may already have a copy of this program. If you don't have it, you can get it from any of a number of sources, including:

- The Berkeley Macintosh Users Group (BMUG) offers ResEdit on a number of disks, including the Utilities R1 disk and the Zen

and the Art of ResEdit CD-ROM. You can contact BMUG at
(510) 549-2684 or, to make an order only, (800) 776-2684. (By
the way, BMUG offers a bunch of great services that any Mac user
will enjoy. We highly recommend that you give them a call and
ask for information about the organization.)

- Apple provides ResEdit for download from its FTP server on the
  Internet. You can use anonymous FTP to get the program from
  the machine `ftp.apple.com`, where it is located in the
  `/dts/mac/tools/resedit` directory.

- Sybex includes ResEdit as one of the
  many resources available on its
  CompuServe forum. Just Go Sybex
  and look in the Macintosh files area.

N O T E

We talk more about SimCity 2000 online and
on the Internet in Chapter 25 of this book.

- Sybex also maintains a World Wide
  Web home page. Just point your Web browser to
  `ftp://ftp.netcom.com/pub/sybex/SC2000.html` and take a look
  around. ResEdit should be easy to find.

Unlike the PC, where any program can and does store information in
its own format in a file, the Macintosh has a rather well-defined and con-
sistent format for files. All Macintosh applications, including SimCity
2000, use files that comply with this format. That's why a program written by Apple can "know" enough about SimCity 2000 data files to allow
you to modify them. ResEdit allows you to edit any file that conforms to
the format Mac applications use.

In this section, we're going to open a SimCity 2000 for the Mac data
file in ResEdit, make some changes to it, and turn it into a SimCity 2000
scenario file. (We owe much of our knowledge of this process to
Kevin Endo.)

1. First you need to pick out a city you already have that you want to
turn into a scenario. This can be any SimCity you've created or ob-
tained. *Don't use the original file for the city—make a backup copy of it,*
for all the reasons we mentioned in earlier warnings on this topic.

2. Double-click on the ResEdit icon to start up ResEdit.

3. With ResEdit running, you are going to open up both an existing SimCity 2000 scenario file and the city you wish to turn into a scenario. Select File ➤ Open.

4. The Open dialog box will appear; in it you should pick the file you want to use (which one you pick doesn't matter; it functions only as a framework to drop your own scenario into). Let's focus on Charleston in this example: The file Charleston is located in the SimCity 2000 folder. Open it.

5. Select File ➤ Open again. This time open up the city you wish to turn into a scenario. ResEdit will ask you if you wish to add a Resource Fork. This is where the information ResEdit can modify is kept. Answer Yes. You should now have both files open in ResEdit as shown in Figure 24.3.

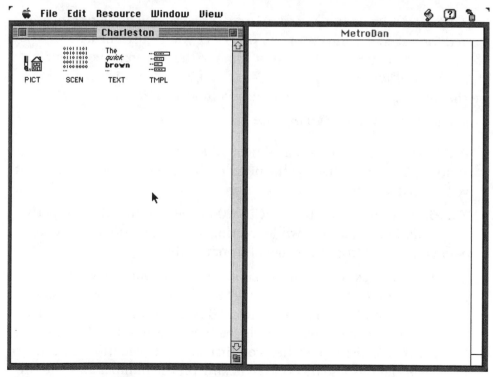

FIGURE 24.3 *Using ResEdit, we have opened both an existing scenario file (Charleston) and the city we want to turn into a scenario.*

6. In the window holding the scenario file, you will see a list of resources:

> PICT
> SCEN
> TEXT
> TMPL

Select Edit ➤ Select All from the menu bar to select all the resources in the window, then select Edit ➤ Copy from the menu bar. This puts a copy of all the resources from the scenario file in the Clipboard.

7. Now click in the window for your city to make that window active and select Edit ➤ Paste from the menu bar. All the resources should appear in the window.

Having completed the preceding steps, you've copied the resources required for a scenario into your city file. Next you'll customize the resources. By changing the content of some of the resources, you control the win condition in the scenario. You don't want your new scenario to be the same as the one you are using as a model, after all.

The resources you can change are

PICT Holds the picture that SimCity 2000 displays in the Scenarios window. You can either use the picture from the existing scenario that you copied, or you can use a paint program to create a new picture.

TMPL Contains data that SimCity 2000 needs to function properly. You should not modify it while creating a new scenario. Just use the data you copied from the original scenario file.

TEXT Holds text that SimCity 2000 displays about the scenario. Double-clicking on this resource will reveal a list of two TEXT resources labeled 128 and 129. TEXT resource 128 contains the text that is displayed in the Scenario selection dialog box. Text resource 129 holds the text that is displayed when you first start the scenario. You can modify either of these by double-clicking on the number and entering the new text into the dialog box that appears.

SCEN Contains all the details about the goal of the scenario. When you double-click on the SCEN resource, you will see a list of the labels listed in Table 24.3, all of which you can change.

TABLE 24.3: *Disaster types*

Scenario Condition	Description
Disaster Type	Controls what disaster will strike in the scenario. You tell SimCity 2000 what disaster should happen by setting this item to a value between 0 and 16. (The meaning of each of the possible values is given in Table 24.2.)
Disaster Xloc and Disaster Yloc	Holds the origin on the map of the disaster. The location 64, 64 corresponds to the center of the map.
Time Limit (months)	Controls the number of months that pass before the end of the scenario.
City Size	Holds the size the city must be at the end of the scenario to win.
Ind Goal	Holds the minimum industrial population at the end of the scenario to win.
Res Goal	Holds the minimum residential population at the end of the scenario to win.
Com Goal	Holds the minimum commercial population at the end of the scenario to win.
Cash Funds–Bonds	Holds the total amount of money, less any outstanding bonds, you must have at the end of the scenario to win.
Land Value Goal	Holds the minimum average land value required to win the scenario.
Pollution	Holds the maximum pollution level allowed to win the scenario.

continued

TABLE 24.3:   *Disaster types (continued)*

Scenario Condition	Description
Crime	Holds the maximum crime rate allowed at the end of the scenario.
Traffic Limit	Holds the maximum traffic level allowed at the end of the scenario.

8. You can make changes to any of the above win conditions by double-clicking on the item and typing in its place the new value.

9. Once you have made the changes to the resources to describe your new scenario, you must change the *file type* so SimCity knows it is no longer a city file, but rather a scenario file. Click on the ResEdit window containing your new scenario to make it active and select File ➤ Get Info. The Get Info dialog box will appear, showing information about the file. In the File Type box, type in SCEN. This indicates that the file is now a scenario file (Figure 24.4).

10. Once you have changed the file type to SCEN, click on the close box to return to ResEdit. When you select the close box, you will be prompted with a dialog box to save changes to the file. Select Yes.

> **N O T E**
>
> On the Macintosh, scenarios must be in the same folder as SimCity 2000. When you've finished the steps described, move your scenario file into the SimCity 2000 folder.

11. Select File ➤ Exit to leave ResEdit. Be sure to answer Yes when you're asked if you want to save the changes you've made.

That ought to do it—the next time you access the list of scenarios in SimCity 2000, your new scenario will appear along with the others.

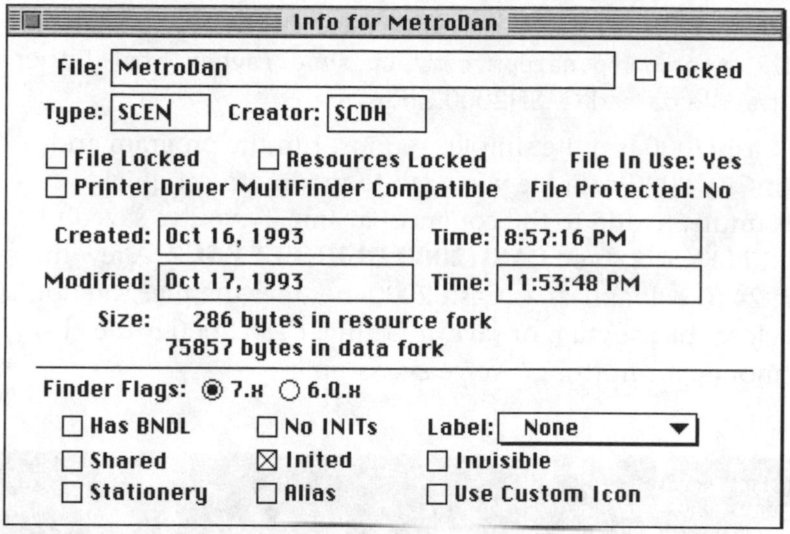

```
╔══════════════════════════════════════════════════════╗
║ ▣ ▤▤▤▤▤▤▤▤▤▤▤ Info for MetroDan ▤▤▤▤▤▤▤▤▤▤▤ ║
╟──────────────────────────────────────────────────────╢
║                                                        ║
║  File: │MetroDan                    │    ☐ Locked     ║
║                                                        ║
║  Type: │SCEN│   Creator: │SCDH│                        ║
║                                                        ║
║  ☐ File Locked      ☐ Resources Locked   File In Use: Yes  ║
║  ☐ Printer Driver MultiFinder Compatible File Protected: No ║
║                                                        ║
║  Created: │Oct 16, 1993│   Time: │8:57:16 PM│          ║
║                                                        ║
║  Modified: │Oct 17, 1993│  Time: │11:53:48 PM│         ║
║                                                        ║
║     Size:    286 bytes in resource fork               ║
║            75857 bytes in data fork                    ║
║  ──────────────────────────────────────────────────── ║
║  Finder Flags: ◉ 7.x ○ 6.0.x                           ║
║     ☐ Has BNDL     ☐ No INITs   Label: │ None    ▼│   ║
║     ☐ Shared       ☒ Inited     ☐ Invisible           ║
║     ☐ Stationery   ☐ Alias      ☐ Use Custom Icon     ║
╚══════════════════════════════════════════════════════╝
```

FIGURE 24.4   *In ResEdit's Get Info dialog box, the file type is changed from CITY to SCEN.*

GETTING MORE MONEY

Everybody wants more money. Playing honestly and well, you'll find your SimMoney coffers max out at around $2 million, but way before you amass that much cash you'll probably find yourself wishing for more. During a simulation you may be tempted to want more Sim-Money to expand your city and its services faster.

> **NOTE**
>
> Okay, everybody's asking for the big-money DOS cheat, and nobody seems to have it. Well, here's a simple way to get a lot of money fast for the DOS and Windows versions of the game.

Throughout this book we give you tips for building up your cash honestly as well as for grabbing it where you can in more nefarious ways. That's always been a lot easier on the Mac than on the PC. There are now handy programs available that read in SimCity 2000 city files for the PC and make modifications to provide more money. Once such program is called (cleverly enough) *Cash 2000*.

Cash 2000 will fork over to any SimCity some very big bucks. It's easy to use and free for you to download from various locations. You can get Cash 2000 from the Sybex forum on CompuServe—in the Games download section—or from the Sybex home page on the World Wide Web via the URL `ftp://ftp.netcom.com/pub/sybex/sybex.html`. Either way, look for the file named CASH2000.ZIP.

The use of Cash 2000 is quite simple. You just run the program and tell it what SimCity 2000 data file you wish to modify to get quick money. For example, to add to the coffers of a SimCity you've saved in a file called BERKELEY.SC2, type **CASH2000 BERKELEY.SC2**. A few lines of text (Figure 24.5) will appear as Cash 2000 modifies the file. You don't even have to close the program or save anything; Cash 2000 is the closest thing to "money for nothing" we've ever seen!

```
C:\SC2000>cash2000 berkeley.sc2
Cash2000 - SimCity 2000 savegame modifier v1.2
by Brian Curnow

File: berkeley.sc2   DateFlag: 1   StrictFlag: 1   MoneyFlag: 1
              W A R N I N G ! ! !

This program will modify your city and may cause trouble.
Do you have a backup and wish to continue?(Y/N)

Your file has been modified!  Hope the guilt isn't
too bad.  Happy Gaming!  (Howdy Sierra On-Line)

C:\SC2000>
```

FIGURE 24.5 *The text output of Cash 2000 might look dull, but the SimMoney you get will be very exciting.*

When you next load and use the city file you've modified, you'll find *$2 billion* (yes, that's two BILLION dollars) for your use. Because the year has changed, too, you'll also have access to some dandy technological advancements.

CHAPTER TWENTY-FIVE

SIMCITY 2000 ONLINE AND ON THE INTERNET

IN DOING THE RESEARCH TO write this book, of course we played SimCity 2000 into the wee hours of the night for months on end, and of course we talked to the folks at Maxis, but we also consulted with other players all over the United States and even in other countries. You can do this, too.

In this chapter, we'll visit (via brief descriptions) each of the services and tell you what sorts of SimCity 2000 information

> **N O T E**
>
> To use an online service, you need a modem. You also need an account with the online service (CompuServe, America OnLine, or Prodigy) that interests you or with an Internet service provider. To find out more about modems and services, check out *Your First Modem* (Sharon Crawford; Sybex, 1995).

you can pick up or trade in each. We'll also tell you how to get directly in touch with the folks at Maxis using electronic means. Sorry to say we can't cover every detail of using the online services in this space; we'll have to just tell you what's there with a few tips on getting and using the stuff.

WHERE TO LOOK

There are a number of "places" for SimCity 2000 enthusiasts to get together online; you'll find gamesters trading tips, ideas, and/or city files on CompuServe, America OnLine, and Prodigy; on plenty of BBSs (bulletin board systems); and on the Internet.

CompuServe, America OnLine, and Prodigy are membership services; the way they work is that you pay a fee for subscribing to the service, and the service dishes up its services, which are wide and varied but basically boil down to e-mail capability, online reference materials, and some sort of bulletin boards, forums, or "chat" features that allow you to interact with other subscribers in an exchange that focuses on some topic (*games*, for example).

These services don't share their information, just as when you subscribe to one magazine you don't get access to another; when you subscribe to CompuServe, for example, you'll get access to its entertainment forums, but you don't get access to Prodigy's game bulletin boards. (On the other hand, you can exchange e-mail with just about anybody—whether they're on CompuServe, American OnLine, Prodigy, or the Internet.)

The Internet is a vast, worldwide system of single PCs and networks (groups of computers cabled together so they can share resources), all interacting via a combination of high-speed communication links and phone lines and modems. This takes special software, of course, and for a (usually) small fee, various companies provide access to Internet service. (This isn't terribly different from a phone company providing access to phone service.) The Internet, which may be the least-expensive option for your online interaction with other SimCity 2000 enthusiasts, is composed of not just machines, modems, and software, but people—more than 20 million of them (and still counting)!

> **N O T E**
>
> The Internet was once (not too long ago) thought to have an ugly and difficult interface—you had to know and type in a lot of commands to do anything, and what you saw on screen was not very pretty. (It was usually a lot of text that was not nicely formatted or presented.) These days the Internet is getting more and more accessible and even more attractive. To get yourself a good deal on an easy-to-use point-and-click Internet service provider that looks and acts more like Windows than DOS, check out *Access the Internet!* (David Peal; Sybex, 1995).

SIMCITY 2000 ON COMPUSERVE

CompuServe provides, among its other services, *forums* for discussion between members on a given topic. You'll find SimCity 2000 stuff in the Macintosh Entertainment Forum and in the Game Publishers B Forum's Maxis section. You can *upload* (send) your cities to these forums, or you can *download* (get) cities people have posted there. You can also trade SimCity 2000 info and files with people on other services via e-mail.

> **T I P**
>
> Sending or receiving files electronically can get expensive. If you *zip* or compress the files using PKZip, LHArc, or Stuff It, you'll save a bit because the size of the file when it's compressed will be smaller, and smaller files travel more quickly over the lines. Versions of all of these utilities should be available for downloading from any commercial online service.

SIMCITY 2000 ON PRODIGY

On Prodigy, you can correspond electronically with SimCity 2000 enthusiasts via the games bulletin board. To get there, Jump Games BBS. Prodigy does not provide a place for the uploading or downloading of city files. You can use Prodigy's Mail Manager to send stuff to other

Prodigy subscribers, however, and there's always e-mail to others outside the Prodigy sphere.

SIMCITY 2000 ON AMERICA ONLINE

America OnLine includes a full-fledged gaming community focusing on SimCity 2000 and loads of other electronic entertainments. Maxis sections are News & Information, Product Information, Frequently Asked Questions, a Software Library, and a lively question and answer section called Let's Discuss. To get there, use the Keyword: Industry Connection. Click on Games, then select Maxis from the list of companies.

SIMCITY 2000 ON THE INTERNET

On most Internet computers, you'll have access to USENET, a messaging system of more than 3,000 "newsgroups" on different topics. Within each topic are subtopics; within each topic and subtopic are thousands of messages passing between participants in a big electronic exchange that can get to be really amazing. For SimCity 2000-related stuff, we like the comp.sys.ibm.pc.games, comp.sys.ibm.pc.games.strategy, and comp.sys.mac.games newsgroups. Check out all of them—SimCity 2000 is so similar running under DOS, Windows, or the Mac that you'll find the information in each of these newsgroups useful whatever version you have.

> **N O T E**
>
> To participate in a USENET newsgroup, you need an Internet service provider, as mentioned in an earlier Note; specifically, you need one that provides a *newsreader*. To upload and download city files, you need FTP (file transfer protocol) capability.

Trading Files via E-Mail

Using e-mail, which comes with your Internet account, you can trade files with SimCity 2000 buddies all over the world. To do this, however, you must make your city file a text file (not binary). You can find out more about doing this from your Internet service provider.

Trading Files via FTP

Using FTP (file transfer protocol), you can trade your city files around the Internet as binary files. A few FTP sites on the Internet specialize in SimCity 2000 files. For example, take a look at the /pub/thx directory on ftp.netcom.com, and don't forget /pub/maxis on ftp.netcom.com, which is where Maxis puts updates to SimCity 2000.

> **N O T E**
>
> FTP is also a great way to get free public-domain software and utilities stored on other machines that are part of the Internet. To do this, you log into the other machine using the name *anonymous*, then use your own e-mail address as the password. Once you're in, you can browse the machine's directories and download whatever SimCity 2000 stuff interests you. To find out more about *anonymous FTP* and other Internet techniques, check out *A Guided Tour of the Internet* (Christian Crumlish; Sybex 1995). To find out more about using Mosaic for FTP and other purposes, check out *Mosaic Access to the Internet* (Daniel A. Tauber and Brenda Kienan; Sybex 1995).

GETTING IN TOUCH WITH MAXIS

Using electronic means, you can even contact Maxis directly. Here's how.

USING COMPUSERVE

Maxis maintains a presence on CompuServe in the Game Publishers B Forum under the Maxis section. A representative of Maxis pops in and out to answer questions as needed.

USING E-MAIL

Maxis is available via e-mail on the Internet and CompuServe; just send your communications via the Internet address support@maxis.com, or via the CompuServe address 71333,1470.

USING PRODIGY

Maxis does not have a representative on Prodigy itself, but you can get in touch from Prodigy using either of the Maxis e-mail addresses. Use the Prodigy Mail Manager, addressing your communications to support@maxis.com or to 71333.1470@compuserve.com.

USING AMERICA ONLINE

Maxis does not have a representative on America OnLine, but you can make contact via AOL using e-mail. Open the Mail menu, select Compose Mail, and in the To: line, type `support@maxis.com` or `71333.1470@compuserve.com`.

USING THE MAXIS BULLETIN BOARD

Maxis maintains its own bulletin board (BBS), and you can call it directly for the latest patches, upgrades, and drivers any ol' time you're willing to pay the long distance phone charges. The phone number for the Maxis BBS is (510) 254-3869. Set your machine to the protocols *no parity*, *8 data bits*, *1 stop bit*, and *full duplex* at speeds of up to *14,400 bps*.

> **N O T E**
>
> **Maxis also maintains a directory (`/pub/maxis` on the machine `ftp.netcom.com`) on the Internet from which you can transfer by anonymous FTP the most current patches and upgrades to the program. Check in here as often as you like to find out what's available.**

SUBSCRIBING TO THE MAXIS DISCUSSION LIST

The Maxis discussion list is not maintained by Maxis, yet it is devoted to discussion of Maxis-produced games, including SimCity 2000. The list, which goes to its subscribers via their e-mail accounts on CompuServe, Prodigy, America Online, or the Internet, is distributed daily at 12:00 AM PST. To subscribe, send e-mail to `majordomo@cisco.com`. Include in your message the phrase `subscribe simlist-digest`. To ask for more info, send e-mail to `simlist-owner@cisco.com`. To send an article for inclusion in the list, send e-mail (with your article in the body of the message) to `simlist@cisco.com`.

THE SYBEX COMPUSERVE FORUM

Last, but by far not least, Sybex maintains a forum (called, predictably, `Sybex`, with a section called `Games`) on CompuServe where you can upload and download SimCity 2000 files. You can even talk to the publishers of this book and ask questions of us, the authors.

INSTALLING SIMCITY 2000

THIS APPENDIX TELLS YOU HOW to install SimCity 2000 on a Mac or on a DOS or Windows PC.

INSTALLING ON A MAC

Installing SimCity 2000 on a Mac requires nothing more than a few mouse clicks. Before you start, however, verify that your Mac is capable of running the program.

WHAT YOU NEED

You can run SimCity 2000 on any of the following Macintoshes:

- LC
- Performa
- II
- Centris
- Quadra
- Color Classic
- PowerBook (160, 165c, 180c, Duo 210, 230)

You'll need a color monitor along with at least 8-bit (256-color) graphics, 4 MB of RAM, and 4 MB of hard-disk space. Apple's System 7.0 or higher is also required.

> ### TIP
> SimCity 2000 officially "requires" 256 colors, but our sources tell us it will run with a 256-grayscale system. Watch out, though—it's hard to tell what's what without the color.

INSTALLING THE SOFTWARE

To install the SimCity 2000 software, do the following:

1. Create a folder on your Macintosh hard disk and name it SimCity 2000. (You can give it another name if you like, but for the rest of our discussion, we'll assume you did what we suggested and named the folder SimCity 2000.)

2. Place the SimCity 2000 Program Disk in your floppy-disk drive.

SimCity2000™.sea

3. Double-click on the icon titled SimCity 2000.sea.

4. Click on the Desktop button in the Select Destination Folder dialog box (Figure A.1).

5. Double-click on the disk on which you want to store the game (your hard drive).

6. Double-click on the folder into which you want to extract the files (SimCity 2000 in this case).

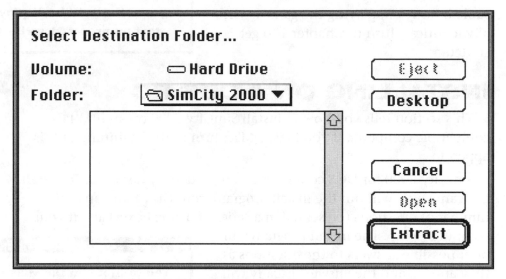

FIGURE A.1   *The Select Destination Folder dialog box*

7. Click on the Extract button. Files will be extracted from the floppy disk into the SimCity 2000 folder.

8. When the extraction is complete, remove the Program Disk from your floppy drive and insert Disk 2. (Disk 2 contains the scenario files.)

9. Double-click on the Cities.sea icon.

Cities.sea

10. Repeat steps 4 through 7 to select the SimCity 2000 folder as the destination folder and extract files from Disk 2 into it.

STARTING SIMCITY 2000 FOR THE MAC

SimCity2000™

With SimCity 2000 now installed on your hard disk, you can start the game by double-clicking on the SimCity 2000 icon shown here.

Installing SimCity 2000 on a Mac is very different from installing it on a PC. Now that you've got the software installed, however, playing the game is virtually identical. Turn to Chapter 1 to get started.

> **NOTE**
>
> The first time you run SimCity 2000 on your Macintosh, you'll be asked to provide your name and the name of your organization. Once you've done this, whenever you start the program your name and the name of your organization will be displayed as part of the start-up process described in Chapter 1.

INSTALLING ON A DOS PC

This section tells you how to install SimCity 2000 on an IBM PC-compatible computer. If you have a Mac, turn to the beginning of this appendix.

SimCity 2000 for DOS comes on two high-density diskettes. To install the game, you will run the install program from Disk 1 and answer a number of questions (presented in a series of dialog boxes) about your computer setup. The install program will offer possible answers to the questions as they appear, and the answers usually will be correct. If you are not sure how to respond to any of the questions, just accept the default response.

> **NOTE**
>
> You cannot run the Macintosh version of SimCity 2000 on a PC, nor the PC version on a Mac.

WHAT YOU NEED

Because of its complexity and wonderful visuals, SimCity 2000 requires more CPU power than some other games. To run the program, you will need the following:

- 386 or better CPU
- 4 MB of RAM

> **TIP**
>
> Although you really do need a color display to make the best of the program, it will run if you have a monochrome VGA monitor attached to your video card. The actual video card must be supported by SimCity 2000 and must be able to display 256 colors.

The faster your computer, the faster you'll see the SimYears tick by. If you want time to really fly, make your city window as small as possible—this will save your processor from working too hard, which will enable it to go faster.

T I P

It is much easier to install SimCity 2000 when your mouse driver is already installed. This allows you to use the mouse to select options and click buttons. If you have been running Windows successfully with a mouse but now find that SimCity 2000 doesn't recognize your mouse, it means the mouse was installed within Windows and not at the DOS level. Exit the Install program and load your mouse driver. (Refer to your mouse manual for information about installing the correct driver.) Now, when you restart the Install program, your mouse should be available.

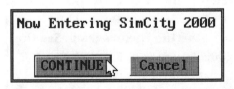

T I P

If the directory you specify already exists, the program will ask if you want to specify a different directory or replace your existing files. Select No to change the directory you are installing into or Yes to replace your existing program files.

- 4 MB of free hard-disk space
- A supported Super VGA (256-color) display adapter and monitor

SimCity 2000 will also use an Ad Lib, Media Vision, Sound Blaster, Roland MPU-401, or 100% compatible sound card, if any of those is present in your machine.

INSTALLING THE SOFTWARE

To install SimCity 2000, first place Disk 1 in your A: drive, type **a:install** (if you use your B: drive, type **b:install**), then press ↵.

The message *Loading…* will appear in a small window in the middle of the screen for a few seconds. Then a screen filled with Maxis logos will appear. When the Install program is finished loading, it will display a dialog box asking if you want to continue installing or stop.

Click on the Continue button to go ahead with installation.

A dialog box will appear asking for the drive and directory into which you want to place Sim-City 2000. Unless you have a compelling reason not to, leave the default values alone and click on the OK button. The program will create (and install itself into) an SC2000 directory on your C: drive.

A dialog box will appear asking you to personalize your copy of the program. Type your name and your organization's name in the space provided, then click OK.

Next, a dialog box will appear displaying the names you entered and asking you to verify that they are correct. If the names are correct, click Yes. You can go back and change your answers to these questions by clicking on the No button and then entering the correct answers.

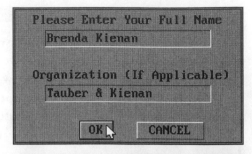

SimCity 2000 and its ancillary files will be copied to C:\SC2000 on your hard disk. This may take a few minutes—how long it takes depends on the speed of your computer.

Once the files have been copied from Disk 1, a dialog box will appear asking you to specify the type of graphics card in your computer. As usual in SimCity 2000, this dialog box will offer a suggested response.

- If the suggested response is correct, click on the OK button to accept it.

- If you don't know what type of graphics card you have, click on the OK button to accept the suggested response—it is almost certainly correct.

- If you know what type of card you have and it is not correctly specified, click on the down-arrow button to see a list of known cards and select your card from the list by clicking on it with the mouse pointer. Click the OK button to continue.

- If your card does not appear in the first list of supported video cards, click on the Not In List button to see an extended list of video cards. If your card is on this second list, select it. If your card is not on this second list, select VESA Super VGA.

> **N O T E**
>
> **If you selected your video card from this extended list of cards, you may need to load a driver before starting the program. See the SimCity 2000 Addendum & Quick Start Guide, DOS Version, for details. (The Addendum comes with the SimCity 2000 program.)**

Once you have selected the proper video card, click on the OK button to continue installing SimCity 2000.

In the dialog box that appears, specify the type of sound card you have in your computer. If you don't have a sound card, click on PC SPEAKER or NO MUSIC.

If you know what type of card you have and it does not appear in the initial list of sound cards in the dialog box, click on the MORE... option to see if your card is listed. Once you see your card listed, click on its name to select it and continue.

Next, you'll select the source for sound effects. A dialog box almost identical to the Sound Card dialog box will appear. This time, the dialog box will be asking for the source for Sound Effects. (This is a separate step from specifying the sound card you're using.) From the list of sound cards that appears in the dialog box, select the sound card by clicking on it, just as you did before.

The installation program will continue to copy files from the floppy disk (Disk 1) to your hard disk. When it is finished copying files, you will be prompted to replace Disk 1 with Disk 2. Do this and select Continue to go on.

When the files from Disk 2 are copied to your hard disk, a window will appear, showing additional information about SimCity 2000 that is not covered in the documentation. Click on the Continue button to see additional details. When you are finished reading this information, click the Exit button. The dialog box will close and the DOS prompt (C:\>) will appear.

> ### N O T E
>
> **If you pick PC SPEAKER, SimCity 2000 will play music with your computer's built-in speaker. It won't sound great, but you can always turn it on now to check it out and disable it later from the Options menu in the City window's menu bar.**

> ### T I P
>
> **If your card does not appear in the list of supported sound cards, try selecting Sound Blaster. Many other sound-card brands can emulate a Sound Blaster card.**

```
SIMCITY 2000 (TM)
Last Minute Info
12/27/93
------------------

Please read _ALL_ of this document! This stuff is important!

It covers a lot about memory, installation, various graphics cards and
sound cards, gameplay issues, importing cities from other versions of
SimCity 2000 and hot keys.

** MOST IMPORTANT STUFF--ABOUT MEMORY

SimCity 2000 requires a lot of memory to run--4 MB total, but also a lot
of free memory in the conventional 640K range. On some machines, even if
you have the required 4 MB, SimCity 2000 may report that you do not have
enough free extended or conventional memory. If this is the case, your
best alternative is to create a boot disk as outlined on page 6 of the
SimCity 2000 DOS Addendum/Quick Start Guide. Another solution that may
help is to install SimCity 2000 with No Sound and No Music selected. If
you have already installed SimCity 2000, you can change your current
```

CONTINUE   EXIT

STARTING SIMCITY 2000

To start the program, from the DOS prompt (C:\>) type **cd SC2000** and press ↵. This will make the SimCity 2000 directory current. Then type **SC2000** and press ↵ again. The game will start as described in Chapter 1 of this book.

> **N O T E**
>
> When you install the program, it will copy VESA drivers for a number of popular video cards into the \SC2000\VESA directory. You can either use a VESA driver from this directory or one provided by your video card manufacturer.

STARTING SIMCITY 2000 WITH A VESA DRIVER

Even if SimCity 2000 does not directly support the video card you have in your computer, you may still be able to run the program by communicating to your video card using a standard called "VESA."

To use SimCity 2000 with a VESA driver, load the VESA driver before you run the SimCity 2000 program. The name of the VESA driver depends on the video card you have. For more information on running SimCity 2000 with a Vesa driver, see the SimCity 2000 Addendum & Quick Start Guide, DOS Version.

RUNNING SIMCITY 2000 ON A 4-MB MACHINE

Occasionally, loading SimCity 2000 on a machine with 4 MB of RAM seems to present problems. If you have 4 MB of RAM and SimCity 2000 still refuses to run—a message will appear saying you don't have enough memory—you will need to create a boot disk.

Follow the directions in the SimCity 2000 Addendum & Quick Start Guide, DOS Version, for instruction on creating a DOS boot disk.

Installing SimCity 2000 for the PC is different from installing it on the Mac. But now that you have the program installed, playing the game is virtually identical. Turn to Chapter 1 to start playing SimCity 2000.

INSTALLING ON A WINDOWS PC

Installing the Windows version of SimCity 2000 is considerably less troublesome than installing the DOS version. SimCity 2000 for Windows comes on two high-density diskettes and installs just like any other Windows program. Read on for more detail.

WHAT YOU NEED

The requirements for running the Windows version are just about the same as those for the DOS version with one caveat: You have to have Windows 3.1 or 95. (Surprise!) Like the DOS version, SimCity 2000 for Windows requires a video card capable of displaying 256 colors at a resolution of at least 640×480. Unlike the DOS version, video resolution is already set in Windows, not by the game. So if Windows is working on your machine, you probably won't have to fuss with the video resolution.

Here's what you need to install and run SimCity 2000 for Windows:

> **NOTE**
>
> **Interestingly, the Windows version of SimCity 2000 is slightly slower than its DOS twin. As is true in the DOS version, a faster computer with more memory will make playing the game smoother and more enjoyable. So if you want fast play, play on a fast machine and jack up the memory.**

- 386 or better CPU
- Windows 3.1 or better
- 4 MB of RAM
- 5.5 MB of free hard-disk space
- A display adapter, monitor, and Windows video driver that allow you to run Windows in SVGA (256-color) mode

INSTALLING THE SOFTWARE

To install SimCity 2000, first place Disk 1 in your A: drive, choose File ➤ Run, type **a:\setup** in the Command Line text box (if you use your B: drive, type **b:\setup**), then press ↵ or click on OK.

Wait a moment while SimCity 2000 starts the setup program (you'll see a note that says *Initializing Setup...* in the **SimCity 2000 for Windows Setup** window). A screen will appear, welcoming you to the game. Click on Continue to get on with it.

In the next window's text boxes, personalize your copy of the program by typing your name (or maybe just a name you like) and, optionally, the name of a company. Click on Continue again. Now you must choose a location—where on the hard disk do you want to store the game? The default location is **C:\SC2K4WIN**. If this drive and directory seem okay (why wouldn't they?), click on Continue. If you would like to install the game in another location, type the new location in the Path text box and then click on Continue. Finally a screen appears asking you to confirm your choices. Click on OK. The setup program copies the program files to your disk, and as it does, it shows you its progress in a status bar. It will even prompt you when it wants the next disk.

STARTING SIMCITY 2000 FOR WINDOWS

When setup is complete, the program will create a new group in Program Manager called Maxis. There you will find three icons:

- Help, which (if you click on it) gets you into the same online Help system you can see during the game

- Readme, which (if you click on it) opens a document containing extra information about the Windows version of the game

- SimCity 2000 for Windows, which (if you click on it) *starts the game*

A Word on Drivers

As mentioned earlier, the setup of video and sound drivers is done separately within Windows. If you don't know the resolution under which you are running your Windows display, you can find out by clicking on Windows Setup in the Program Manager's Main group. The information you are looking for (the name of the specific video driver you are using) is in the *Display:* line. If you are not running in

> **NOTE**
>
> **The first time you start SimCity 2000 for Windows, a window with red and green boxes in it will appear. Not to worry—the game is testing your video card and making some choices based on the information it gets. This may also occur if you change the video driver you are using under Windows and start the game afterward.**

a mode that supports 256 colors, you need to change drivers. This can be a bit tricky, and it all depends on how your machine is set up, so for more on this check the documentation that came with Windows and your video card.

TESTING YOUR VERSION

Want to know which version of the program you're running? On either a DOS PC or the Mac, just type **vers** anytime you've got the program running. On a DOS PC, if you type **test**, or on a Windows PC, if you press Ctrl-Alt-t, you'll learn something similar.

INDEX

Note to the Reader:

Boldface numbers indicate pages where you will find the principal discussion of a topic or the definition of a term. **Boldface** words indicate Easter egg words you can type to get some surprising results. *Italic* numbers indicate pages where a topic is illustrated in a figure.

Tools for Quickly Seeing
Information Windows

Maps   Structures
Zones

 Roads
Rails
Traffic

 Power

 Water Supply

 Density
Rate of Growth

 Crime Rate
Police Power
Police Depts

 Pollution

 Land Value

 Fire Power
Fire Depts
Schools
Colleges

**Population
Window** Population
Health
Education

Graphs City Size
Residents
Commerce
Industry
Traffic
Pollution
Value
Crime
Power%
Water%
Health
Education
Unemp.
GNP
Nat'l Pop
Fed Rate

Over a
Span of:
1 Year
10 Years
100 Years

**Industry
Window** Ratios
Tax Rates
Demand

**Neighbors
Window**

**Budget
Window** Property Taxes
City Ordinances
Bond Payments
Police Department
Fire Department
Health & Welfare
Education
Transit Authority